SERIES EDITORS:
Stewart R. Clegg &
Ralph Stablein

ADVANCES IN ORGANIZATION STUDIES

Eric-Hans Kramer

Organizing Doubt
Grounded Theory, Army Units and Dealing with Dynamic Complexity

Liber & Copenhagen Business School Press

Organizing Doubt
– Grounded Theory, Army Units and Dealing with Dynamic Complexity

ISBN 978-91-47-08705-1 (Sweden)
ISBN 978-82-15-01158-5 (Norway)
ISBN 978-87-630-0197-7 (Rest of the world)
© 2007 Eric-Hans Kramer and Liber AB

Publisher's editor: Ola Håkansson
Series editor: Stewart Clegg and Ralph Stablein
Typeset: LundaText AB

1:1

Printed in Slovenia by
Korotan Ljubljana, Slovenien 2007

Distribution:
Sweden
Liber AB, Baltzarsgatan 4
S-205 10 Malmö, Sweden
tel +46 40-25 86 00, fax +46 40-97 05 50
http://www.liber.se
Kundtjänst tel +46 8-690 93 30, fax +46 8-690 93 01

Norway
Universitetsforlaget AS
Postboks 508
0105 Oslo
phone: +47 14 75 00, fax: +47 24 14 75 01
post@universitetsforlaget.no www.universitetsforlaget.no

Denmark
DBK Logistics, Mimersvej 4
DK-4600 Koege, Denmark
phone: +45 3269 7788, fax: +45 3269 7789
www.cbspress.dk

North America
International Specialized Book Services
920 NE 58th Ave., Suite 300
Portland, OR 97213, USA
phone: +1 800 944 6190
fax: +1 503 280 8832

Rest of the World
Marston Book Services, P.O. Box 269
Abingdon, Oxfordshire, OX14 4YN, UK
phone: +44 (0) 1235 465500, fax: +44 (0) 1235 465555
E-mail Direct Customers: direct.order@marston.co.uk
E-mail Booksellers: trade.order@marston.co.uk

Advances in Organization Studies

Series Editors:
Stewart Clegg
Professor, University of Technology, Sydney, Australia

Ralph E. Stablein
Professor, University of Otago, New Zealand

Advances in Organization Studies is a channel for cutting edge theoretical and empirical works of high quality, that contributes to the field of organizational studies. The series welcomes thought-provoking ideas, new perspectives and neglected topics from researchers within a wide range of disciplines and geographical locations.

www.organizationstudies.org

Preface and Acknowledgements

'(...) I know that wider circles of readers have been content to reduce the contents of the book to a catch word ('wish-fulfillment') which can be easily remembered and conveniently misused.'

Sigmund Freud (1960, p. 197) on The Interpretation of Dreams

The fact that this book has grown out of my doctoral dissertation puts me in a somewhat different position compared to many other writers of books. One of the differences is that I have already experienced the reaction of numerous readers. There were many positive reactions from readers, both from within and outside the military organization. Eventually, these reactions led me to submit the manuscript to a publisher. Of course, critical comments were made; often by the same people that formulated positive reactions. Some took the trouble of intensely reviewing parts of this study and worked out some critical notes. After these experiences I know that being criticized is a form of being taken seriously. These reactions helped me to progress further with the subject.

Apart from what one might call 'normal academic reactions', there are the reactions that were 'different'. My standard reaction has been that these reactions confirm the claims being made in the study. I experienced that if a study is considered controversial, many people voice an opinion on it, whether they have read it or not. Indeed, it seems that many find it convenient to reduce the content of the book to a catch word which can be easily remembered and conveniently misused. More than once people have, with superior disdain, formulated reactions like: 'there is more to military operations than doubt'.

Another difference between me and many other writers of books is that I am in a way being offered a second chance. There is a positive and there is a negative side to this. On the one hand, this second chance was inevitable, as the editor demanded that some changes should be made. Particularly the basis of the argument in organizational literature has been extended. I consider these comments to be valuable, they improved the work considerably. I also took the opportunity to use the critical comments of my previously mentioned 'academic critics'. On the other hand, however, there was the ever present lure to go over every single formulation again and again, to incorporate quotes from the latest books I read. A distinct risk of such changes is that the new version drifts away from the original version. For this reason, I only gave in to this lure in modest amounts, on a few occasions.

Without the dedication and support of others I would not have been able to finish this project. As this study grew out of my dissertation, I first want to thank the members of my Ph.D. project committee: Prof dr H. Kuipers, Prof dr. R. van der Vlist, Prof. dr. A. Vogelaar, Prof. dr P. Van Amelsvoort and Dr F. van Eijnatten. Prof dr H. Kuipers, Prof dr. R. van der Vlist, Prof. dr. A. Vogelaar supervised me during the process of developing this thesis. On the one hand, they helped me with their profound knowledge of the subject of this thesis. On the other hand, they provided me with every opportunity to follow the sometimes very twisty paths towards this thesis. Most importantly perhaps, they were always prepared to discuss extensively and critically any topic that was related to this study. Such broad minded supervision of dissertations is the exception rather than the rule. In the later stages of the process Prof. dr. Van Amelsvoort and Dr F. van Eijnatten made invaluable contributions. Second, I want to thank Stewart Clegg for providing me a thoughtful review of the original manuscript of the dissertation and for providing me the opportunity to publish the study within this series.

Third, I want to thank the members of the project group *Leiderschap in Crisisomstandigheden*. Together they developed the exploratory case studies that are the basis of this study. Over the years a great number of people have contributed to the project: Max Metselaar, Jolanda Bosch, Annemarie Witteveen, Coen van den Berg, Frans Nederhof, Ed de Bruin, Nancy Kensmil, and Tessa op den Buijs.

Fourth, I could not have finished this dissertation if the Military Academy in general and the Social Science Department in particular had not provided me every opportunity. Not only have I been given the freedom to pursue my own interests, I always have been able to devote many working hours to the thesis. Apart from these matters of time, the Social Science Department also provided a stimulating intellectual climate in which a critical and creative research attitude has always been wholeheartedly supported. In this sense the department has been somewhat of an oasis within the Military Academy. Some members of the Social Science Department particularly helped me by critically reviewing (parts of) this thesis or by providing me the opportunity to discus certain controversial issues: Rudy Richardson, Frans Ramakers, Jolanda Bosch, Axel Rosendahl Huber, Erna Rijsdijk and Nancy Peters.

Fifth, I would like to thank a number of people who made an important contribution outside the realms I have mentioned previously: Georgia Zara who commented on early drafts of a couple of chapters, Jeroen Jansz who advised me in the early stages of this thesis, Anniek van Bemmelen who made an invaluable contribution to the improvement of my English, Yorrick van der Voort van der Kleij who produced some photo-shop pictures.

Finally, I want to thank my family and friends who always lovingly stimulated me during the entire process, if only by commenting in characteristic fashion ('are you *still* not ready?'; 'will I live to see the finishing of this?').

Table of Contents

PART III
Analytical framework:

PART IV

PART V

Introduction

Asserting that military organizations need to operate in complex environments is one of the least controversial statements one can make in the realm of military studies. In fact, it is a truism that military organizations need to operate in difficult circumstances. During their deployment, armies are confronted with dangers, cunning enemies, unexpected changes, and a general level of uncertainty. The obvious implication is that armies need to be able to deal with complexity, or *dynamic complexity* as it will be labeled in this study.

Not surprisingly, the general theme of the turbulence and chaos of war is important in military literature, although the actual phrase 'dynamic complexity' is never used. For example, Von Clausewitz (1968, p. 162) remarked: 'Great part of the information obtained in War is contradictory, a still greater part is false and by far the greatest part is of doubtful character.' Von Clausewitz (1968, p. 140) stated furthermore that: 'From this uncertainty of all intelligence and suppositions, this continual interposition of chance, the actor in War constantly finds things different from his expectations; and this cannot fail to have an influence on his plans, or at least on the presumptions connected with these plans. If this influence is so great as to render the predetermined plan completely nugatory, then, as a rule, a new one must be substituted in its place; but at the moment the necessary data are often wanting for this, because in the course of action circumstances press for immediate decision, and allow no time to look for fresh data, often not enough for mature consideration'.

In these quotations Von Clausewitz emphasizes the effects of chaos on the *individual* actor. However, he also recognized the *organzing* problems with which military organizations are confronted as a result of dynamic complexity (1968, p. 165): 'Theoretically all sounds very well: the commander of a battalion is responsible for the execution of the order given; and as the battalion by its discipline is glued together into one piece. (…) But it is not so in reality, and all that is exaggerated and false in such a conception manifests itself at once in War.' Von Clausewitz referred to this phenomenon as *friction* (1968, p. 168): 'This enormous friction, which is not concentrated, as in mechanics, at a few points, is therefore everywhere brought into contact with chance, and thus incidents take place upon which it was impossible to calculate, their chief origin being chance.' These quotes show that already in the 19th Century military thinkers grappled with subjects that are currently of the highest importance in organizational studies.

This study focuses on the *organizing* problems that result from the problem of dealing with dynamic complexity. However, the focus is not on conventional military operations. This study will use the concept of dynamic complexity to focus on a new type of military operations: Military Operations Other Than War, or peace operations[1]. In recent years the Dutch Armed Forces, for example, have been involved in more than 25 peacekeeping operations, peace-enforcing operations, humanitarian operations, or UN-monitor functions (Klep & Van Gils, 1999). In fact, in the last decade the Army has continuously been involved in such operations. Because of the sheer number of such operations and the number of units involved in those operations, peace operations constitute an important part of the daily business of the Dutch Armed Forces. In fact, The Ministry of Defence indicated that peace support operations are to be considered the core business of the Dutch Armed Forces (Ministerie van Defensie, 2000). One can imagine that all this constitutes a significant transformation for the Army.

The introduction will briefly touch upon the main themes in this study. The staging of central themes in this study already hints at the main conceptual positions taken by this study, although the different themes are more thoroughly worked out in the chapters. The introduction should enable the reader to grasp the complicated structure of this study. Subsequently, the following topics will be discussed:

- The central issues of this study;
- The concept dynamic complexity;
- The experiences of military organizations in dealing with dynamic complexity;
- The similarities and differences between peace operations and conventional military operations;
- The main thereotical position of this study, summarized by the statement 'organizing doubt';
- The methodological approach used in this study.

Finally, an overview will be given of the structure of this study.

Central issues

At first, this study will argue that in peace operations the Army needs to be able to deal with a dynamically complex environment. For this reason, this study will perform a theoretical exploration of useful ways of thinking about dynamic complexity are explored. The theoretical exploration carried out in this study will address theoretical questions like:

- What is meant by dynamic complexity and what is dealing with dynamic complexity?

---

[1] The phrases 'peace operations' and 'crisis operations' are used interchangeably in this study.

- How can operators deal with dynamic complexity in the best possible way?
- How can an organization organize its ability to deal with dynamic complexity?

Second, the Army's ability to deal with a dynamically complex environment in peace operations will be analyzed. The theoretical exploration is used to support an analysis of three existing exploratory case studies of Dutch Army units operating in Bosnia. These case studies show that Army units deployed in Bosnia in different periods did confront dynamic complexity and did find ways to deal with dynamic complexity. The analysis of the experiences in the case studies will explore the capabilities of the units in the cases to deal with dynamic complexity. Finally, on the basis of this analysis it will be attempted to develop insight into the ability of the Army to deploy units that are able to deal with dynamic complexity.

The concept of dynamic complexity

Within organizational studies, dynamic complexity is regarded as one of the most fundamental problems organizations are confronted with. This is of small wonder as dynamic complexity represents the very antithesis of organizing. Organizing refers to forgetting and reducing variety (Weick & Westley, 1996), in other words to developing control and order within a system. On the other hand, manifestations of dynamic complexity (for example uncertainty, ambiguity, equivocality, see Weick, 1995) threaten existing forces of 'order'. Not incidentally, organizing and dynamic complexity are often defined in reference to each other. In a sense, therefore, *organizing* and *dynamic complexity* refer to Nietzsche's Apollonian and Dionysian forces, i.e. the forces of order and disorder, which are active in and upon organizations.

At this place I want to roughly define the problem of dealing with dynamic complexity by delineating its abstract structure. This definition will be extensively discussed in Part Three. Dynamic complexity refers to a *problematic environment* that organizations are confronted with. Its *indeterminate nature* is the environment's main problematic characteristic. The organization's environment is not an object with an underlying 'true' and 'fixed' structure that can be revealed by analysis. At the same time, however, the environment confronts the organization with a *necessity to act*. The environment is not a mere object for observation but the area in which the organization should accomplish its goals. The organization cannot postpone action and devote itself to abstract theorizing about the problematic environment until it is absolutely certain. To be more precise, the environment becomes problematic because of the necessity to act. The organization cannot ignore the indeterminate environment; somehow it needs to deal with it. Subsequently, the 'problem of construction' arises. *The organization needs to find out 'what is going on'* in order to be able to deal with the problems it is confronted with. In the rest of this study organizing activities and 'dealing with dynamic complexity' are considered to be synonymous. All in all, dynamic complexity confronts an organization with a control problem.

Quite deliberately the elementary problem for organizations is named *dynamic* complexity. Senge (1992, p. 71) distinguished between *detail* complexity and *dynamic* complexity. Detail complexity is complexity constituted by many variables. Dynamic complexity refers to situations in which 'cause and effect are subtle, and where the effects over time of interventions are not obvious'. In other words, mathematical problems can be complex but these are problems for which there is only one correct solution. The complexity of mathematical problems belongs therefore to the *detail* kind. When the solution is found, the problem is solved. The particular kind of complexity this study is interested in continues to exist after a – for the moment – workable solution has been found (Weick, 1979).

Experiences of military organizations with the challenges of dynamic complexity

Throughout history, military organizations have tried to find solutions for the problem of dealing with dynamic complexity. It will be of no surprise that there are examples of armies that have been rather successful and armies that have been unsuccessful at dealing with dynamic complexity. A typical reaction to the threats of dynamic complexity is the tendency of aiming to transform all uncertainties into certainties by trying to develop perfect systems of planning, perfect ways of data-gathering, perfect ways of monitoring and controlling troops, etc.[2].

Experience has taught us that strategies that rely on a totalitarian transformation of all uncertainties into certainties tend to be short-lived when confronted with the first un-planned uncertainties. World War I has arguably shown the most penetrating examples of the perverse nature and potentially devastating effects of this strategy (Van Creveld, 1985). Although the aim to transform uncertainties into certainties is in a certain sense understandable it ignores the fact that dynamic complexity is considered a *fundamental* problem for organizations that are challenged by the chaos of war. Fundamental means that it provides a problem that *in principle* cannot be overcome, although organizations can be prepared for it in better and worse ways.

Apart from many bad examples there are examples of armies that have been rather successful at developing practical solutions for dealing with dynamic complexity. Van Creveld (1985, p. 270) also recognized the problem

---

[2] Cohen & Gooch (1990) make clear that it is more fruitful to view these problems from an organizational perspective, than from the perspective of individual psychopathology.

dynamic complexity confronts military organizations with and pointed to an important implication: 'The fact that, historically speaking, those armies have been most successful which did not turn their troops into automatons, did not control anything from the top, and allowed subordinate commanders considerable latitude has been abundantly demonstrated'. The example that has particularly captured the mind of both military commanders and military scientists is – perhaps surprisingly – the German Army in World War II. They applied a system of command that was later labeled *Auftragstaktik*. The system of Auftragstaktik, which was developed and applied by the German armed forces during World War II, although the first experiments had already been conducted in World War I, or even earlier (Wilson, 1989; Nelsen, 1992; Van Creveld, 1985; Naveh, 1997). Autragstaktik can be considered a system of decentralization *avant la lettre*.

This system of command proved to be very effective during the early years of World War II. The chaotic and unpredictable nature of situations during war was taken as a point of departure. It was reasoned that because of this level of uncertainty not every action at the operational level could be prescribed. Rather, units at the operational level were considered to be the ones that were most aware of all recent developments and consequently in the best position to decide how to act. In this respect this system of command implies autonomy at the operational level. Top-down there were only rough guidelines formulated, i.e. objectives to be met, the deployment of a unit in its wider context, and units were supplied with adequate means to accomplish the goal (see for example Vogelaar & Kramer, 1997; Kramer & Kuipers, 2002). Within this framework of general rules, units were supposed to perform their *Auftrags* or Missions. Many contemporary Western armies developed systems of command that are based on the essentials of *Auftragstaktik*, usually under the name of Mission Command. The advantages and disadvantages of different ways operationalizing the essential ideas of *Auftragstaktik* are permanently discussed within the realm of military sciences (see for example Vogelaar & Kramer, 2004).

What I perceive as lacking in most accounts of Mission Command is a clear link to organizational theory. Although the historical experiments with decentralization in military organizations are certainly very interesting, the theoretical underpinning of the system rarely goes beyond: 'because of chaos, you should grant operational units autonomy by providing broad assignments and rough guidelines instead of detailed orders.' In this study I want to approach this subject the other way around, so to speak. The starting point is organizational theory in general and the issue of dealing with dynamic complexity in particular.

Peace operations and conventional military operations

Quite obviously, the actual everyday challenges of military units in peace operations are quite different from the challenges of conventional military operations. In these respective operations, the tasks and environment of military units are very different. Already in 1976 Moskos has described the main differences between conventional operations and peace operations (1976, pp. 130–131) 'In contrast with standard armed forces, the constabulary and peace soldier are concerned with the attainment of viable political compromises rather than with the resolution of conflict through force'. This difference between roles can lead to particular problems for soldiers[3]. They are conceptualized as *identity* problems by Franke (2003). To clarify this problem of identity he quotes Winslow for example who claims (1997, p. 210): 'because civilized military training incorporates into its standards the notion that it is permissible to kill certain people but not others, feelings of ambivalence are likely to result among combat troops when faced with their ROE (rules of engagement, ehk). This ambivalence may create an environment within which concepts of morality and legality become abstract, subject to varying situational definitions.' One could say that compared to conventional military operations there is a distinctive 'political' side to the operational tasks in peace operations. In the last decades the differences between peace operations and conventional military operations have been intensely discussed (Britt & Adler, 2003).

Although there are obvious differences between conventional military operations and peace operations it is not accidental that military organizations are supposed to perform these missions. One could say that peace operations most of the time involve some kind of danger. It might be that units are supposed to protect a part of a civilian population, or are to enforce a peace treaty, or there might be a certain threat of escalation in a certain area. Notwithstanding the differences between conventional military operations and peace operations, the problem of dealing with dynamic complexity can be considered manifest in both types of operations. Although the specific problems military units are confronted with may be different, both in peace operations and in conventional military operations, military units can be said to be confronted with a problematic environment, with a necessity to act and have to find out what is going on. This is also recognized by Britt & Adler (2003, p. 3): 'These international peacekeepers must often do their job in a chaotic and uncertain environment.' One could say that dynamic complexity in peace operations manifests itself in different ways compared to conventional military operations. In other words, although there are obvious differences between conventional military operations and peace operations, *the organizing challenge can be considered quite comparable.* For an

---

[3] See also Avant & Lebovic (2000); Miller (1997); Segal & Tiggle (1997).

15

organization like the Army it is sensible to assume that it will encounter dynamic complexity. Therefore it is sensible for the Army to organize units they deploy in such a way that they can meet the challenges resulting from dynamic complexity in their operations. This challenge is at the center of attention in this study.

The methodological approach

The methodological approach used in the research project is an example of the 'grounded theory' framework (Glaser & Strauss, 1967). In 1968, the grounded theory approach (GT-approach) was introduced as a type of qualitative research to 'uncover and understand what lies behind phenomenon about which little is known' (Strauss and Corbin, 1990, p. 19). After 1968, many publications about this approach have addressed its underlying and operational logic and, most of all, its (differences in) procedures (Glaser and Strauss, 1967; Glaser, 1978; Glaser, 1992; Straus and Corbin, 1990; Wester and Peters, 2004). The methodological logic of this study resembles the logic of the grounded theory approach.

The grounded theory approach is appropriate for this study for several reasons. To start with, the existing exploratory case studies that this study analyses were conducted in order to develop insight into the everyday problems of operational units during peace operations. At the time the case studies were developed, peace operations were a relatively new phenomenon, so little was known about these everyday problems. This study can be said to take up issues that were generated by the case studies. One of the issues that emerged from the case studies was indeed the problem of dealing with dynamic complexity. Further insight into this problem appeared to be relevant given the problems the operational units in the case studies experienced.

An issue that followed from this was the question of the particular way in which organizational characteristics stimulated or hindered dealing with dynamic complexity at the operational level. All in all, an analysis of existing case studies, combined with an analysis of 'stable' characteristics of the mother-organization will add up to insights into the ability of the Army to deploy units that are able to deal with dynamic complexity. The result of the reflection is a substantive theory, which is a theory that is specific to the field of study (Strauss & Corbin, 1998, p. 23). Substantive theory is to be distinguished from formal theory. Compared to substantive theory, formal theory is less specific to a group and place and therefore more generally applicable (Strauss & Corbin, 1998, p. 23). Formal theory refers to the 'existing theoretical insights'.

Organizing Doubt

As has been emphasized, formal theory about dynamic complexity is not explored for its own sake in this study. Formal is used in order to facilitate the process of developing a substantive theory. Nevertheless, the development of an analytical framework is one of the main activities in this study. An analytical framework is a construction of theoretical ingredients to tackle specific questions. It is not merely assembled to conduct interesting theoretical explorations. Generally speaking, the analytical framework of this study will be built up of theoretical ingredients that specify what the nature is of dynamic complexity, of dealing with dynamic complexity and of dealing with dynamic complexity in the best possible way. That means that this study is orientated to a normative question.

Although the analytical framework is constructed from existing formal theory, in certain respects this study interprets this existing theory in a specific way. Starting from systems theory as a macro-theoretical framework, the problem of dealing with dynamic complexity is developed using the organizing model of Karl Weick which he described in *The Social Psychology of Organizing* (1979). According to the interpretation in this study, a 'logic of hypotheses' is central in this model: systems deal with the demands of a dynamically complex environment by *acting* to deal with immediate challenges and subsequently by developing 'workable' hypotheses aboutthe nature of the environment. The model essentially describes the process of developing *and discrediting* these 'workable' hypotheses. Because this study is orientated to normative issues, the model is analyzed for its normative aspects. It will be argued that 'doubt' occupies a normative role in this model. This is an interpretation that is not made explicitly by Weick himself. The importance of doubt can be made clear by means of the following deceptively simple statement: 'if the environment is dynamically complex it is impossible to know and understand everything in advance, therefore you need to be able to doubt your existing insights.'

'Doubt' is described here as an abstract function necessary for dealing with dynamic complexity. The ideas of social psychologist Michael Billig on *argumentation* as he formulated them in *Arguing and Thinking* (1996) are used to characterize the nature of the process that is behind the abstract function. It is concluded that if organizations want to organize doubt, they need to develop a process of *meaningful* argumentation. The emphasis on *meaningful* argumentation as opposed to argumentation in general implies in this study that the organizational context in which argumentation is taking place can have a profound influence on the process of argumentation. A subsequent deceptively simple statement follows therefore: 'if the ability to doubt is of crucial importance for organizations dealing with dynamic complexity, organizations need to organize their ability to doubt'. It will be argued that – what Michael Billig calls – a spirit of contradiction should be 'organized' within an organizational system that is confronted with dynamic complexity.

The two deceptively simple statements constitute the rationale for the title of this book: organizing doubt. In order to establish whether doubt was organized in the operational units in the cases, the organizational structure of these and the style of leadership that was employed will be analyzed. Subsequently, the limitations on the organization of doubt that result from the characteristics of the mother organization (which provides the prerequisites for the deployed crisis organization, i.e. the Army in the Netherlands) will be analyzed. All in all, it will be concluded that certain structural (meaning 'stable') characteristics of the mother-organization have a negative influence on 'doubt'. It is not implied that it is absolutely impossible that a process of meaningful argumentation can be established in the operational units of crisis organizations. It implies that the chances for such a process are negatively influenced by certain stable characteristics of the Army. One of the conclusions will be that these stable characteristics make the development of successful systems of decentralization, such as Mission Command, rather problematic.

The different parts of this study

In a sense it is ironic that this study advices a military organization to organize doubt. An organization that has the image of strict orderliness, tight planning and obeying orders to the letter is advised to build in forces of disorder, so to speak. It is furthermore advised to locate this ability at the very front of the operations not in some shady staff bureau. As such, this study challenges what are often considered as obvious truths in the military organization. Personally, I have considered this to be a goal in itself.

This study consists of six parts, which each consist of a couple of chapters. Part One discusses the architecture of this study in detail. Furthermore, the relevant methodological aspects of this study are dealt with. Part Two is orientated to the development of the abstract parts of the analytical framework. The macro theoretical framework is discussed, the process of dealing with dynamic complexity is modeled and the normative element in this model is identified and discussed. Part Three is orientated to the development of the concrete parts of the analytical framework. The necessary conceptual tools are discussed which will be used to analyze the cases. In Part Four the existing exploratory case studies are analyzed. Part Five will discuss the influence of some characteristics of the mother organization on the organization of doubt. Part Six is the final part and summarizes the most important conclusions and discusses directions for further research. To facilitate reading, only the male pronouns 'he' and 'his' are used throughout this study. They do, however, refer equivalently to 'she' and 'her', respectively.

PART I
The architecture of this study

Part One consists of two chapters and is dedicated to the architecture of this study. Chapter One discusses the background and goal of this study and the central questions. Chapter Two discusses the crucial methodological questions.

Chapter 1

The architecture of this study

In this chapter, the architecture of this study is discussed. To start with, the background from which this study started is discussed, followed by an exploration of this study's central problem. Subsequently, the goal of this study and the specific research questions are formulated. The next chapter will go into the details of the methodological characteristics of this study.

1.1 The background

In 1995 a research project was started at the Military Academy entitled *Leiderschap in Crisisomstandigheden* (Leadership in Circumstances of Crisis). The project started with the involvement of the Dutch Armed Forces in former Yugoslavia in operations before and after the Dayton Peace Agreements in 1995 as part of a UNPROFOR and NATO intervention. Involvement in such operations was, partly, the result of a change in military strategy in the Netherlands from a 'cold war military strategy' to 'modern military action' as a consequence of the East-West détente in 1990. These operations will be referred to as peace operations. Peace operations involve the range of military operations under United Nations or NATO responsibilities in certain regions in the world like: conflict prevention, humanitarian actions, peace-keeping, peace-building, peace-restoring, and peace-enforcement. The project was induced by the then relatively new phenomenon of peace operations and the fact that the Military Academy trains cadets who may become involved in such operations. The main goal of the research project was to develop insight into the experiences of Dutch units working in peace operations. The results of the research project were (and are) worked out in various publications and used in the officers' education.

This study is part of the research project. It can clearly be distinguished from other projects within the research project and this study is located in a different methodological phase compared to the rest of the projects within the research project. This can be clarified by distinguishing between different phases in the Grounded Theory process. Wester (1993) argued that the 'grounded theory process' can be split up into four phases: the exploration phase, the specification phase, the reduction phase and the integration phase:

- The *exploration phase* aims at becoming acquainted with the field of study, and at the development of an analytical framework (Wester, 1993, p. 56). The research project started with two exploratory case studies. The goal of these case studies was to develop insight into the nature of the experiences of the soldiers that had been deployed in peace support operations. As such they provide a picture of the everyday life of military units at the lowest hierarchical levels.
- The *specification phase* is more aimed at analysis of material than at gathering material (Wester, 1993, p. 63). After the analytical framework had been developed, the material was subsequently analyzed using this framework ('selective coding'). The framework consisted of categories of 'problem situations' junior leaders engaged. The categories were worked out by discussing the ins and outs of the 'problem situations' and the different ways in which the junior leaders handled them.
- In the *reduction phase*, the emphasis is on explicating the core of the grounded theory that is being developed (Wester, 1993, p. 64). In the grounded theory approach, such theory is called 'substantive theory' because it is orientated to the field of study (i.e. theory on military units in crisis operations). The core of the grounded theory is represented by what is called a core concept. Identifying and developing such a core concept is the main activity in the reduction phase (Wester, 1993, pp. 63–69). The *core concept* is a concept that characterizes a central process in the field of study (Wester, 1993, p. 64).
- In the *integration phase*, the core concept is used to develop a theory about the field of study (Wester, 1993, p. 69). In the grounded theory approach, such theory is called 'substantive theory' because it is orientated to the field of study (i.e. theory on military units in crisis operations). Substantive theory should be distinguished from formal theory, which is orientated to a general subject (for example, theory on organizational structuring) (Strauss & Corbin, 1998).

It will be argued that the most important other activities in the research project are located in the first two steps: the exploration and the specification phase. This study focuses on the last two steps: the reduction phase and the integration phase. One can also say that this study works out specific issues that have emerged after the first steps of the research project.

1.2 The starting point of this study

The exploratory case studies have a value in themselves because of the general picture they drew of everyday life during a crisis operation. However, the case studies were inherently limited. Although the experiences were categorized into groups of typical problems that junior leaders experienced, and some attempts at theoretical reflection were made, the emphasis of the case studies was on recording experiences. **Since recording experiences was the main emphasis of the case studies, the researchers mainly 'listened' to the stories of interviewees, but did not 'react' (or 'talk back').** That is to say, the researchers described the experiences of the interviewees in cleverly constructed categories, but they did little more than superficially reflect on the experiences. They did not systematically use theoretical knowledge to put the experiences into perspective. This limitation of the case studies is inherent in their being exploratory case studies and should not be seen as criticism on the case studies. Nevertheless, the first motivation for this study was to do more than listening and recording experiences. In other words, this study progressed to the reduction and integration phase of the grounded theory approach.

Due to their exploratory nature, the case studies provided broad insight into the everyday affairs at the operational level. Therefore, the cases provided many possible topics for reflection. The operational units were confronted with stress, different cultures, danger, international cooperation, a worried home front, accidents, etc. As such, the cases provided various possible perspectives for further analysis. In this study, dynamic complexity will be identified as a core concept that fits the experiences in the cases ('emergent fit').

1.3 The relevance of the core concept

In introduction the centrality of the problem of dealing with dynamic complexity in organization studies was discussed. This study was induced by the apparent relevance of this topic. This section is orientated to arguing why 'dynamic complexity' is considered to be a relevant core concept. It will be discussed why this core concept has been chosen in the reduction phase. Subsequently, the implications of using this core concept in this study will be discussed. After these steps will have been taken, the design of this study will be explicated.

The problems of operational units in the cases

Notwithstanding the general acknowledgement of the importance of the issue of dealing with dynamic complexity in organization theory, it is important to see how it manifests itself during peace operations, in order to illustrate why it was chosen as a core concept. In this section, specific practical problems experienced by operational units will be interpreted as problems of dealing with dynamic complexity. The case studies discuss everyday practical problems of leaders and how they were dealt with. It is argued here that the problem of dealing with dynamic complexity can be recognized in the case descriptions. For example, the convoys of Logtbat were confronted with dangerous situations such as shootings. Necessarily they were confronted with questions such as:

- When will the shootings occur again?
- Were they really directed at us?
- Why are the shootings taking place?
- What must we do when we are confronted with shootings?

When such everyday practical questions are asked, units are dealing with the indeterminate nature of the environment, the problem of (re)construction of this environment and the organizational issue of dealing with these problems. Furthermore, the answers to these questions are no eternal truths nor are they ultimately objective. Rather, they are based on everyday ideas and everyday structures that units recognize in their environments. It should be emphasized that not all practical problems involve dealing with dynamic complexity. Some practical problems can be dealt with on the basis of rules. The life of operational units would – after all – become pretty difficult if every practical problem involved dealing with dynamic complexity, and reality would have to be re-invented in every step they would take. Nevertheless, it is argued here that the most important and the most difficult, and therefore the most interesting, practical problems involve dealing with dynamic complexity.

If one asks people about their experiences in these operations, they are not likely to answer that they experienced difficulties with the ambiguity of the environment and the subsequent problem of the construction of reality. Nor are they likely to answer that they experienced their neutral role as paradoxical or that they had trouble with questions regarding the objectivity of minefields. Besides, people can become annoyed if one claims that their ideas are mere constructions ('If I step on a mine I will die, I did not imagine that!') or indeed if one claims that the environment is the construction of the organization itself ('I did not plant the mines myself!'). People are, of course, quite right to become annoyed if their experiences are branded constructions in such a primitive way. They are certainly not mere constructions because, as this example shows, the lives of the members of the units may depend on it. Below, a number of practical problems of operational units and how they were dealt with will be discussed. It is attempted to recognize the abstract behind the concrete[4].

(Potential) danger

Military units are often deployed in dangerous areas. Actually, the reason that military units are deployed is precisely because the situations are dan-

---

[4] The examples originate from the two earliest case studies that were conducted within the research project.

gerous and not very stable or certain. If a situation is safe other types of organizations could also be deployed. In the exploratory case studies it was found that operational units often had to deal with shootings, mines, and an aggressive local population. What makes a situation even more uncertain is that dangerous incidents can potentially occur at any time. Potential danger is, therefore, a continuous stressor for operational units.

Unforeseen situations

The situations military units are deployed in are mostly very unstable. As with (potential) danger: the reason why military units are deployed in certain areas is the instability in these areas. For operational units this means that they have difficulty to understand the complexity of a conflict and therefore the complexity of the situation they engage in. The convoys of Logtbat in the UNPROFOR period can be used as an example of the problem of unpredictability. It was their job to transport goods from one point to another. While doing this, they saw quite a large part of the Bosnian area. What they did not expect and at first did not understand was that in one part of the area the Muslim and Croatian population were at war against each other, while in another part the Muslim and Croatian population teamed up against the Serb population. There are further examples. Logistic units in Bosnia, for example, had problems with roadblocks, shootings, mine incidents, everyday accidents like cars skidding of the road, sometimes witnessed atrocities, and saw the deplorable living conditions of the local population, but they also witnessed many people who did not seem to be in need at all. When a unit went on a convoy or on patrol, it did not know what situations it would encounter. The preparation of units is also a problem, because the complexity of the conflicts is often poorly understood beforehand. It is generally difficult to prepare units for a situation that is unpredictable and changes continuously. Sometimes operational units are even pioneers in an area, and thus the first witnesses of change.

The problematic neutral position

In some way, life in 'normal wars' is at least clear because there is an identifiable enemy. In peace-supporting operations, however, units are often deployed as a neutral, third party. This neutral position is more straightforward on paper as it is in the everyday experience of units. Suppose the units of the crisis organization are shot at. It can be far from straightforward how units should deal with such situations. Rules of engagement tell them not to shoot back immediately, but instead to wait and see (Was the shooting 'really' aimed at us? Was it a 'shooting' or a 'firing close'?). How they are supposed to act depends on the exact formulation of the Rules of Engagement (ROE) in a certain operation, but most often it means that they must act counterintuitively ('wait and see') when they are shot at. Such rules make that soldiers have to think 'politically', which is something they have not been extensively trained for. A further complication is that although there are often extensive ROEs, but there still remains substantial room for interpretation (Kroon, Heesakkers, Jacobs, Van der Veer, 1997). Another problem of neutrality is that the different parties in the conflict can potentially misuse the neutral position of units. Patrols of Dutchbat were sometimes shot at by the Muslim population who they were supposed to disarm and defend. The Muslim population, however, wanted to make it look like the Serbs were the ones that were doing the shooting. This game of 'pretending to be the other' was also played by the Serbs. One can imagine the frustration of units that are shot at by both parties in a conflict without being able to respond (apparently due to restrictive ROE), and without being able to fully understand the political games behind the incidents. Fighting parties sometimes try to use the neutral element in the environment as a cover to surprise the opposing force. There have been occasions in which military units used the passing of the Logtbat convoys to change positions.

No consistent effects of operations

Dutch logistic units sometimes had to deal with a hostile local population at roadblocks. Sometimes it was helpful to approach them informally, starting with a light conversation about the weather or something like that. This could also have an adverse effect if it caused the locals to take the Dutch soldiers no longer seriously. Sometimes it was therefore helpful to approach them formally, asking for an equal in rank at the roadblock to negotiate on the situation. This, however, could have the effect of the locals finding the Dutch too arrogant (which was the theory of the Dutch units themselves). Contrastive lessons were learned from this situation. On the one hand 'locals only have respect for formal authority', and on the other hand 'it is important to be able to communicate with locals on a fair and friendly level'. Surprisingly, the same respondent could sometimes defend both rules[5]. This is an example of the response uncertainty of operational units. One could believe that this is only a temporary discomfort: after getting used to the specifics of their situation, units will learn how to deal with their problems. However, the nature of experiential knowledge is not that it provides simple rules to deal with every situation. On the contrary, the importance of experi-

---

[5] This is one reason why an orientation on drawing lessons on the level of concrete behavior is not very useful for Army research institutes. Studies that aim to draw general lessons regarding "the approach of a roadblock" run the risk that they become too much entangled in the specifics of a given operation. The specifics of operations differ so much that lessons on that level are difficult to generalize to other operations. Another possibility is that lessons become so general that they become rather too obvious ("stay alert!").

26

ential knowledge is probably that it teaches that there are no simple rules to deal with every problem.

A dispersed way of operating

Characteristic of peace operations is that crisis organizations have a role as third party in a conflict. For operational units in the cases, this meant that they needed to be present in the area, which implied that they had to operate relatively dispersed. This way of operating had many consequences for the way units had to deal with dynamic complexity. For example, the superior officers were often not present at the scene of action when operational units went on patrol or on a convoy. This meant that on-scene commanders had great responsibility both for safety of the units as for the goods. In the Logtbat case on-scene commanders had to deal with all kinds of problems themselves, without being able to ask a superior what to do. Interestingly, and a point that will be worked out later in this study, superior officers did try to control the behavior of operational units when the situation in Bosnia had stabilized significantly. Due to the calmer circumstances and the improved means of communication they had better abilities to do so in this operation.

The foregoing will have made it clear that dealing with dynamic complexity is a problem that can – quite easily – be observed in the everyday experiences in the cases. It was certainly recognizable that, on the one hand, units struggled to determine the nature of the environment and the meaning of events, and on the other hand struggled to determine what to do. The practical problems **reveal the abstract structure of dealing with dynamic complexity**. On the basis of this observation it is assumed that peace operations are operations in which military units can be confronted with dynamic complexity. Therefore, I conclude that dynamic complexity is a relevant core concept. It follows that these military units need to be able to deal with dynamic complexity[6].

1.4 The implications of choosing 'dynamic complexity' as a core concept

The previous section has made it clear that 'dynamic complexity' can be recognized as a central theme in the experience of operational units and can therefore be used as a core concept in this study. This choice repre-

---

[6] The following note should be added to this line of reasoning: the importance of the problem of dealing with dynamic complexity is not only deduced from the case material, it is known from theory as well. If the problem of dealing with dynamic complexity might not have been visible in the case studies, this theoretical knowledge would have been a sufficient reason to justify the choice for dynamic complexity as a core concept.

sents the *reduction phase* of the development of a grounded theory and it is the starting point for this study. However, before the goal and central questions of this study can be presented, this section needs to address two crucial issues. What are the implications of stating that dynamic complexity is a central theme? In other words, if one states that dynamic complexity is a central theme, what does that mean for the units that are (to be) engaged in this situation? What are the implications for this study? After clarifying the consequences of taking dynamic complexity as a core concept, the central issues at stake in this study can be identified.

The implications of choosing dynamic complexity as a core concept

In order to pinpoint the implications of using dynamic complexity as a core concept, attention should be paid to a particular aspect of the presented abstract structure of this problem. If units are confronted with dynamic complexity, they are confronted with problems for which no clear-cut rules or procedures are available. That is to say, there are no rules available that make the problem of dealing with dynamic complexity a matter of mere rule-following. The essential nature of the problem of dynamic complexity is that such rules and procedures are in principle not available.

Due to the nature of dynamic complexity, operational units cannot be told in advance how to deal with every single problem. Furthermore, a central commander removed from the scene of action, lacks the insight into the local circumstances in order to make direct supervision a likely option. He depends on the operational unit for a description of the situation (which is inevitably colored by interpretation). Also, if such a central commander does formulate an order, the implementation of this order is still something that inevitably requires interpretation on the side of the operational unit. Different kinds of rules help to create a *workable level of certainty* (Weick, 1979). However, due to the elementary nature of dynamic complexity, rules cannot transform all uncertainties into certainties[7]. This implies that it is impossible to design a rule system that makes dealing with dynamic complexity a job of mere rule-following. If the activities of operational units could be totally submitted to a set of rules, then indeed there would be a perfect science of dealing with dynamic complexity. The consequence of this is that dealing with dynamic complexity necessitates *thinking* instead of rule-following (see for a justification for this distinction, Billig, 1996).

---

[7] Shalit (1988, p. 147) formulated this dilemma as follows: 'The more confusing the situation, the greater our dependence on predetermined patterns of behavior. However, the greater our dependence on prelearned and unquestioningly accepted routines, the greater the danger that we will be unable to adapt to unexpected conditions that do not fit our routines. What is gained in terms of coherence of perception may be lost in terms of incongruence of response.'

The consequences for this study: the issue of design

Because of the nature of dynamic complexity, operational units possess a particular degree of 'natural' autonomy. Autonomy is defined here as 'freedom that exists to deal with problems'[8]. This definition indicates that a system possesses a certain degree of freedom in reacting to the environment[9]. Consequently, both the crisis organization and the mother organization do not have absolute control over the operational units. This is a statement of logical necessity: if the environment is dynamically complex, then the organizational context does not have absolute control[10]. As a consequence, the Army as an actor in such environments is confronted with different problems: (1) the operators in the operational units are confronted with the need to act meaningfully (one certainly does not want them to act randomly). Meaningful action refers to the fact that units need to be able to react sensibly to the challenges of their environment without there being a set of prescriptive rules that can be applied straightforwardly; (2) the larger crisis organization is confronted with the problem that they need to design and control units that are confronted with such an environment; (3) the mother organization is presented with the problem that it needs to be able to design crisis organizations and operational units that can deal with such environments. If the Army engages in circumstances in which it cannot control its operational units in an absolute way, it should design units that can deal with this natural autonomy in a sensible way. This is a normative stance: if the environment necessitates thinking, then operators should be able to think.

---

[8] It should be added that in particular ways the autonomy of operational units is limited. In important ways, operational units are dependent upon the organizational context. One could say that operational units also possess a 'natural lack of autonomy' because they are part of a larger organization and because this larger organization is performing a complex operation. Although the autonomy of operational units is limited it is inevitable, as a consequence of the nature of dynamic complexity. This has important consequences for the position of operational units and their necessary competences. Therefore De Sitter (2000) would call them 'semi-autonomous'.

[9] De Sitter (2000, p. 72) stated that autonomy of a system refers to the issue that "an external influence can eventually cause a local change in the internal structure of system x, but that the nature of the resulting [change] (...) is also determined by something 'typical' in the internal structure of the system itself" (my translation).

[10] This argument shows how the organizational context can regain control over operational units: it can turn down its level of ambition. However, it is assumed here that this option is in principle impossible for an organization as the Army, since this organization is made for difficult circumstances.

At this stage I want to introduce a concept that will become important in the rest of this study, namely the concept of self-organization[11]. In this study, self-organization is understood in its abstract sense: because of the nature of dynamic complexity, operational units have to perform these organizing activities themselves. In a literal sense they are therefore self-organizing[12]. The Army should be concerned with creating operational units that are able to deal with dynamic complexity in the best possible way[13]. In light of the previous discussion this claim means that the Army should be concerned with designing operational units with capabilities for self-organization[14]. This is an issue of design: the Army should equip the units in a particular way in order to enhance their capabilities of self-organization. It is supposed that this design issue is located at the levels of the crisis organization (which directly designs operational units, f.e. Logtbat) and the mother organization

---

[11] This concept is also popular in the complexity research within the natural sciences. It refers to the phenomena of self-assembly that many systems display in order to adapt to complex environments. In this case, the phrase *systems* is understood in a broader sense. This kind of self-organization refers to emergent order in computer programs (Holland, 1995), biological systems (Kaufmann, 1995), natural systems (Prigogine, 1996), and even piles of sand (Bak, 1999).

[12] The sociotechnical approach uses this concept to describe the crucial qualities of self-managing work groups (Kuipers, 1989a; Kuipers & Van Amelsvoort, 1990; Morgan, 1997). Within sociotechnical literature, self-organization is often understood in a concrete sense. It refers, for example, to planning systems that workgroups can use in order to have a certain amount of grip on the proceedings in their jobs (Kuipers & Van Amelsvoort, 1990).

[13] This seems to contradict the earlier assumptions that were expressed. After all, how can one judge whether a unit dealt with dynamic complexity in the right way if at the same time one claims that it is a problem for which no right solution exists? How can one speak of "the best possible way" if the defining characteristic of the environment is that certainty itself is unavailable? On the more practical side of doing research: how is it possible to criticize the way operational units dealt with practical problems from such a distance? Furthermore, "constructionist" theory frequently is very cautious, if not outright dismissive of normative questions as they appear to import an "objectivist" way of thinking. Notwithstanding the theoretical, practical and methodological prohibitions, it is obvious that the question whether or not units dealt with complexity in the best possible way is very important for the Army. If one claims that "it is impossible to tell", one condemns the organization to apathy regarding this crucial part of its operations. Therefore this question will not be avoided in this study, but rather, the issue will be taken up.

[14] Generally speaking, the essence of the position in this study is that no attempts will be made to criticize the tactics that units used for dealing with practical problems. In other words, no attempts are made to take a normative stance towards the content of this process as they are exhibited in the case studies. Instead, attention is focused on the characteristics of the organizational system that is active in the dynamically complex environment. It will be claimed that although it is impossible to design a closed system of rules for dealing with dynamic complexity, it is possible to develop rules for the design of the organizational system involved.

(the Army in general)[15]. The capability of designing such units marks one of the most crucial qualities of the Army organization as an organization that is serious about performing a certain type of mission. This issue will be taken up in this study and the existing case studies form the basis of the analysis. Since the cases draw a picture of everyday life during peace operations, they also give a picture of the possibilities and limitations operational units experience in dealing with certain problems.

1.5 The goal and central questions of this study

The various exploratory case studies not only show the practical problems that units were confronted with, they also provide information on how these units were organized and show the insights of operational units, but also show what was lacking in that respect. They show what units could decide for themselves, but also when central commanders intervened. To put this into a general statement: the cases provide clues about how the Army organization engages dynamically complex environments. The goal of this study can therefore be formulated as follows:

Developing insight into the ability of the Army to deploy units that are able to deal with dynamic complexity in peace operations. This insight will be developed by:

1. **Analyzing the way in which the design of the operational units in the exploratory cases influenced their ability to deal with dynamic complexity;**
2. **Reconstructing the influence of the mother organization on the design options of crisis organizations.**

The first characteristic of the 'substantive theory in progress' implies that it is attempted to find 'deep structures' in the case descriptions, which means performing a meta-analysis of the case studies. The second characteristic means that the influence of the mother organization on the crisis organization needs to be reconstructed. This implies the gathering of extra data on the characteristics of the mother organization.

The relevance of the study

As this study has an ambitious goal, it is necessary to address the scope of its ambition. There are certain limits inherent in the reflection. The case studies were never meant to provide insight into the self-organizing capabilities of operational units. The emphasis in this study is therefore on *explor-*

---

[15] Later in this study this will be referred to as the *direct* and *indirect design* of operational units, respectively.

ing available case material. In other words, the emphasis is on *finding clues* in the cases about the influence of the design of the operational units on their ability to deal with dynamic complexity, and on *reconstructing* how the mother organization influences crisis organization. One may state that this enterprise is limited by the fact that the cases were never intended to perform such analyses. This study is therefore, one could say, located in the *context of discovery* rather than in the *context of justification* (Kelle, 1995). In other words, this study is not focused on testing hypotheses, but on developing (discovering) *useful hypotheses* about the ability of the Army to deploy units that are able to deal with dynamic complexity. The substantive theory is therefore made up of such hypotheses. The relevance of developing such a substantive theory is that it should support the Army in developing itself as an organization that is involved in crisis operations. The final chapter of this study is therefore devoted to the identification of topics of further research and of topics for the development of the Army as an organization that is involved in peace operations.

Central questions

In order to develop a complicated substantive theory, formal theory is needed. The concept of self-organization needs to be clarified. It needs to be identified what is the nature of dealing with dynamic complexity and how it can be organized in the best possible way. Furthermore, theoretical reflection should explicate how to observe this abstract ability in the case studies. The necessary formal theory needs to be abstract enough to grasp complicated concepts as 'dynamic complexity' and 'self-organization' and concrete enough to be able to apply it to the existing cases. Furthermore, the formal theory needs to be normative because it is explicitly the object to study how the ability to deal with dynamic complexity is influenced by (1) the crisis organization in the cases and (2) the mother organization in general. The formal theory will be gathered by developing an analytical framework. This framework will be built up of existing theoretical insights. All in all, this goal of this study can be achieved by answering the following questions:

Questions referring to the development of an analytical framework:

1. **How can a system deal with dynamic complexity in the best possible way?**
2. **How can the organization of doubt be observed in the cases?**

Questions referring to the analysis of the cases and the mother organization:

1. **How was the problem of dealing with dynamic complexity influenced by the design of the operational units?**

2. **How is the possibility of designing self-organizing units in crisis organizations influenced by characteristics of the mother organization?**

This study consists of six parts. In parts two, three, four, and five, a specific research question will be at center stage.

Conceptual model

The different analyses that are performed in this study can be represented in a conceptual model:

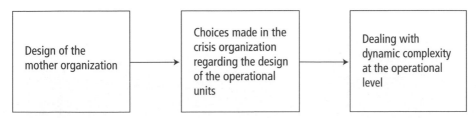

Model 1.1

The conceptual model describes the structure of the substantive theory that will be developed: it should provide insight into how the mother organization *structurally* influences (*all*) crisis organizations. Furthermore, it should provide insight into how the crisis organizations *in the cases* influenced the ability of the operational units to deal with dynamic complexity. As such, it provides insight into how characteristics of the *general* (the Army) influence proceedings in the *local* (the operational units). It should be emphasized that this conceptual model reverses the logic of the various analyses, so to speak. After finding clues in the local (the experiences of the operational units), this study explores how the design of the units influenced these experiences. Subsequently, it is explored how the proceedings in the crisis organizations were influenced by constraints in the mother organizations. In other words, the conceptual model suggests top-down logic, while this study performs a bottom-up analysis. This is a deliberate 'reversal'. For the substantive theory to be relevant beyond the local level, it should be orientated to 'general' mechanisms. Subsequently, the general is relevant so far as it can be defended that it has influence on the local.

Important definitions

At this moment it is necessary to pin down the meaning of a couple of central phrases used in this study. I should emphasize that I formulated these definitions. In this study, a distinction is made between the operational, the tactical, and the strategic level of an organization: the operational level is the level where the actual work is done, the tactical level is the level where

33

the various operational units are designed and controlled, the strategic level is the level where the general direction of the organization is established.

It should be added that this is a conceptual distinction that does not refer to a specific idealized division in hierarchical levels. In an organization events can have operational, tactical, and strategic consequences and therefore operational experiences are extremely relevant for strategic discussions. These definitions differ from military definitions in important ways[16]. Following the distinction in organizational levels, I will use a distinction between operational units, the crisis organization, and the mother organization.

- An operational unit is considered to be a unit at the shop floor. This means that an operational unit is the one that does the actual work (going on patrols, transporting goods, etc.). The operational unit is the part of the organization that is most directly confronted with operational complexity. Therefore, it is the center of attention here. What makes these units particularly interesting is that they are in direct contact with the environment. The problem of dealing with dynamic complexity will be perceived from the perspective of the operational level.

- A crisis organization is an organization that is designed for the purposes of a specific peace operation. As will be discussed in greater detail later in this study, crisis organizations are task forces. Task forces are organizations that are built up from the mother organization for the specific purpose of a particular operation. As such, task forces are temporary organizations. The operational units are a subsystem of this crisis organization and are in many ways the tentacles of the crisis organization in the environment. To clarify this distinction with an example: Dutchbat was a crisis organization; the various platoons of Dutchbat were operational units. It is the crisis organization that designs and controls these units and divides tasks among them. Therefore the crisis organization is the immediate organizational context for the operational units.

- The mother organization refers to the Army in the Netherlands. The Dutch Armed Forces consist of the Navy, the Air Force, the Army and the Military Police. The Army is the part of the organization I am interested in. It is relevant for this study because the crisis organizations in the cases were assembled from the Army. They were designed for the purpose of a specific operation. The mother organization is the remote organizatio-

---

[16] According to the military doctrine, the military strategic level is the level where the systematic deployment of military means of a state is discussed. The operational level is the level where the strategic goals are translated into the design and control of campaigns. The tactical level refers to the deployment of units in order to reach the operational goals. The technical level refers to the deployment of small units and sometimes even individual soldiers (Military Doctrine, 1996, pp. 12–16). What is called "operational" and even "tactical" in this study is called 'technical' in the military doctrine.

nal context for units and supplies the basic building blocks for the crisis organization.

1.6 An overview

The first part focuses on explicating the architecture of this study and on justifying the different methodological steps. The second and third part focus on the theoretical issues of this study. In these parts, the analytical framework will be explicated. The reflections upon the existing cases will be performed in part four. The reflections on the mother organization as a provider of means will be conducted in Part Five. Part Six is not really a part as such because it consists of just one chapter, but it can be logically separated from the previous parts. In this final part, there will be a reflection on the results of the analyses in this study.

Chapter 2

Methodological considerations

This chapter consists of three distinctive parts. The first part discusses relevant methodological aspects of the original case-studies. In the second part, the methodological structure of this study is worked out. This part explicates the various methodological choices and should clarify how they are connected. The third part positions this study's methodological structure. In this part, the methodological position of this study will be dealt with.

2.1 Methodological characteristics of the case studies

This study aims to build a substantive theory upon the foundations of the original exploratory case studies. These cases are part of the exploratory phase and specification phase of the research project. As will be discussed, these cases have certain structural weaknesses for the purposes of analysis. The major structural weakness is that the cases were exploratory and were never designed to be used for the sort of analyses that are made in this study. That means that at certain points some clever reconstruction work needs to be done. Apart from certain structural weaknesses the case studies posses an important structural strength. The cases provide an interesting insight into the everyday experiences of the military units during different peace operations. Multiple member checks confirmed the validity of the picture that emerged from these cases.

Research projects at the Military Academy

In order to understand the nature of the research project this study is part of, first it is important to become familiar with the position of the Royal Netherlands Military Academy (to be called Military Academy in the rest of this study) as a research institute. The Military Academy in Breda educates cadets for officer positions in the Army, the Air Force, and the Military Police. It is the Academy's ambition to provide education at an academic level, and because of these academic ambitions, the Military Academy has a research program. The position of this program within the organization is different from the position of staff departments conducting 'policy research', i.e. research that is performed on the basis of explicit needs of policymakers. The scientific staff has the freedom to study a variety of topics with relevance for the Dutch Armed Forces and has the freedom to publicize the results openly. The research program is not directed by policymakers, which implies that the research program at the Military Academy possesses a particular kind of independence. One can imagine that this independent position is essential for the Military Academy. On the one hand it is important because of the scientific pretension of the research program; on the other hand it is important because it grants the scientific staff a position that is independent from 'office politics' at the Ministry of Defence in The Hague (in colloquial speech referred to as 'The Hague'). This means that scientists can take up topics that are not 'popular' in 'The Hague' or that run against the personal interests of individuals within the organization. In other words, a scientist at the Military Academy is at the same time an insider and an outsider and one can imagine that this position is of particular importance to both the scientists and the organization. This last kind of independence has been of particular importance for this study. Before this study was conducted it had already been clear that the style of thinking used in this study differs significantly from 'mainstream' thinking within the Dutch Armed Forces. An implicit goal of this study has been to confront the organization with such a different way of thinking, and to show what becomes visible if this way of thinking is applied to the central topics of this study. The results of this study are directly used in the cadets' educational program. Indirectly this study is used to confront the organization with this different way of thinking and to inspire new research.

Exploratory phase

The research project started with two exploratory case studies. The goal of these case studies was to develop insight into the nature of the experiences of the soldiers that had been deployed in peace support operations. During this phase the project group conducted the following activities:

- Research questions for the first exploratory cases were formulated[17];
- The first cases were two Dutch units that had been engaged in peace operations. The criterion for selecting these cases was quite straightforward: Logtbat and Dutchbat were the only two integral units that had been

---

[17] 1. What are the problem situations junior leaders in crisis situations are confronted with? 2. How do they handle these problems? 3. How effective was the way in which they handled these situations? 4. What lessons can be drawn from the way in which junior leaders handled problem situations? (see Vogelaar 1996a, p. 2.)

deployed in peace operations at that time. Dutchbat was an infantry battalion that had been was deployed in the Safe Area of Srebrenica. Logtbat was a transport battalion that had transported humanitarian goods in the first half of the 1990s. These two battalions will be discussed in greater detail later in this study;

- Members of the organizations were individually interviewed after their return to the Netherlands. In the interviews, the respondents reflected upon their time in Bosnia on the basis of the leading questions of the research project. All members of the project group conducted interviews (one or two interviewers interviewed one respondent);
- Data was gathered for both Dutchbat and Logtbat[18]. The interviews were open; the research questions were used as a guideline. The respondents were soldiers from various ranks (from private to lieutenant-colonel);
- The material was transcribed;
- It was attempted to develop a framework for understanding the experiences. It was decided to first focus on the Dutchbat case and to attempt to interpret the events using an existing theoretical model. This attempt was disregarded because the members of the project were of the opinion that the theoretical categories did not do justice to the experiences as they emerged in the interviews.

A second attempt was made to develop an analytical framework. In a group discussion, the researchers came to an analytical framework that was in direct line with the experiences in the cases. The categories of the framework referred to specific 'problem situations' of junior leaders and the way they dealt with these ('dealing with danger', 'dealing with shortages of supplies', etc.).

Specification phase

After the analytical framework had been developed, the material was subsequently analyzed using this framework ('selective coding'). On the basis of this analysis and after a member check, a first exploratory case study was published (Vogelaar c.s., 1996a). After this publication, the Logtbat case was worked out. Firstly, additional interviews were conducted, using the analytical framework of Dutchbat as a topic list. On the basis of the interviews it was decided to drop certain categories of the Dutchbat framework (e.g. 'dealing with shortages in supplies') and to add a couple of categories with which the experience of Logtbat (e.g. problems en route) could be covered. Using the Kwalon instrument (Wester & Richardson, 1989), the transcribed interview material was analyzed. After a member check, the second

---

[18] For the Dutchbat case a total of 18 people were interviewed and for the Logtbat case a total of 28 people.

case study was published (Vogelaar c.s., 1996b). After both exploratory case studies were finished, they were published together (Vogelaar c.s., 1997a). This is relevant because in this publication the case descriptions were reflected upon in an epilogue. In this epilogue the topic of 'environmental uncertainty' was used to reflect on the experiences (using the classification of McCaskey, 1985).

At a later stage a third case study was worked out. This case was orientated to a particular SFOR rotation. At the time more units were active in peace operations, but the reason for selecting SFOR was that (a) again, it involved a larger unit, (b) the operation was in a sense 'riskier' than, for example, a peace operation in Cyprus, which was also an option at that time. In other words, dynamic complexity was more likely to be a problem in Bosnia than in Cyprus. The methodological procedure used before was also used for the SFOR case. Interviews were conducted with members of different ranks in the organization[19]. The interviews were topic-guided, using the topics that were used for Logtbat. Subsequently, the interviews were analyzed using the existing system of categories (selective coding). Again, it appeared that the existing analytical framework did not quite match the experiences of the SFOR battalion. After a group discussion, the analytical framework was adjusted to fit the experiences of SFOR. The interviews were subsequently analyzed using the adjusted system of categories. Eventually, again after a member check, this resulted in the publication of the third case (Vogelaar, c.s, 2001).

2.2 Methodological structure of this study

As was mentioned in chapter one, this study is located in the reduction and integration phase of the Grounded Theory process. The methodological structure of this study is discussed by addressing a number of topics. Subsequently, the ins and outs of the research strategy, the method of data collection, the procedures for data analysis, and the analytical framework are discussed.

Research strategy

In order to clarify the design of this study a – what Verschuren & Doorewaard (2000) called – *research model* is presented here. This model consists of three basic ingredients. First, the *goal* of this study is presented at the right hand side. The research activities should result in reaching the goal of the study. Secondly, the *object of study* is specified. Thirdly, the *research perspective* is specified. This perspective refers to the way the object of study

---

[19] For the SFOR case, a total of 26 respondents were interviewed.

is perceived. Central to the research strategy of the approach in this study is what Verschuren & Doorewaard (2000, pp. 50–51) called 'a confrontation'. This confrontation should eventually result in insight into the ability of the Army to deploy units that are able to deal with dynamic complexity in peace operations. The case studies and the mother organization constitute the research object. This research object is 'perceived' from an analytical framework. Applied to this study, two research models can be distinguished, one for part four and one for part five:

Part Four

Research design:

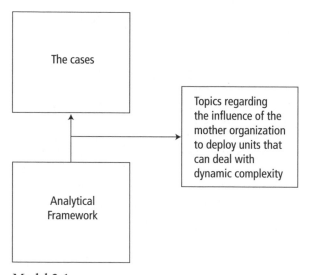

Model 2.1

From the perspective of an analytical framework, cases are explored, resulting in *topics*. These topics are organizational aspects of the mother organization considered to have an influence on the ability of crisis organizations to design self-organizing operational units.

Part Five

Research design

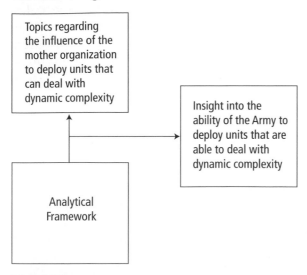

Model 2.2

The topics identified by the analysis in Part Four are explored are analyzed in Part Five in order to develop insight into the ability of the Army to deploy units that can deal with dynamic complexity. Again, the analytical framework developed in Part Two and Part Three is central in this analysis.

Selection of the cases

All the exploratory case studies that were performed by the research group are analyzed. One could therefore say that this study chooses a 'no selection' criterion of selection.

Data collection

In order to develop the substantive theory, various types of data need to be collected. These types of data can be deduced from the conceptual model displayed in Chapter One:

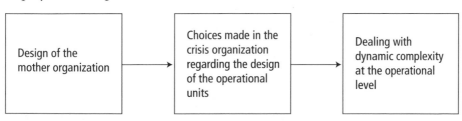

The conceptual model indicates that three types of data need to be collected: (1) data about dealing with dynamic complexity at the operational level, (2) data about the design of the operational units, and (3) data about the mother organization. For the data types (1) and (2), the original case studies are the sources of data. For data type (3), various types of data have to be collected. Here the various types of data are discussed in more detail[20]:

1. The original case studies described the problems leaders of operational units were confronted with and how they were dealt with. As such, they provide insight into the daily affairs of the operational units, also (but not exclusively) about the problem of dealing with dynamic complexity. In order to collect data about dealing with dynamic complexity events should be selected. Theory is used to select the relevant events from the cases. As this theory has not yet been discussed, for the specific way in which this type of data is extracted from the cases please refer to the discussion on this subject in section 10.7;

2. Although the case studies were not orientated to analyzing the design of the various crisis organizations, there is information available about the organizational context that operational units operated in. With the use of theory, this information about the organizational context can be selected. This means that theory fulfills an important function (a) in developing an idea about what the crucial design characteristics of operational units are, and (b) in selecting relevant information about the relevant characteristics of the design of the operational units. As this theory has not yet been discussed, for the specific way in which this type of data is extracted from the cases please refer to the discussion on this subject in section 10.7;

3. The third type of data is of a different nature. Data about the nature of the mother organization cannot be derived from the cases. Again, theory is used to select the relevant characteristics for the mother organization. The selected characteristics are analyzed for their influence on the design of operational units. Data will be gathered from different sources (military doctrine, articles, intranet, etc.) in order to obtain the required picture. It is important to develop a non-controversial characterization of the mother organization. The specific way in which information about characteristics of the mother organization is collected is specifically discussed in the various chapters of part five.

---

[20] In the discussion of all three types of data, the importance of the analytical framework as a tool of selecting data is underlined. The implication of this is that only after the development of the analytical framework the data that will be collected can be specified in more detail. This will be the topic of section 10.4.

Data analysis

As the two research models indicate, there are two different 'analytical moments' in this study. In the data analysis the influence of both the direct design and the indirect design on dealing with dynamic complexity at the operational level is explored.

- *Analysis of the influence of the direct design.* This analysis focuses on how the design of the operational units influences their ability to deal with dynamic complexity. This adds up to an exploration of the possibilities and limitations of operational units to deal with dynamic complexity (that is to say, the possibilities and limitations relating to their design). The hypotheses resulting from these explorations are considered to be *specific* for the cases;
- *Analysis of the influence of the indirect design.* This analysis focuses on the constraints that crisis organizations experience when designing operational units. The characteristics of the mother organization that can function as a constraint will be determined after the analysis of the case studies. The hypotheses resulting from these explorations are considered to be *analytical* and *general*. They are analytical because the claims are based on logical implication: *if* the Army has characteristics X, *then* the effect on a crisis organization is Y. They are general because they are considered to be relevant for all crisis organizations deployed by the Army.

Central to the data analysis of this study is the idea of *exploration*. The objects of study (the cases and the mother organization) are explored to find clues about the ability of the Army to deploy units that can deal with dynamic complexity. This means that the data analysis goes beyond the technical categorization and description of the data itself (Coffey & Atkinson, 1996)[21]. Theoretical insights function as a *heuristic* in the process of developing hypotheses[22].

---

[21] On this subject, Coffey & Atkinson (1996, p. 155) said: 'Our important ideas are not 'in' the data, and however hard we work, we will not find those ideas simply by scrutinizing our data ever more obsessively. We need to work at analysis and theorizing, and we need to do the intellectual, imaginative work of ideas in parallel to the other tasks of data management.' Kelle (1995, p. 41) argued that although the general sentiment within the grounded theory approach is against using theoretical concepts for analyzing the empirical world, '(…) an open mind does not mean an empty head'.

[22] This process functions by combining abstract theoretical notions and observations made in the cases (Kelle, 1995). Data is collected about facts in the cases and about the mother organization. These facts are linked together using theory. In a way, *data is gathered* about a possible pattern (influence of design on dealing with dynamic complexity), and *theory is used* to interpret the nature of the pattern that becomes visible. In this study, the analytical process is called 'analytical abduction', in order to capture that theory is used to explore the object of study. The finer details of analytical abduction will be dealt with in the second part of this chapter.

Miles & Huberman (1984) emphasized that the human mind has an enormous ability to find patterns. For that reason they proposed that when patterns are recognized, researchers should (1) be able to recognize real added evidence of a pattern, and (2) be open for disconfirmation (Miles & Huberman, 1984, p. 216). This study takes this advice at heart by (1) selectively searching for specific patterns (not just any possible association is branded a pattern); (2) interpreting the patterns by using theory (a pattern should make sense); (3) formulating the conclusions in the form of hypotheses (the study is located in the context of discovery); (4) studying more than one case before the step from the local to the global is made, and (5) supplying an extensive system of references to the events in the original case studies. Points 1, 2, 4, and 5 refer to the fact that the process of finding patterns is guided by procedure, and point 3 refers to the nature of the claims of this study.

Analytical framework

The previous discussions on data collection and data analysis have made it clear that the analytical framework takes a central role in this study. It has two main functions (comparable to the two functions of theory that Wallace brought forward (Wallace, 1969, p. x)): it is used for *selecting data* and as a framework for *interpreting patterns*. Formal theory is therefore used as a tool to give meaning to experiences and to provide reference points for learning (see Gustavsen, 1996). In the Introduction it was stated that an analytical framework is a construction of theoretical ingredients to tackle specific questions. As such, it is assembled from elements that enable one to answer specific questions. This characterization of an analytical framework implies that its ingredients are collected because of their *function*. The development of this framework has been a study in itself: a substantial part of the time that was devoted to this study was used to develop this framework. The main challenge in developing an analytical framework is that the required elements need to be identified and the various elements need to be connected coherently. This means that the discussion has an exploratory tone.

First, the necessary ingredients of the analytical framework will be discussed, which will be followed by a discussion of the analytical framework. The analytical framework consists of 6 basic ingredients:

1. *Theoretical exploration of the concept of dynamic complexity.* The Introduction provided a general characterization of dynamic complexity. As a first step, the concept of dynamic complexity is discussed against the background of the theoretical context it originates from. The theoretical exploration should also provide a formal description of meaningful

action, and thus a picture of 'the thing to be organized'. This first ingredient will be worked out in Chapter Three and Four;

2. *The characterization of the problem of dealing with dynamic complexity using an abstract model.* The discussion on meaningful action will be advanced in a systematic way using the organizing model of Weick. This description is necessary in order to identify the normative elements of dealing with dynamic complexity. This second ingredient will be worked out in Part Two, Chapter Five;

3. *The identification of the 'normative element' in the abstract model.* The capability of self-organization was identified in Chapter One as being essential for operational units in order to be able to deal with dynamic complexity. However, this claim does not reveal anything about how to deal with dynamic complexity in the best possible way. This third ingredient will also be worked out in Part Two, Chapter Six;

4. *A description of the normative element.* The normative element that is identified is functionally defined, which means that it is defined by virtue of what it should accomplish. In such a definition, the content of the process remains a black box. In Chapter Six it is attempted to provide a description of this black spot. This fourth ingredient will be worked out in Part Two, Chapter Seven;

5. *The issue of 'organizing the normative element'.* After the normative element of the formal model of dealing with dynamic complexity has been identified, attention will be turned to 'organizing the normative element'. This discussion should make it concrete how an abstract normative ability can be influenced by organizational factors (i.e. can be 'organized'). This fifth ingredient will be worked out in Part Three;

6. *Finding indicators that can be used to analyze the cases.* After an idea has been developed of how the normative element can be organized in a system, the issue of how to observe it in the cases should be dealt with. This point should follow logically from the previous point, but it is a distinct step in the development of the analytical framework. This sixth ingredient will also be worked out in the various chapters of Part Three.

After the ingredients of the analytical framework have been worked out, the way the analytical framework is used to study the cases and the mother organization will be discussed. In other words, it will be discussed how the various ingredients are applied to study the object of study. This will be the topic of section 10.7.

Research Process

The previous sections focused on the formal characteristics of the methods used in this study. Here, I want to briefly discuss the process of developing this study. There are two topics that are important in this respect. In the first place, the study started in 1996. About half of the period since has been devoted to the development of conceptual tools. So, in a sense this 'conceptual journey' has been an important part of the research process. An important experience from this study is therefore that, 'developing a way of thinking' about the topic of dealing with dynamic complexity is not a straightforward process. That is why the 'journey to develop the analytical framework' is also presented here as a journey and not as a tight set of analytical tools. In the second place, the analyses of the cases were worked out and reworked in several steps. An essential role in this process was 'peer debriefing'. Two of the three supervisors of this study worked at the Military Academy at the time the study was developed. They can therefore be seen as representatives of the Army, although their influence on the process was not limited to this role. The analyses in this study, however, were *not* presented to members of the original crisis organization (a procedure that is generally known as a 'member check')[23]. One reason for this is that this study is orientated to the development of hypotheses, rather than at testing hypotheses. However, there is a second, perhaps more important reason for not performing member checks. Previously, it was indicated that one of the underlying reasons to conduct this study was to present the Army with a different way of thinking. A member check could have undermined this goal. An example can show why this is a crucial point. During the development of the original case studies, commanders were used if they applied the doctrine. Most of them enthusiastically reported about the way they aimed to let people think for themselves. However, the analyses in this study result in the hypotheses that (a) the doctrine does not claim what it appears to claim, which results in (b) misunderstanding about the doctrine. The fact that various 'members' claimed to have applied the doctrine is exactly one of the matters that are considered to be problematic in this study.

2.3 Methodological position

Section 2.2 outlined the methodological structure of this study. Some of the topics that were dealt with demand further discussion. This section is orientated to taking up these topics in order to clarify the methodological position of this study.

Pragmatism

The claim that hypotheses are important in order to 'conquer' the unknown is not uncommon in science and, indeed, philosophy. This idea was central to the thinking of the 'founding father' of Pragmatism, C.S. Peirce. Abduction consists in studying facts and devising a theory to explain them

---

[23] A member check **was** part of the development of the exploratory case-studies.

(Cunningham, 1998, p. 833). Postmodern theorists emphasize, of course, that what counts as fact is also the result of a construction process. A fact is, in that sense, observed from a theory (indeed 'believing is seeing' (Weick, 1979, p. 135)). That does not preclude, however, that there is an underlying reality consisting of raw material to which the edited 'facts' refer. This is an assumption of critical realism. It is claimed here that this study shares assumptions with the philosophical traditions of pragmatism and critical realism. Pragmatism is a philosophical school of thought in which the idea of usefulness of knowledge is at center stage. Rescher (2000, p. 2): 'The characteristic tactic of the philosophical movement that has come to be designated as pragmatism was to pivot legitimization on success by adopting efficacy in application and implementation as the salient criterion of adequacy.' Not truth as such is considered to be crucial, but the question what one can do with the insights. The functional aspect of knowledge is underlined (Van der Vlist, 2003, p. 149). One can imagine that a concept such as usefulness is bound to be controversial. Based on an original paper of Lovejoy, Rescher (2000) made it clear that the field of pragmatism is rather diverse, sometimes based on rival contentions. In this study, pragmatism is interpreted according to Peirce's 'root idea'. Rescher (2000, pp. 59, 60): 'The root idea was that (1) the meaning of a term or conception is constituted by the use that we make of it in the course of our communicative operations and other activities; and (2) it is appropriate and warranted to class a proposition involving such conceptions as true insofar as and to the extent that such applications are successful and effective in enabling us to realize the correlative aims and purposes.'[24]

Selectivity: heuristics and maps

Theory is used in this study as a heuristic to select relevant data and interpret patterns in the selected data. Dennett (1995, p. 210) emphasized that a heuristic search is a 'risk worth a try'. It is a risk because of the inevitable selectivity involved in such a search; it is worth a try because of possible results. The selectivity of theory can be illustrated by the analogy of map-making. Essential in this analogy is that of the same area (i.e. object of study) many different maps can be drawn (Christis, 1998, p. 25). Depending on one's specific interest, one can draw maps about climatic characteristics, demographic characteristics, the roads, geological features, industrial develop-

---

[24] Claiming that this study endorses a pragmatist approach may lead to some confusion. This study is also interested in pragmatic affairs at the operational level. The operational units were not dealing with problems on the basis of superior abstraction or a closed system of rules. As such, one could say that the operational units used a 'pragmatic' approach. They attempted to find a way that worked and tried to learn from experience. As will be seen in the next chapter, meaningful action will be described using the logic of abduction. This means that this study uses a pragmatic approach in studying pragmatic problems.

ment, differences in height, historical development, etc. All those different perspectives cannot be portrayed in the same map, because this map would become unreadable[25]. The map-making analogy shows that a map is only useful when it leaves out certain elements, e.g. when it sensibly reduces complexity. Other maps can be made to observe the environment from another perspective. Just as it is impossible to portray all complexity of a geological area in one single picture, it is considered to be impossible to cover the complexity of a subject area in an all-explaining model. One determines a way of looking, depending on one's specific interest[26]. In this study the topic of dealing with dynamic complexity is at center stage. The analytical framework can be seen as a map of this problem with which the cases can be observed[27].

Because of the dominant role of the analytical framework, one could consider the methodological strategy of this study an example of a *pro-theoreti-*

---

[25] Van Boxsel (1999), also reasoning from a map-making example, stated that in order to be successful, every structure must anticipate its own shortcomings. After all, a map that looks like the terrain of which it is a map is hardly practical and indeed misses the point. Similarly, a study that wants to explain, for example, stress problems with an all-explaining model will become as complex as the phenomena it wants to explain and thus misses the point (Christis, 1998).

[26] A geologist has a different interest in a certain area than a tourist, and therefore their maps of the same area will differ considerably. In this way a map, like a theory, is used as a tool for a specific purpose. The question whether it is good to portray a process in a particular way can only be answered by asking whether it is useful to do so. Christis (1998) emphasized that a model provides a certain perspective on the problem in hand. This perspective can make certain problems clear and can provide insight into how to solve these problems. If this proves to be useful in everyday practice, one can consider the portrayal to be useful and therefore successful. This is evidently a pragmatic criterion. Also Sayer, who defended critical realism, indicated that practical adequacy is an important criterion for truth (2000, p. 43): '(...) truth may be better understood as 'practical adequacy', that is in terms of the extent to which it generates expectations about the world and about results of our actions which are realized.' This shows that pragmatism and a pro-theoretical strategy are essentially on a par.

[27] The metaphor of the map might give the impression that theory is interpreted here as a deductive tool. A map – after all – helps a traveler because it shows how reality looks like. A map shows 'the truth'. A traveler is, in that sense, not an explorer because reality is displayed on the map and is not discovered through exploring. The journey of the traveler does not teach anything new about reality. If in this study theory is perceived as such a map, then the exploration will not lead to new insights. The conclusions are, after all, already available on the map. In that case, this study would use a deductive style of reasoning: specific cases are judged on the basis of general laws. I want to contradict this possible criticism. The map-making metaphor was specifically used to clarify the issue of selectivity. The same area can be observed from different perspectives, depending on one's interest in the area. In that particular sense, theory is a map. The metaphor of the map should not be seen as a characterization of the logical structure of this study. The theoretical ingredients that are being used constitute an abstract model of the process of dealing with dynamic complexity. These insights might be helpful to make sense of the complex and 'messy' reality in the cases. In that sense it is a tool to explore areas that have *not* been explored before.

cal strategy as Christis (1998) described it. A pro-theoretical strategy states that the explication of theory, i.e. the definition of essential concepts and how they are related, should come before empirical study (Christis, 1998). This strategy is used as a way to make sense of the complex reality[28]. The analytical framework should inform where to look for available material and how to relate the information in the various boxes. It therefore is orientated to the content of the various boxes of this study's conceptual model: the characteristic of the mother organization, the choices regarding the design of operational units, and the dealing with dynamic complexity by the operational units. It should furthermore provide sufficient insight to enable the drawing of relations between these various boxes.

Analytical abduction

Abduction is the type of inference that can be used to describe this process of exploration. Coffey and Atkinson (1996, p. 155) stated that: 'abductive reasoning lies at the heart of 'grounded theorizing'. Abduction is orientated towards finding explanations for observed facts. These explanations are hypothetical (which is relevant for the nature of the substantive theory that will be developed). According to Peirce, a hypothesis is: 'Any proposition added to observed facts, tending to make them applicable in any way to other circumstances than those under which they are observed, may be called a hypothesis' (Peirce, 1955, p. 150). This is exactly what is done in this study. The facts that are observed here are the cases. The observation of the cases (I prefer 'exploration') should lead to insights into the Army as a crisis organization ('making them applicable in any way to other circumstances'), i.e. the substantive theory. In the second part of this chapter, the concept of abduction is worked out further[29].

---

[28] Sayer (2000, p. 19) about this: 'The objects that social scientists study, be they wars, discourses, institutions, economic activities, identities, kinship or whatever, are concrete in the sense that they are the product of multiple components and forces. Social systems are always open and usually complex and messy. Unlike some of the natural sciences, we cannot isolate out these components and examine them under controlled conditions. We therefore have to rely on abstraction and careful conceptualization, on attempting to abstract out the various components or influences in our heads, and only when we have done this and considered how they combine and interact can we expect to return to the concrete, many-sided object and make sense of it.'

[29] Abduction is therefore a "bottom up type" of inference: individual facts are collected and linked together in order to develop hypotheses. The particular is the starting point (Coffey and Atkinson, 1996). It seems perhaps that theory has no place in such an approach, which would contradict earlier claims about the importance of the analytical framework. However, Coffey and Atkinson (1996, p. 157) emphasize that formal theory is not 'forbidden' in such an approach: '(…) we can also recognize that theories usefully can be thought of as heuristic tools. In other words, we *use* concepts, theories and ideas constructively and creatively. (…). Regularities in data – whether of form or content – must be associated with ideas that go beyond those data themselves.' (italics in original).

Abduction can be contrasted with both deduction and induction. The method of *deduction* is about applying general rules to specific cases. Formally, this style of reasoning looks as follows (Shank, 1998, p. 847):

> 'Rule. – [It is true that] All the beans from this bag are white.
> Case. – [We know that] These beans are from this bag.
> Result. – [Certainly, it is true that] These beans are white.'

In deduction, cases are judged on the basis of rules. This is for various reasons not the type of inference that is central to this study[30]. The traditional counterpart of deduction is *induction*. Formally this type of reasoning looks as follows (Shank, 1998, p. 847):

> 'Case. – [We know that] These beans are from this bag.
> Result. – [We have observed that] These beans are white.
> Rule. – [Probably, then] All the beans from this bag are white.'

Induction is the inferior counterpart of deduction, because it always leads to conclusions that are only probable (Shank, 1998, p. 845). It might also be

---

[30] In a way, the logical structure of this study might resemble deduction because theoretical insights (rules) are applied to cases. This would mean that theory would occupy an arrogant position. This is, for various reasons, not the case.

- One can only answer the demands of deductive reasoning if one has at one's disposal a system of perfect rules and an objective account of the circumstances. Not incidentally theory is called an analytical framework here. An analytical framework is composed of various theoretical ingredients that might be helpful to deal with the specific issues in this study. This implies that there is no theory available that can serve as deductive tool. Instead, searching intelligently for useful theory is one of the main parts of this study.
- Furthermore, in order to make deductive conclusions valid, a perfect and unquestionable account of the cases should be available. That is not the case, here. This has to do with the fact that the cases were not constructed with the core concept in mind. Sometimes there might be little information available on the topics that are important according to the analytical framework. Theory can be useful to reconstruct experiences with few clues in the case material. Theory can also be used to search for clues that, without theory, would have remained insignificant.
- In deductive reasoning there is a one-way traffic between theory, cases and conclusions. In deductive syllogisms this is possible because theory is unquestionable. Although such a one-way traffic is indeed recognizable in this study, the logical structure is not deductive because the one-way traffic is not considered to be one way in principle. One can imagine that the results of this study can lead to theoretical discussion.

Josephson & Josephson (1994, p. 17) claimed that deduction is not necessary for explanations. They claimed that there is a difference between explanations that are *causally* sufficient and explanations that are *logically* sufficient. Josephson & Josephson (1994, p. 17) concluded that: 'Thus, we conclude that explanations are not deductive proofs in any particularly interesting sense. Although they can often be presented in the form of deductive proofs, doing so does not succeed in capturing anything essential or especially useful and tends to confuse causation with logical implication. An alternative view is that an explanation is an assignment of causal responsibility; it tells a causal story. Finding possible explanations is finding possible causes of the thing to be explained'.

thought that the logical structure of this study resembles induction because of the issues of probability and generalization (developing a substantive theory on the basis of observations in cases). Induction is orientated towards finding statistical generalizations (a number of observations leads to conclusions about the way the world works) (Emery & Emery, 1997, p. 120). It is a method for testing theories when these theories are already there[31]. There are various reasons why the logical structure of this study is not inductive. However, this study does not use theory in order to generalize this specific theory; it uses one kind of theory (i.e. formal) to develop another kind of theory (i.e. substantive). Although finding suitable theory is an important part of this study, this study is fundamentally *orientated to* developing meaningful conclusions in a particular case (the substantive theory)[32].

Besides the traditional two formal ways of reasoning, there is a third way called *abduction* or retroduction. This type of logic was originally meant for capturing the nature of scientific progress (finding new explanations for phenomena). Formally this logic looks as follows (Shank, 1998, p. 847):

> 'Result. – [We have the experience that] The beans are white [but this experience lacks any real meaning for us].
> Rule. – [The claim that] All the beans from this bag are white [is meaningful in this setting].
> Case – [Therefore, it is both plausible and meaningful to hypothesize that] These beans are from this bag.'

One can see that a new idea or hypothesis (these beans are from this bag) is added to two 'givens' (the rule and the result). According to Cunningham (1998, pp. 833–834), abduction is the appropriate method for making sense of new (or unknown) situations[33].

---

[31] Shank put this matter as follows (1998, p. 845): '(...) inductive methods are only useful in settling issues of empirical truth when the meanings of these empirical phenomena are first rendered non-problematic. That is, in order to use inductive methods, we first have to make sure that we know what all of our phenomena mean, and that there is general agreement on these meanings. In science, the question of prior meaning is most often resolved by the use of theory.'

[32] The nature of induction is often misunderstood. The economist Brian McArthur is one of the researchers that advocated the importance of induction in contrast to deduction: 'Much more often the players (chess players, ehk) operate in a world of induction. They try to fill the gaps on the fly by forming hypotheses, by making analogies, by drawing from past experience, by using heuristic rules of thumb. Whatever works, works – even if they do not understand why. And for that reason, induction cannot depend upon precise, deductive logic.' (quoted in Waldrop, 1992, p. 253). This study agrees with McArthur with respect to the way everyday thinking works. However, what McArthur is talking about is not induction but abduction.

[33] According to Bateson (2002, p. 134), abduction is rather important because: '(...), all thought would be totally impossible in a universe in which abduction was not expectable.'

To capture the analytical structure of this study, I want to introduce the concept of *analytical* abduction (to be distinguished from analytical *induction* (Lindesmith, 1947); see for a description Vaughan, 1996)). Explanations are sought using analytical material. Theory for observed facts is being developed (hypotheses about the cases) by using general insights theory (the analytical framework). Model 2.3 displays the structure of the analysis in this study:

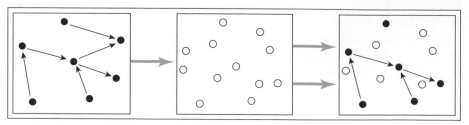

Model 2.3. Analytical abduction.

The analytical framework (left square) functions to make meaningful structures (right square) in the cases (middle square) visible[34].

Normative claims and causation

Given the topic of this study, the analytical framework is necessarily normative. Not only is it described how units dealt with dynamic complexity, it is also discussed how their ability to do so was influenced by design characteristics of both the crisis organization and the mother organization. Furthermore, the analyses made in this study are supposed to be useful for the Armed Forces as a crisis organization. I do not study reality just as an

---

[34] One could ask why this study does not just use some sort of checklist to observe self-organizing potential in the units. Such lists are available in existing theory. Why is such a complex analytical framework constructed? There are two arguments for this. In the first place, it has to do with the phrase "analytical abduction". The case studies were originally not constructed to make an analysis of the self-organizing potential possible. The case studies should therefore be explored in an intelligent way, in order to locate the relevant material. The reflection is, in other words, more complex than merely applying a checklist. In the second place, a relationship is studied between dealing with practical problems and design characteristics. It is not merely attempted to assess the self-organizing potential of units, it is also attempted to draw a link between the design characteristics and the actual descriptions (the original case studies were orientated at practical problems units were confronted with).

aquarium, that is to say, not just for the joy of observation or out of curiosity[35].

However, this study does not try to develop a perfect system of rules for every imaginable problem, in which the best way of dealing with that problem is specified. It will not be stated that design characteristic X always and invariably leads to dealing with complexity in a Y manner. The influence of design characteristics of operational units on their ability to deal with dynamic complexity is of a different causal nature. Instead, this study adopts a realist view on causation. Sayer (2000, p. 14) explained the realist view on causation as follows: 'Consequently, for realists, causation is not understood on the model of regular succession of events and hence explanation need not depend on finding them, or searching for putative social laws. The conventional impulse to prove causation by collecting data on regularities, repeated occurrences, is therefore misguided; at best these might suggest where to look for candidates for causal mechanisms. What causes something to happen has nothing to do with the number of times we have observed it happening. Explanation depends instead on identifying causal mechanisms and how they work, and discovering if they have been activated and under what conditions.' In other words, the causal claims of this study are *not* 'A always, necessarily and invariably causes B', but 'A has the potential of causing B'[36].

The analytical framework of this study explicates causal mechanisms that do not need to materialize in everyday reality. With the causal mechanisms in mind, the cases are studied in order to give meaning to the experiences. What the analytical framework claims is that organizational systems with particular design characteristics are better at dealing with dynamic complexity than others. The implication of this is that well-designed operational units not always operate successfully. Furthermore, when units do not operate on the basis of this philosophy, there is no guarantee that things will always turn out badly. The idea of the normative claims developed in this study is that the chances of dealing successfully with dynamic complexity are greater when one operates according to this philosophy. The analytical framework reflects, in other words, on the potential of operational units to deal with dynamic complexity. Because of these characteristics it is possible to form an opinion regarding cases. It is, for example, possible to state that

---

[35] There appears to be a paradox in these normative aims. The apparent contradiction is that this study appears to ask what it claims to be unable to answer. This study claims that the nature of dynamic complexity operational units have to deal with is such that one cannot develop rules that specify the best possible way for dealing with specific problems. There is no ultimate manual available. Therefore, it seems strange to claim that one can determine that a unit dealt with dynamic complexity in the best possible way.

[36] This would necessitate an absolutist idea of causality, comparable with what has been called 'a map that is as complex as the topic of study'.

the Army might have been successful in a certain case but that this success came about in spite of their way of operating. It is therefore possible to attribute success to luck, or failure to bad luck. This is an essential characteristic of the reflection if it wants to be able to do more than merely recording experiences.

The substantive theory and usefulness

The resulting substantive theory consists of hypotheses about the nature of the various relations this study is interested in. The substantive theory that is developed is orientated to '*insight into*'. However, insight is not only sought for the sake of insight. The insight into the various relations in the conceptual model should be useful. Usefulness is therefore the criterion to evaluate the substantive theory. Or, as Rescher (2000, p. 60) claimed: 'Practice (*praxis*) is to serve as the arbiter of theory (*theoria*)'. The hypotheses that are the result of this study should therefore be evaluated on the basis of their usefulness. The 'real world' evaluation of the reflection is, of course, a matter that lies outside the realm of this study; however, it is possible to reflect here on the kind of insight this study is after. Because of this pragmatist orientation, the usefulness of the substantive theory to be developed can be put as follows:

1. *The insights of the substantive theory are valuable if the resulting insights were not totally obvious beforehand.* For example, the insight that the Army is rather a hierarchical organization is not very valuable. However, the insight that this hierarchical nature influences dealing with dynamic complexity in unexpected ways is valuable.
2. *The insights of the substantive theory are valuable if they provide clear indications for further research.* As has constantly been emphasized, this study consists of an *exploration* and *hypotheses* about the relations in the conceptual model. The substantive theory is valuable if it hits upon certain possible relations that need to be studied more thoroughly. Therefore, the final chapter will discuss various directions for further research.

The insights of the substantive theory are valuable if they provide insight into how the Army can improve itself as an organization that is involved in peace operations. The substantive theory is therefore useful if, due to the specific nature of the analyses (a specific theoretical perspective, an exploration of specific relations), particular strengths and weaknesses of the Army become visible. Therefore, the final chapter will discuss various directions for organizational change.

PART II
Analytical framework:
Dealing with dynamic complexity

Both Part Two and Three are dedicated to the development of the analytical framework. The various chapters of part two and three all formulate a necessary ingredient of this analytical framework. Parts Two and Three are focused on a qualitatively different part of the analytical framework. Part two concerns the theoretical foundation of the analytical framework. Central in part two are discussions on systems, environments, and dynamic complexity. On the basis of these discussions a crucial quality in dealing with dynamic complexity is identified. Part Three is orientated to finding indicators for analyzing the cases. Part Two should result in an answer to the question:

How can a system deal with dynamic complexity in the best possible way?

This question is important because it is explicitly orientated to the normative issue of this study. The following chapters discuss the first four ingredients of the analytical framework:

1. The theoretical exploration of the concept of dynamic complexity.
2. The characterization of the problem of dealing with dynamic complexity using an abstract model.
3. The identification of the 'normative element' in the abstract model.
4. A description of the normative element

Chapter Three will discuss the choice for systems theory as a macrotheoretical framework. Subsequently, the historical developments within systems theory are described in order to provide a theoretical background. Chapter Four will focus on the finesses of the problem of dealing with dynamic complexity. Chapter Five will discuss the central model this study will use to characterize the problem of dealing with dynamic complexity. Chapter Six will focus on the normative aspects of the organizing model. The final chapter of this part, Chapter Seven, will discuss the similtarities and differences between the theoretical insights of Weick and Billig.

Chapter 3

Systems theory as background

In Chapter One, dynamic complexity has been introduced as the core concept of this study. Dynamic complexity was roughly defined as a problem which occurs when organizations are confronted with an environment that is *problematic*. Its indeterminate nature was considered to be the environment's main problematic characteristic. The environment furthermore confronts the organizational system with a *necessity to act*, while at the same time *the best way to act is unclear*. This chapter focuses on discussing the macro theoretical background of the concept of dynamic complexity[37], 'systems theory', which is a well-established tradition in organizational theory (see for example Reed, 1999). There are two main reasons to discuss this macro theoretical background.

To start with, three levels of analysis are at the centre of attention in this study. Scott (2001) emphasized that one needs theoretical frameworks that are sufficiently wide in order to be able to connect different levels of analysis. In the first place, the level of everyday experience at the operational level is discussed. This is the level that is described in the exploratory case studies. In the second place, the design characteristics of the crisis-organizations are brought into focus. The analysis will explore in what ways design characteristics of the crisis organization influence the experiences at the operational level, because these characteristics constitute the context of action at the operational level in important ways. In the third place, the level of the mother-organization is explored. The ways in which characteristics of the mother-organization influence the design choices made at the level of the crisis-organization will be investigated. The first section of this chapter discusses why – according to my interpretation – systems theory can connect these different levels in a satisfactory way. The second section summarizes the different reasons why systems theory is a suitable macro theoretical background for this study.

Furthermore, it was emphasized in Chapter Two that this study uses

---

[37] Van Strien (1986) would refer to this as level A theory: the level of abstract theorizing. This level is distinguished by Van Strien from level B theory, the level of problem-orientated theory, and level C theory, the theory of the individual case.

theory as a tool. Theoretical ingredients are gathered in order to come to grips with the topic of dealing with dynamic complexity and with design issues related to that topic. Chapter Two furthermore explicated the kind of theoretical ingredients that are necessary in this study. However, these ingredients should be more than an opportunistically collected mosaic of theoretical pieces that happen to be useful for a specific purpose. A macro theoretical framework should provide the basis for the different theoretical ingedients.

After clarifying the function of the macro theoretical background, the history of systems theory in organizational studies will be briefly sketched. Actually, I should say 'a' history, because it involves a description that suits the purposes of this study (i.e. placing the concept of dynamic complexity against its theoretical background). This involves a description of the development from early 'technical approaches' to more recent insights, which emphasize the importance of 'chaos' and 'complexity'. Finally, the abstract nature of the problem of dealing with dynamic complexity will be disussed using concepts from systems theory.

3.1 Connecting multiple levels of explanation

The issue of linking different levels of explanation can be considered as a familiar analytical problem in sociological theory. It has to do with the relations between the local and the global, more commonly framed as the relation between 'structure' and 'agency'. According to Latour (1999), this relation is problematic as a result of a *double explanatory dissatisfaction.*

The first type of explanatory dissatisfaction that is distinguished by Latour (1999) is dissatisfaction with descriptions at the micro-level. A narrow focus on the sociological micro level is insufficient to make sense of this micro level. Latour (1999, pp. 16–17) says on this that 'when social scientists concentrate on what could be called the micro level, that is face to face interactions, local sites, they quickly realize that many of the elements necessary to make sense of the situation are already in place or come from far away; hence the urge to look for something else, some other level, and to concentrate on what is not directly visible in the situation but has made the situation what it is.' This type of dissatisfaction is relevant for this study. One of the most important reasons for conducting this study was that the descriptions of experiences at the operational level are not considered to be satisfactory. There is a pragmatic reason for this dissatisfaction. The Army is not only confronted with the question 'What happens at the operational level in crisis operations?' They are also confronted with the question: 'How can we design operational units that are able to cope with the challenges of crisis operations in the best possible way?' This shifts the attention not to the unique problems at the operational level, but to something like the 'existing structures' lying behind the unique, influencing the unique. In a second analytic step, structures behind the design choices made at the level of the crisis-organization are explored. So again, there is dissatisfaction with the choices-as-such, made at the level of the crisis-organization. However, the research projects started with case-studies into the experiences of operational units exactly because it was thought that insight into these experiences has an extra value. In order to understand what crisis operations are about, the research project aimed to develop insight into what Giddens (1984) would call the "practical consciousness" of operational units.

Opposed to this micro-level dissatisfaction, Latour notes a second dissatisfaction of social scientists that is equally relevant for the purposes of this study (1999, p. 17): '(...), once this new level has been reached, a second type of dissatisfaction begins. Social scientists now feel that something is missing, that the abstraction of terms like culture and structure, norms and values, seems too great, and that one needs to reconnect, through the opposite move, back to the flash-and-blood situations from which they have started.' This second dissatisfaction is relevant for this study as well. After all, the exploratory case studies explicitly focused at everyday experiences at the operational level. Subsequently, the choice for dynamic complexity as a core concept indicates that the unique nature of problems at this operational level was appreciated. 'Dealing with dynamic complexity is more than rule following' is one of the most important conclusions of the first chapter. It follows from the way that dynamic complexity is defined, that operators are not considered the victim of fully determining structures. There is a tension between the two dissatisfactions, according to Latour (1999, p. 17): 'Once back to the local sites, however, the same uneasiness that pushed them in the direction of a search for social structure quickly sets in.'

It follows from the analysis of Latour that there is a distinct risk of becoming trapped in an 'eternal shift' between the micro and macro level of explanation. Latour has formulated Actor Network Theory (ANT) in order to give attention to the dissatisfaction of the eternal shift between levels[38]. The conceptual model of this study indicates that the operational level is 'influenced by' design choices at the level of the crisis-organization. If I claim that this 'influence' actually implies that the local is 'determined' by design choices, while at the same time I claim that 'dealing with dynamic complex-

---

[38] Law (1999, p. 3) claims that: 'Actor Network Theory is a ruthless application of *semiotics*. It tells that entities take their form and acquire their attributes as a result of their relations with other entities. In this scheme of things entities have no inherent qualities: essentialist divisions are thrown into the bonfire of the dualism' (italics in original). The division between agency and structure is one of these divisions that are according to Law explained away by ANT as an effect or outcome, rather than something that is given in the order of things (Law, 1999).

ity is more than rule following', I am at risk of building a fundamental contradiction into this study, one which can give rise to such an eternal shift.
Because I want to avoid this eternal shift one could say that I take stance
against both voluntarism and structural determinism (Becker, 2005)[39].

The circularity of agency and structure

The problem described in the previous section has to do with the relation
between structure and agency. Becker (2005, p. 230) emphasizes that: 'One
of the most fundamental issues of any social theory is the question of how
it addresses the topics of structure and agency, and how these topics are related'. The explanatory dissatisfaction can be considered to be a result of a
simple dichotomy between agency and structure (Law, 1999). Structuration
theory of Giddens has proposed a way to formulate the relation between
agency and structure. The next section will show that Giddens account of
structuration theory in my opinion avoids a simple distinction and indeed
appears to emphasize a co-evolution of agency and structure[40]. In order to
underline the relevant indications in the following passages I will add italics
to the original text of Giddens.

In his conceptualization of social systems Giddens (1984, p. 25) emphasizes the interplay between structures, systems and structuration: 'Structure,
as recursively organized sets of rules and resources, is out of time and space,
save in its instantiations and co-ordination as memory traces, and is marked
by an 'absence of the subject'. The social systems in which structure is recursively implicated, on the contrary, comprise the situated activities of human
agents, reproduced across time and space. Analysing the structuration of
social systems means studying the models in which such systems, grounded
in the knowledgeable activities of situated actors who draw upon rules and
resources in the diversity of action contexts, are reproduced in interaction'.
Essentially, Giddens claims that structures are created by the (joint) activities
of agents and – the same time – the activities of human agents are constituted by existing structures. Giddens (1984, p. 25) on this: 'Crucial to the idea

---

[39] Layder (1997, p. 110), in focusing on the problem of social relations, formulates this
issue in a way that comes close to the position of this study: "Thus in each circumstance of
everyday life the individual is both applying 'routine' or established behavioral formulations
to interactional problems at the very same time as creating new 'solutions' or ways of dealing
with the emergent unpredictability of face-to-face encounters. However, this creativity
is not unfettered by social structures (and systems) and is not entirely free-form as some
interactionists (Blumer and the Chicago school) have implied or suggested."
[40] In my opinion Giddens avoids simple dichotomies that are criticized by Law. I interpret the
point made by Law, and the position of ANT not as a position against structuration theory
such as it is formulated by Giddens. I interpret ANT as a theory that is critical of simple
dichotomies that are unable to rise above the fundamental dissatisfaction formulated by
Latour.

of structuration is the theorem of the duality of structure, which is logically implied in the arguments portrayed above. The constitution of agents and structures *are not two independently given sets of phenomena*, a dualism, but represent a duality. According to the notion of the duality of structure, *the structural properties of social systems are both medium and outcome of the practices they recursively organize*. Structure is not 'external' to individuals: as memory traces, and as instantiated in social practices, it is in a sense more 'internal' than exterior to their activities in a Durkheimian sense. Structure is not to be equated with constraint but is always constraining and enabling. This, of course, does not prevent the structured properties of social systems from stretching away, in time and space, beyond the control of any individual actors' (italics added). The macro theoretical network in this study should conceptualize this interplay between levels in a comparable way.

3.2 Systems theory as a macro theoretical framework

The study will use systems theory as a general framework. There are four arguments for choosing systems theory. The first two arguments have nothing to do with the issue of connecting theoretical levels or with the issue of the relation between structure and agency, but with the status of systems theory. According to Clark (2000, p. 59): 'Systems theories are the heartland of orthodox and much current organisation theory.' That means that many useful theoretical insights within organizational studies are based on, or somehow related to systems theory. Furthermore, the problem of dealing with dynamic complexity is considered to be the main issue within systems theory (Blom, 1997). This is important because this study is interested in a social system involved in a specific context with specific characteristics. As such systems theory seems in particular suitable for this study. The third argument has to do with the ability to connect multiple levels of analysis. Blom (1997) emphasized that one of the main characteristics of systems theory is indeed its abstract nature and emphasized that exactly this provides systems theory a potential to tackle many different theoretical issues. The fourth argument is connected to the topic of structure and agency. Although systems theory does not use the concepts "agency and structure" as such, a comparable viewpoint on the relation between the local and the global. Becker (2005, p. 233) formulates this as following: '(…) the relation between structure and action in theories of social practices is equivalent to the relation between operations and structure in systems theories. Structures are structures only insofar as they function as structures. They are virtual in existence and do not have any ontological status beyond the mere operations of the system they structure (...). Moreover, Luhmann considers the relation of structure and operations a relation of mutual dependence. By explicitly referring to Giddens, Luhmann perceives the relationship of structure and "agency" (operations) as "one of reciprocal enabling". In other words, systems theory moves beyond unidirectional relations between explanatory levels, *although one particular direction may be of the centre of attention in a specific study*[41].

3.3 A history of systems theory

Elements of systems thinking can be found in a diversity of scientific approaches. *As early as 1971* Von Bertalanffy remarked that: 'System-theoretical approaches include general systems theory (in the narrower sense), cybernetics, theory of automata, control theory, information theory, set, graph, and network theory, relational mathematics, game and decision theory, computerization and simulation, and so on' (1971, p. 30). Here, systems theory is interpreted as a tool that can be used to think about organizational issues. In organizational studies, organizations or groups in organizations are portrayed as a system, or as a system consisting of systems (Van der Vlist, 1981). As such, systems theory provides researchers a tool to focus on particular organizations or parts of an organization and, depending on how this focus is defined, particular problems become visible or remain out of focus (In 't Veld, 1987). It is, in other words, a metaphor one can use to interpret reality (Van Eijnatten, 2002)[42].

---

[41] I want to argue that systems theory provides organizational studies a diversity of tools that can be used to tackle a diversity of problems. Contrasting two approaches may illustrate this point. De Sitter (2000) and Christis (1998) attempted to supply the traditional open sociotechnical systems theory with a theoretical foundation that is orientated on the recent self-referential paradigm in systems theory. The emphasis of the resulting Sociotechnical Systems Design theory is a theory that can be used to design organizations that are confronted with a 'problematic' environment. Thus, systems theory is used to create an order that is better suited to the kinds of problems this order encounters. However, insights from systems theory can also be used to 'break down' order. For example, Van Galen and Van Eijnatten (2002) discussed how insights from chaos theory had helped an organization to become aware of and understand problems they had previously been unaware of. Kramer & Kuipers (2002) argued that the success of the Israeli Army in the 1960s and 70s could partly be attributed to the 'out of control' character of their operational units. Because of this 'out of control' character and the resulting 'chaos', the Israeli Army was 'truly' able to learn. If one considers systems theory to be a tool to model organizational problems, then the way the model is applied depends on one's specific interest, which, indeed, may be creating a new order or breaking down an existing one. This means that the definition of a core concept such as dynamic complexity should be tailored to suit the study's specific interests.

[42] One's exact understanding of the metaphor determines, of course, one's perception of reality. In organizational theory, all the different system theoretical paradigms have been

In order to place the concept of dynamic complexity against this theoretical background, I will briefly describe the history of systems theory. It should be noted that I refer here to *general* systems theory. Von Bertalanffy (1971, p. 24) emphasized that systems thinking had emerged as an alternative to the paradigm of classical science, which explained complex phenomena in terms of *isolated* elements and unidirectional causal relations. Instead, systems theory proposed to focus on the organization of the elements in order to explain complex phenomena (Von Bertalanffy, 1971, p. 25; presumably on the basis of an Aristotelian dictum). Rapoport (1968) identified the crucial elements of systems thinking as:

– 'something consisting of a set of entities
– among which a set of relations is specified, so that
– deductions are possible from such relations to others or from the relations among the entities to the behavior or the history of the system' (see also, Van der Vlist, 1981).

One can say that different paradigms in systems thinking differ in opinion about all of these points: the nature of the components of a system, the nature of the relation between the components, the nature of the relation between the system and the environment, etc. For the present description I will use a distinction between three different 'paradigms' in systems thinking used by Blom (1997): the paradigms of 'classical' systems theory, open systems theory and self-referential systems theory. Although Blom (1997, p. 20) admitted that a distinction like this is arbitrary, it is at least useful to sketch the theoretical background of the concept of 'dynamic complexity'.

Three paradigms

'Classical' approaches were equaled by Blom (1997) with the structural functionalist approach of theorists like Talcott Parsons and Ratcliffe Brown, which originated from anthropological research. Societies were considered as a structured whole, with each part accomplishing a necessary function. The main criticism on this approach was that it was orientated to stability and at the issue of preserving existing structures. This approach relied, therefore, on the assumption of a uniform and generally accepted system of values (Blom, 1997, p. 14). In other words, classical approaches were

applied. Many are familiar with Katz and Kahn's (1978) account of what open systems theory means for organizational studies, but also the more recent insights on chaos and complexity have found their way into organizational studies. Van Eijnatten (2004) has extensively documented how these recent insights (which, on a closer look, are not so recent, according to Van Eijnatten) are used within organizational studies. Within the confines of this study it is, obviously, impossible and unnecessary to present a complete account of how systems theory has found its way in organizational studies.

considered to be too much orientated to the 'static' properties of systems in order to be able to account for phenomena like variability and change.

In response to the classical approaches, theorists like Von Bertalanffy, Ackoff and Ashby developed the 'open systems paradigm'. In this approach, open systems are distinguished from closed systems (or a system/environment distinction replaced a whole/part distinction, Luhmann, 1995, p. 6). Open systems are typically not just *located* in an environment; they entertain a *dynamic relationship* with this environment (Blom, 1997, p. 18). A closed system, like a clock, is located in an environment but its internal processes proceed relatively independent of external forces, or can be understood to proceed like that. The behavior of open systems, however, was understood to be the result of an interaction between a system and its environment. According to Blom (1997, p. 18) this resulted in the 'primacy of the environment', and phenomena like 'change' and 'development' were understood to be adaptive reactions to the environment. This open systems approach has achieved an important status within organizational theory (for example the 'open sociotechnical systems approach'). One specific problem challenged the open systems paradigm. If systems adapt to the environment, the question was 'how do they adapt?' (Blom, 1997). In other words: adaptation presupposes a *strategic selection* of relevant information from the environment and a *strategic change* of the internal composition of the system. In that case, adaptation depends on the existing structures within a system, which means that a system is not 'open', nor does it 'adapt' in a simple way. Systems apparently can deal with change and the unknown if they are somehow equipped to recognize and therefore anticipate the unknown. However, how unknown is the unknown if it is anticipated?

One can recognize a problem of circularity in this line of reasoning: a system can only adapt to relevant new developments in the environment if it is somehow equipped to recognize these relevant new developments. This criticism of circularity was the stepping-stone for the development of the paradigm of self-referential system theories. The paradigm of self-referential systems theories is orientated to the issue of how dynamical systems organize this circularity (Blom, 1997, p. 20). Luhmann (1995, p. 9) states: 'The theory of self-referential systems maintains that systems can differentiate only by self-reference, which is to say, only insofar as systems refer to themselves (be this to elements of the same system, to operations of the same system, or to the unity of the same system) in constituting their elements and their elementary operations.' According to Blom (1997, p. 21) all theories that are orientated on circular models are counted among the self-referential theories. This includes the 'recent trend' in science: chaos and complexity theory. Complexity science, for example, studies how, and under what conditions, order (distinguishable integrated wholes; i.e. a system/environment distinction) can emerge out of chaos (Waldrop, 1992). Within the paradigm of self-referential systems theories, the concept of *autopoiesis* has become a central issue. Autopoiesis is a concept from biology that Maturana and Varela used to capture the essence of living systems, namely that living systems are able to produce and reproduce the elements they are constituted from (Blom, 1997). Autopoietic systems are systems that reproduce the elements that they are constituted from through the elements they are constituted from (Blom, 1997, p. 24). It should be emphasized that they do not essentially reproduce the physical or chemical reality of their elements but reproduce themselves *as a system* or as an organization of selectively interacting elements. The systems level cannot be reduced to its material basis, i.e. the systems level has characteristics that are *emergent*. In complexity science, a frequently mentioned example of emergent characteristics that cannot be reduced to a material basis is *water*. The characteristic of fluidity cannot be reduced to characteristics of individual water molecules. A *swarm* or system of water molecules possesses a characteristic that is emergent upon the material basis.

By postulating such an 'emergent identity', the paradigm of self-referential systems theories re-introduces an idea of 'closure'. Systems need a particular kind of 'closure' in order to be able to be open (Blom, 1997, p. 27). However, according to the interpretation of Blom (1997, p. 27), self-referential systems need to open themselves for information from the outside. If closure would imply a 'direct circularity' (a system can only see what it already knows) a system would be essentially closed. A solution to the *'totally open but empty/totally closed but blind'* paradox lies hidden in the definition of the concept of autonomy. Autonomy in self-referential systems theory refers to the ability of a system to regulate its dependence and independence (Blom, 1997, p. 26). That means that the environment can 'irritate' or 'trigger', but the environment cannot determine change in the system (see the definition of autonomy given in Chapter One). If one reflected casually on this line of reasoning, it might appear that a new form of essentialism is proposed: the 'true core' of the system (its closure) determines its identity. This would take systems theory back to square one: the classic idea of shared values. However, the order in systems that are studied by this paradigm is not one that is based on a design blueprint or the design actions of a central controller. For example, an issue that is frequently underlined in complexity theory is the issue of 'order for free' (Kauffman, 1995). 'Order for free' refers to order that emerges out of (selective) local interactions between elements without there being a central controller or blueprint. A biologist like Kauffman studies under what conditions such order can come into existence, i.e. 'the laws of self-organization'.

3.4 Dynamic complexity and the problem of openness

The previous discussion will have made it clear that systems theory in its most recent formulation is neither fundamentally based on an assumption of stability nor is it based on a naive idea of adaptation. My interpretation is that, as a consequence of the transition from the open systems paradigm to the self-referential paradigm, a difference in focus on a system's essential problems has emerged. Instead of assuming the openness of the system (open systems theory), the issue of openness of the system becomes the essential problem for *self-referential* systems theory. The problem of openness is one of the main issues of this paradigm.

This interpretation can be justified by discussing the nature and place of the concept of complexity in social systems theory (systems operating on the basis of communication, Knodt, 1995, p. xxiii). According to Luhmann (1995, p. 27), the self-referential paradigm is based on a different conception of complexity compared to earlier paradigms: '(…) one that must be formulated entirely as a difference in complexity. One must distinguish the incomprehensible complexity in a system (or its environment) that would result if one connected everything with everything else, from determinately structured complexity, which can only be selected contingently. And one must distinguish environmental complexity (in both forms) from system complexity (again in both forms); the system complexity is always lesser and must compensate by exploiting its contingency, that is, by its patterns of selection.' From this portrayal it follows that *both* system and environment are considered to be complex. Systems are 'organized complexity' (complexity with selective relations among its elements (Luhmann, 1996, p. 24)). Moreover, a system is complex because it is incapable of observing its own complexity (Luhmann, 1995, p. 28). Blom (1997, p. 38) explains this problem by emphasizing the paradox of self-observation: a system can observe itself, but it cannot observe itself while observing itself. Furthermore, it follows that *reduction* of complexity is the basis of system formation, in other words, reduction of complexity is constitutive of a distinction between system and environment. Knodt (1995, p. xvii) underlined that this difference is of crucial importance: 'Without it, there would be nothing, no world consisting of discrete entities, but only undifferentiated chaos.' Besides, Knodt underlined that the relation between system and environment is asymmetrical and simplifying. Luhmann (1995, p. 25) stated further that: 'Establishing and maintaining the difference between system and environment then becomes the problem, because for each system the environment is more complex than the system itself.' From this I conclude that openness to the complexity in the environment is the essential problem in this paradigm of systems theory.

The foregoing has consequences for the way in which the concept of dynamic complexity is perceived in this study (as stated in chapter 1, I use the phrase *dynamic* complexity instead of complexity). Given the central issues of self-referential systems theory, dealing with dynamic complexity is not a matter of simple adaptation. In this study, dynamic complexity refers to an identified system (here a military unit) that experiences problematic environmental conditions. Given the main topics of self-referential systems theory, the *essential* problem of dealing with dynamic complexity becomes the way in which such units can be open to the problematic environment in order to be able to adapt strategically to these conditions. This issue is therefore the cornerstone in modeling the problem of dealing with dynamic complexity.

Making a system/environment distinction

In this study, dynamic complexity has been roughly defined by identifying an abstract structure. The previous discussion will have made clear that this abstract structure is not 'innocent' in the sense that it implies a choice for a particular system/ environment distinction. The abstract structure emphasizes an organizational system that is confronted with a problematic environment and a necessity to deal with this environment. This description implies that the operational units deployed in crisis operations are considered to be 'the system'. The actors that operate in the operational environment of the system are considered to be 'the environment'. The 'organizational context' of the operational units occupies a special place in this description. It designs and controls 'the system' but is not considered to be part of 'the operational environment'. Operational units can be considered to be subsystems of the crisis organization. The relation between the system and its organizational context crucially influences the system's ability to deal with dynamic complexity. It should be emphasized that this distinction is 'pragmatic', i.e. the system/environment distinction is drawn in this particular way because it logically follows from the central issues in this study (one can image that in other studies the system/environment distinctions may be drawn in a different way). In this description, dynamic complexity is something that is perceived by the system as being located in the environment. The system is consequently confronted with the necessity to deal with dynamic complexity.

The *origin* of the concept of 'dynamic complexity' as it is used here can be found in the open systems paradigm. Here, I want to argue that although this study uses a traditional system/environment distinction and indeed certain ingredients from open systems theory, this choice is made on the basis of a modern interpretation of systems theory. This interpretation implies that insights from earlier paradigms of systems theory are not considered useless, but are, however, not seen as capturing the essence of systems thinking. For example, classical systems theory is orientated to stability of structures. Of course, systems sometimes show interesting signs of stability, but that does not mean that they are essentially orientated to stability. Equally, the phenomenon of adaptation to a dynamically complex environment is something that is important and interesting, without necessarily claiming that it is a system's essential act.

3.5 Final remarks

This chapter discussed the choice for systems theory as a macrotheoretical framework and discussed the most relevant historical developments within systems theory. The next chapter aims to relate these abstract concerns to the problems organizations are confronted with.

Chapter 4

The concept of dynamic complexity and the organizing problem

This chapter focuses on the previously introduced 'abstract structure' of dealing with dynamic complexity. In the introduction it was specified that this abstract structure was made up of a *problematic environment* that characterized by *indeterminacy*. It was, furthermore, specified that this environment confronts the organization with a *necessity to act*. This chapter specifies what is exactly meant by the phrases 'a problematic environment', 'dealing with the problematic environment'. Furthermore, 'the organizing problem' that these environments confront organizations with, is specified. The previous chapter described the essence of the challenge of dealing with dynamic complexity as a problem of openness. This chapter relates the abstract structure of dealing with dynamic complexity to this problem of openness.

4.1 The basic problem of dealing with dynamic complexity

To underline the subtleness of the problem of dealing with dynamic complexity, the following example is presented, which originates from a discerning scientific experiment conducted by Alex Bavelas. The following account is paraphrased from a discussion by Jay Haley (1986, pp. 145–147):

In his theory building experiment, Dr. Bavelas would tell his subjects that he wished them to develop a theory in an area where they had no knowledge. He confronted his subjects with pictures of cells. The subjects' task was to guess whether a particular cell was sick or healthy. Subsequently, they received feedback if their guess was right or wrong. After that, they were presented a second picture, made a guess, received feedback and were presented with the next picture, etc. However, none of the cells in the pictures were particularly healthy or sick. Furthermore, regardless of their choice, the experimental subjects were told 60 % of the time that they were right and 40% of the time that their guess was wrong. The feedback they received was therefore independent of the actual choices the experimental subjects made. In so doing the subjects developed an implicit theory about the characteristics of healthy and sick cells. They would, for example, theorize that a sick cell had a round body with a thing hanging down, etc. After the experiment they were asked to write their theory down. This theory was presented to a next generation of experimental subjects, which used the theory to make guesses about the nature of cells. The second generation also wrote its theory down and this 'second-generation theory' was presented to a third generation. The third generation used the theory to make guesses about the cells, they wrote down their theory, and so on. The design of the experiment made it, of course, impossible to develop a theory that was perfect. Instead, the typical pattern that emerged from the experiment was a theory that became increasingly complex over generations. Bavelas was interested in the development of theories. A typical pattern that emerged from the experiment was that if someone from about the fourth generation looked at the extraordinarily complex theory, he would say 'the hell with it' and disregard the theory. He would start from scratch and develop a more simple theory based on his guesses; this theory would be passed on to a next generation and so on.

Bavelas was interested in the development of theories. His experiment showed that theories tend to grow more complex until a revolution throws them over (Haley, 1986). The experiment can also be used to illustrate the paradoxes of dealing with dynamic complexity.

A problematic environment

In Bavelas' experiment, the problematic nature of reality (i.e. the diagnosis of the cells) was the essential problem the subjects had to deal with. The fact that only 60 % of the guesses were right ensured that this was a problem for which no objective solution existed. Applied to organizational theory, a quotation from Karl Weick illustrates the nature of a problematic reality (1979, p. 6): 'The basic raw material on which organizations operate are informational inputs that are ambiguous, uncertain, equivocal.' Weick (1995, p. 95) emphasized three different types of uncertainty that organizations are confronted with. The first type refers to a lack of understanding of the way in which the context of the organization changes ('state uncertainty'). In other words, the environment hides 'the unknown'. Secondly, organizations are unaware of the precise impact of environmental changes on the organization ('effect uncertainty'). The third type refers to uncertainty with regard to the best way to react towards changes ('response uncertainty'). Ambiguity refers to the problem that elements in the context of an organization can be understood in different, even opposing ways. Weick (1995, p. 92): 'Ambiguity (...) means that the assumptions necessary for rational decision-making are not met. The problem in ambiguity is not that the real world is imperfectly understood and that more information will remedy that. The problem is that information may not resolve misunderstandings.' In this respect, ambiguity differs from uncertainty. Equivocality is the phenomenon of multiple meaning. Weick (1979, p. 174): 'Things that are equivocal do not lend themselves to definite classifications. They can always be classified as indications of two or more different objects and meanings. Equivoques are indeterminate, inscrutable, ambivalent, and questionable, and they permit multiple meanings.' Ambiguity, in other words, refers to 'confused meaning' and equivocality to 'multiple meaning'[43].

The problems for Bavelas' experimental subjects only arose after they attempted to develop a theory. The pictures of the cells were not problematic in themselves; they became problematic as a result of attempts to develop a theory. 'The environment' became complex as a result of the ambitions of the 'organizational system', i.e. the 'closure' (the ambitions) of the system was necessary to see problems at all. Equally, dynamic complexity is not a straightforward characteristic of the environment. The environment of an organization is – in a sense – the construction of the organization. An environment gets constructed as a result of the organization's ambitions and it gets shaped as a result of the actions of the organization (Weick, 1979). This, of course, does not imply that the environment is dependent on the organizational system. The environment has a *causal texture* (Emery & Trist, 1969) independent of the organization, but the relevance of this environment is dependent on the organization's involvement in that environment[44]. Dynamic complexity is therefore the result from the interaction of purposeful behavior of a system in an uncertain ambiguous, equivocal but reactive environment.

There are two distinctive ways in which the nature of the organization's environment differs from the tasks of the subjects in Bavelas' experiment. Bavelas' experiment may even be a little misleading. Throughout Bavelas' experiment the environment did not react to the actions of the subjects and neither did it change. Regardless of the choices of the experimental subjects, the pictures of the cells stayed the same and the good/bad answer ratio stayed the same as well. This is quite unlike the complexity organizations are

---

[43] Different approaches within organizational theory emphasize that "uncertainty", "ambiguity" and "sensemaking" are crucial problems for organizations. One can even claim that there is a diversity of approaches that emphasize themes like the "uncertainty principle" and the subsequent problem of "constructing reality" (Alvesson & Deetz, 1996). Although scientists interested in these general problems study comparable phenomena and define comparable concepts, their concepts have different names and slightly different contents, emphasizing slightly different aspects of the same problem. Alvesson & Deetz (1996) called these "postmodern approaches" and emphasized that critical theory can also be added to this general category.

[44] Emery & Trist (1969) distinguished four types of causal texturing: the placid randomized environment, the placid clustered environment, the disturbed reactive environment, and turbulent fields. Dynamic complexity could be located in type 4, the turbulent field.

confronted with. The organizational context is *reactive* (competitors alter strategies in reaction to the choices of the organizational system; Emery & Trist, 1969) and *dynamic* (the environment changes independently of the organizational system: 'the ground is in motion'; Emery & Trist, 1969, p. 249). In the second place, the development of a workable theory was made impossible for Bavelas' experimental subjects. That is quite unlike the picture of dealing with dynamic complexity that I would like to draw. If reality is fundamentally chaotic or unstructured and no insight is useful to get a grip on things, then thinking is useless because it offers no extra value (Emery & Trist, 1969). In that case the environment is random. This is not characteristic of dynamically complex situations that are of interest to this study. They are *problematic*, but *not necessarily fundamentally chaotic*. As has been said, dynamically complex situations are not necessarily completely ordered as well. Dynamic complexity probably refers, therefore, to a state on the edge of chaos (see Waldrop, 1992).

The organizing problem

Bavelas' experimental subjects were confronted with a problem of construction (building a theory in order to make better guesses) given the problematic nature of their reality. The efforts of Bavelas' experimental subjects were in vain. A closer look, however, reveals an interesting function of the theories. In the experiment, the subjects used the theories in order to raise themselves beyond the stage of guesses. The theories helped to observe new cells in a more structured way by drawing attention to some characteristics, but at the cost of drawing attention away from other characteristics. They helped to make **meaningful choices** (not random) and acted as an anchoring point to add new insights. One can imagine situations in which an organizational system is right 80 %, or even 90 % or 100 % of the time. These situations are less dynamically complex. A 100 % situation is absolutely stable. Theories will never be disregarded in a 100 % situation. Opposed to that, in a 0 % or 10 % situation, no theoretical insight will be sustained for very long, perhaps only the crudest rule of thumb.

In a way, dealing with dynamic complexity involves making increasingly better guesses while absolute certainty is not available. Weick's definition of organizing implies this (1979, p. 3): 'Organizing serves to narrow the range of possibilities, to reduce the number of 'might occurs'. The activities of organizing are directed toward the establishment of a workable level of certainty.' Furthermore he claims that: 'To organize is to assemble ongoing interdependent actions into sensible sequences that generate sensible outcomes.' One can therefore say that organizing activities help an organization to overcome the level of mere guessing and help an organization to act meaningfully. Weick's definition indicates that organizing is considered to be a process. Weick frequently emphasized that organizing is a verb rather than a noun. In line with Weick, this study considers the informational inputs in organizations to be elementarily ambiguous, uncertain and equivocal. With 'elementary' I mean that it is a problem that cannot be solved. The informational input of organizations is such that it cannot be transferred into certainty. That is to say, it is possible to transform it into a workable type, but not into an absolute type of certainty[45]. As a consequence, organizations are never finished thinking. At the same time, however, 'thinking' has its limitations. An interesting point that follows from this is that in **more** complex situations only theories that are **less** complex are workable and sustainable[46]. In absolutely chaotic (0 %) situations no theory is workable[47]. Note that this line of reasoning is the consequence of defining 'chaos' in a certain way[48].

Many understand organizing as involving 'developing rules to deal with all possible situations'. This can be compared to the task of developing a perfect theory about the cells. In Bavelas' experiment developing such a the-

---

[45] The cornerstones of postmodern philosophy in particular remain under fierce discussion, especially centering on the topic of relativism. If one wants to abolish the idea of "one objective truth", does one claim that nothing can be considered as certain (extreme relativism)? Or is such a position the consequence (result??) of conceptual confusion? Such themes are central in the discussions between "social constructionists" and "critical realists" (Shotter, 1993; Parker, 1998; Sayer, 2000, etc.).

[46] In crisis organizations, 'scenario thinking' is particularly popular. It refers to the practice of building different operational scenarios based on "what ifs". This is, of course, a sensible practice, but the previous point makes it clear that in more complex situations scenarios can only be less precise. In the most complicated dynamic situations, scenarios will probably involve some critical procedures that should be applied if things get terribly out of hand. In dynamically complex situations, scenarios built up of more complicated procedures can lead to an illusion of certainty. If one aims to remain purely rational in circumstances in which the nature of reality is problematic, one can fall victim to a sort of endless rational regression (ever more complex theories). Apart from an illusion of certainty, an orientation on pure rationality can lead to apathy (no ability to make choices between cells). In an environment that is complex, striving for total control and absolute insight in order to find 'the one and only right solution for a problem' leads to nothing.

[47] Karl Weick, as can be understood from the following quotation, made the same point. 'The greater the perceived amount of equivocality present in the input, the *fewer* the number of rules used to compose the process. Conversely, the smaller the perceived amount of equivocality in the input, the greater number of rules used to assemble a process. If an input is judged to be highly equivocal, there is uncertainty as to exactly what it is and how it should be handled: this makes it more difficult to judge what the appropriate cycles would be or how many should be applied. As a result, only a small number of rather general rules are used to assemble a process. However, if the input is judged to be less equivocal, there is more certainty as to what the item is and how it should be handled; hence a greater number of rules can be applied in assembling a process to deal with this input' (italics in original; Weick, 1979, p. 114).

[48] As has been said, other approaches in systems theory underline the importance of chaos in organizations (Van Eijnatten, 2004) on the basis of an orientation on different kinds of organizational problems (for example, issues of organizational change).

ory was impossible in principle. A workable theory was the best the subjects could achieve. Inherent in the structure of Bavelas' experiment is that such a workable theory does not remain stable. It becomes more refined and parts are disregarded ('the hell with it'). One can set approaches that emphasize the importance of dynamic complexity apart from classic organizational theory. The latter aimed to establish the one best way of organizing (Perrow, 1985; Morgan, 1997).

4.2 The problem of openness as the essence of the organizing problem

In the previous sections, the nature of dynamic complexity has been characterized using Weick's theory and Bavelas' experiments. Here, the implications of this portrayal of dynamic complexity are discussed by clarifying why the problem of openness is the essence of the organizing problem. The theories of Bavelas' experimental subjects functioned by recognizing the common (lessons from experiences with earlier cells) in the unique (the new cells). The experimental subjects were 'open' to new information by comparing it to existing abstract structures. Although this is a common strategy in dealing with dynamic complexity, there is an obvious risk related to this procedure: the illusion of certainty. Systems are not truly open if they compare 'the new' on the basis of 'the existing'. The problem of this 'lack of openness' is that new situations may be unlike the old, and focusing on the common may lead one to overlook the unique.

Sense-making is an essential process in dealing with complexity ('narrowing the range of possibilities'), but at the same time it is a dangerous process. A sensible observer focuses therefore also on structures that disconfirm existing insights. One could say that sense-discrediting is a process that is as important as the process of sense-making (Weick, 1979), because it functions as a balancing force. Dealing with dynamic complexity demands therefore rather paradoxical qualities of operators: systems confronted with a dynamically complex environment need to be able to develop intelligent ideas about that environment (sense-making) but at the same time need to be able to criticize their ideas (sense-discrediting). Since there is a tension between sense-making and sense-discrediting, an organization cannot overcome the organizing problem by optimizing one basic quality (for example, sense-making). More detailed information or more thorough analysis on the basis of ever more sophisticated analytical models will not result in solving the organizing problem in an absolute way (see Weick's description of ambiguity). That does not, however, mean that more information and more thorough analyses will be useless in principle. They will just not provide *the* final answer[49].

However, sense-making coupled with sense-discrediting as a balancing force does not provide the system 'real openness'. Sense-discrediting without action, or without 'real world' experience, is little more than an isolated intellectual game. This is not real openness because isolated intellectual games proceed from 'the known' and can therefore be blind to 'the unknown'. Real openness implies that a system is open to information that it has never thought of before. For this reason, *action* is an important informer for systems. In fact, action provides the system with a stream of data that is necessary for the development of further insight. In Bavelas' experiment, acting and thinking were interwoven in a complex way. The experimental subjects had no choice but to build ideas upon previous actions, while these previous actions were based on (first less, then more educated) guesses. The theories result from actions: making choices and see what happens. Acting and thinking are therefore closely related if a system is dealing with dynamic complexity. Actions necessitate thinking (otherwise actions would be based on blind guesses), and thinking necessitates action (given their hypothetical nature, the theories need experimentation). If presented with the unknown, systems can be confronted with circumstances in which they need to act before they can think. New experiences are therefore the source for discrediting.

Again, it is questionable whether action coupled with sense-making and sense-discrediting provides the system with 'real openness', i.e. an observation of the outside world and its complexities without any preconceptions. After all, if new experiences discredit existing insights the new experiences still have to be interpreted. In a way, existing structures are used for interpretation, which implies that new information is processed on the basis of a certain 'closure'. A system cannot be open in a fundamental way, as the preceeding makes clear. In that sense there is no perfect way of dealing with dynamic complexity. At the same time, however, it makes clear that systems that are prepared to act and are able to make sense of their experiences and are able to discredit their existing insights are better able to deal with dynamic complexity than others. After all, they are more orientated to 'being open'. Such a system may not be open in an absolute sense, but an orientation to openness can make a huge practical difference. In this sense these systems are 'dealing with complexity in the best possible way' while this

---

[49] This can perhaps be compared to the problem of weather forecasts. No matter how sophisticated the means of analyses, the weather can still surprise all forecasts (chaos theorists have shown that the weather is unpredictable in principle (Lorenz, 1996)). However, forecasts are still useful and most of the time quite adequate, especially if the forecast is limited to one or two days. Weather forecasts provide a workable level of certainty (e.g. for farmers) but no *eternal* level of certainty.

does not provide a system with any guarantees that they are truly open and are able survive. Systems are never 'open' in an absolute sense, but they can try to be as open as they can possibly be.

4.3 Final remarks

This chapter related abstract notions from systems theory to the problems organizations experience when they are confronted with dynamic complexity. The next chapter will refine these ideas by discussing a model for dealing with dynamic complexity. This model – Karl Weick's organizing model – incorporates these basic notions on organizing. In not every instance, however, are the subtleties that are discussed in this chapter recognized by Weick. In a way therefore, one can say that the next chapter extends the model used, by developing it further.

Chapter 5

A model of dealing with dynamic complexity

The first part of this chapter aims to provide an abstract description of 'meaningful action'. In the second part of this chapter, Weick's model will be described (i.e. this description implies both the normative and descriptive element). The final section of this chapter is devoted to a critical discussion of the main features of Weick's thinking on organizing and organizations, in an attempt to position Weick within the field of organizing studies in general. The next chapter will identify a distinction between the descriptive and the normative element of Weick's model. Subsequently, the normative element will be elaborated.

5.1. A description of meaningful action

Previously, the importance of meaningful action was underlined. The phrase 'meaningful action' refers to the issue that an organization that is confronted with dynamic complexity should advance beyond the level of mere guessing. However, it has not yet been discussed how the logic of 'not being absolutely sure and not totally guessing' should be more formally expressed. In order to deal with dynamic complexity, a system should neither act on the basis of a closed system of rules, nor should it act totally at random. Between the extremes of perfect rationality (a totalitarian system of rules) and perfect irrationality (no rules whatsoever) there exists a third option: the level of hypotheses. To act neither on the basis of guesses nor on the basis of absolute certainty is to act on the basis of hypotheses. Meaningful action can therefore be described 'as acting on the basis of hypotheses', which implies acting on the basis of fallible, partial, and preliminary knowledge of the environment.

The same type of logic that can describe the structure of the methodology used here can, in other words, describe the specific character of everyday thinking. Both deduction and induction cannot characterize the typical character of everyday thinking. As has been said in Chapter Two, one can only answer the demands of deductive reasoning if one has a system of perfect rules and an objective account of the circumstances at one's disposal. Deduction, therefore, is an unsuited style of thinking in complex circumstances or, in other words, is typical of dynamically complex environments that deduction is not possible. For some scientists the 'probable character' of inductive conclusions is a point in its advantage because it reminds them of the way people think in everyday reality. However, to think that induction resembles everyday thinking is a misunderstanding of the nature of everyday thinking or the nature of induction.

The logic of abduction is used out of necessity: because of the dynamic nature of the circumstances, an operator cannot rely on a closed system of rules, as this denies that circumstances are ever-changing and dynamically complex. The logic of abduction does offer a description of meaningful action, but it does not provide a normative perspective on the issue. This chapter aims to present a model that can be used for this purpose.

5.2 A model of organizing

The model that will be used to describe the dynamic between system and environment is the so-called 'organizing model' that Karl Weick explicated in *The social psychology of organizing* (1979). For the purposes of this study, one could also name it the 'self-organizing model'. The organizing model describes the organization process within a system, which is in this study an operational unit:

- It assumes that a system deals with dynamic complexity by using hypotheses; it describes how a system engaged in a dynamically complex environment develops hypotheses. This implies that Weick's model is presented here as a model that describes the process of abduction's organizing model. To my knowledge, this is the first time this link is explicitly made, although Weick has hinted at the importance of hypotheses[50].
- It explains how a system can deal with dynamic complexity in the best possible way. Therefore it adds a normative element to the idea of abduction.

In Weick's thinking, organizing is synonymous with 'dealing with dynamic complexity'. On this subject Weick stated (1979, p. 6): 'The basic raw materials on which organizations operate are informational inputs that are ambiguous, uncertain, and equivocal. Whether the information is embedded in tangible raw materials, recalcitrant customers, assigned tasks, or union demands, there are many possibilities or sets of outcome that might occur. Organizing serves to narrow the range of possibilities, to reduce the number of 'might occurs'. Indeed, hypotheses about the nature of a situation help to narrow the range of possibilities. The model is inspired by evolution theory

---

[50] 'In effect, interacting with one another, employees generate hypotheses about what is going on, what can be done, and what the long term, system-wide consequences of proposed actions might be' (Weick & Sutcliffe, 2001, p. 60).

(Weick, 1979, p. 122) and the elements are functional elements of natural selection. The simple variant of Weick's model looks as follows (1979, pp. 132–133):

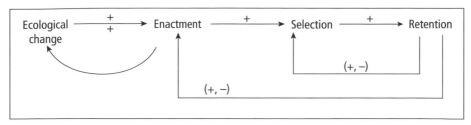

Model 5.1. Organizing model.

The various elements in the model

The various elements of the organizing model and their connections will be explained (Weick, 1979, pp. 130–132).

- *Ecological change.* This refers to raw change in the environment (that is, independent of the system's interpretation[51]). Raw input, ecological change, necessitates action. Raw input from the environment is not meaningful; it will only become meaningful after the subsequent steps in the model. To translate this into the experience of military units: their environments consist of uncertain elements and unexpected happenings. Suppose a unit experiences that it is being shot at. In itself an event such as this is not meaningful. It can be mere intimidation or it can be an outright assault. To be able to determine whether it is one or the other, however, one needs more than the raw input.
- *Enactment.* Enactment refers to 'action'. Action is therefore a necessary part of the organizing process. Weick described enactment as an 'act of bracketing'. Through acting, attention becomes focused on a particular part of the environment. As a result of acting the environment can react and provide further raw material (the arrows between ecological change and enactment). There are a number of implications that follow from this definition of enactment. A first implication is that a system by acting to some extent constructs its own environment: the system's actions can become an anchor for the environment to react to and an anchor for the organization for further acting and interpreting. The second implication is that, although by acting some equivocality is reduced (an interpretation inherent in the action) the result of an enactment is still equivocal

---

[51] The acknowledgement of a reality that exists independently of the system's interpretation makes it clear that Weick's model is also based on a realist's assumption. The acknowledgement that this reality is only accessible through a system's interpretations is further proof of a realist assumption.

79

and still needs interpretation. It is not meaningless as with ecological change, but has multiple meanings. When a military unit runs away from a shooting is that an act of outright cowardliness? Is running away a sensible way to deal with a hostile environment? The fact that the number of shootings subsequently increases is that a sign that the competitors in the environment have found out that the units are cowards? Or is it further proof that the environment is dangerously aggressive, which necessitate a different kind of measure?

- *Selection.* Enactment provides 'edited' raw material. Selection involves the imposition of various structures on enacted equivocal displays in an attempt to reduce their equivocality. Or, to use Weick's words: it generates answers to the question of 'what is going on there?' (1979, p. 175). The selection process makes the world more orderly, if not fully unequivocal (that is, in the mind of the organizing system). To recapture the previous example: the military unit that is being shot at can impose the interpretation that the 'local population is not to be trusted' and 'they shoot to kill' so 'we should get away as fast as one can', or 'it is just mere intimidation'. In an equivocal environment it is not sensible to entertain an unequivocal scheme of interpretation. The process of selection is therefore Janus-faced: one needs a reasonable degree of unequivocality in order to be able to act meaningfully. Too much unequivocality can make one blind to the complexity of the environment.

- *Retention.* This refers to the memory of an organization. It is the relatively straightforward storage place of the products of successful sense-making (1979, pp. 131–132). The input for the memory comes from the selection process (the arrow from selection to retention). On its part, retention influences subsequent selection (the arrow from retention to selection) and subsequent enactment (the arrow from retention to enactment). The content of the memory of organizations consists of 'cause-maps'. That means, an interpretation of the different elements in the environment and their relations. One could consider the memory to be the storage place of the various hypotheses. Also memory is Janus-faced: memory is necessary, but relying too much on memory can be very dysfunctional (signified by the plusses and minuses next to the arrows that leave retention).

The dynamic process portrayed by the model

The dynamic of the model can be described as follows. A system deals with the dynamic complexities of its environment (ecological change) by acting to meet the demands of the environment (enactment) and by developing insight into the nature of the environment on the basis of these actions (selection, retention). Note that the 'raw input' into the organizational system is 'equivocal', which makes the processes of enactment, selection and retention arbitrary in principle. Insight influences the environment that is enacted (the arrow that runs from enactment to ecological change). This is useful because it helps a system to act meaningfully, at least to raise itself beyond random action. 'Insight' is equaled here with 'hypotheses'. For that reason, dynamic complexity is dealt with by using hypotheses (previous insight influences subsequent action) and it is therefore considered to be a model that describes how hypotheses are developed (results of actions influence the development of hypotheses). **That means that Weick's model is interpreted here as a model that assumes abduction as the dominant logic in dealing with dynamic complexity.**

As a result of this dynamic, there is an inherent danger that the system becomes 'closed off' from the environment. This is the case when actions become increasingly influenced by existing insights. In order to prevent that a system can only see what it already knows, the system must be able to 'deny' or 'discredit' its insight. This is the trigger for identifying the normative element in this model. In other words, in an environment that is equivocal, ambiguous and uncertain, a system's existing knowledge is not sufficient. This means that it needs to possess a 'certain openness' towards the environment. The openness of a system is, in the first place, established by its actions and the resulting experiences. In the second place, the openness of a system is established by its ability to discredit what it already knows, i.e. doing something intelligent with new information (the plusses and minuses).

The process of dealing with dynamic complexity is very much depicted as an imperfect process by the organizing model. Weick's depiction shows a system that – through a process of developing insight – tries to get a grip on an environment. If a system would not attempt this, one could not say that it was acting sensibly. A system that would not attempt to develop insight in order to improve its ability to deal with the challenges of the environment would act randomly. However, attempts to get a grip on the environment have a simplifying effect (underestimating the complexity of the environment). Furthermore, present insights are always limited and are unaware of future developments. This portrayal of an imperfect process is inherent in the concept of hypotheses. If hypotheses were certain, they would not be hypotheses but perfect rules. The opposite is true as well. If hypotheses lacked any certainty, they would be merely random[52].

The connection between acting and thinking

One crucial feature of the organizing model is that knowledge and action are conceptualized as being interwoven[53]. According to the organizing model, knowledge does not come into existence by means of abstract reflection on the nature of things, but is influenced by previous action. Both knowledge and action are necessary for self-organization. Building up knowledge starts when practical needs give reason to do so. Ecological changes are the starting point of the model. The 'thought elements' of the model, selection and retention, only become active after enactment, i.e., after the organization has acted towards the changes in the environment. Changes are the reason attention is triggered and the process of organizing begins (Weick, 1979, p. 130). Consequently, meaning is retrospective, or action precedes thought (Weick, 1979, p. 194). In later stages of the model, previous moments of sense-making influence subsequent action. This subsequent action provides the occasion for further sense-making. Knowledge and action then become interwoven. In new situations (for example, when an operational unit arrives in its area of operation) there is no previous direct experience to base actions on. In such cases, enactments may be based on far-fetched analogies or rules of thumb or perhaps primitive instincts such as lust and fear. Subsequently, self-organization makes more self-organization possible (the strong become stronger, as chaos theorists would say). This, however, can

---

[52] An important implication of the particular relation between acting and thinking is that units are not considered to be rational decision-makers. Units do not act after a finite analysis of the relevant cues in the environment. Rather, they are confronted with change that necessitates action. Previous training and knowledge will influence action, indeed by thinking, but action is not dominated by thinking. Dynamically complex circumstances demand acting without too much scientific analysis. Weick (2001) emphasized that this notwithstanding, organizations and operators frequently have the illusion that action indeed is dominated by thinking. In an environment in which a system cannot know everything in advance, the system should be open to the environment. Action is an important constituent of this openness because it confronts an organization with the reality of the situation.

[53] As has already been concluded from Bavelas' experiment, when dealing with dynamic complexity or when engaging in organizing activities, acting and thinking are interdependent. This can be illustrated by a quotation. Weick (2001, p. 225): 'If action is a means to get feedback, learn, and build an understanding of unknown environments, then a reluctance to act could be associated with less understanding of unknown environments and more errors.' Later in this study (in the discussion of the Dutchbat case) it will be seen that an organization can become alienated from the environment by not acting.

be deceiving. As one gains experience, one becomes more orderly, but one can equally gain professional blinders to different interpretations as well[54].

Contradiction in the body of hypotheses

One particular important feature of Weick's organizing model is the position attributed to contradiction in the body of hypotheses. The hypotheses represent the system's knowledge about the environment. One can imagine that the knowledge of a system becomes increasingly elaborate in a dynamically complex environment. In order to appreciate the complex patterns in the theories, the concept of 'theories of action' is interesting. This is a concept that is introduced by Hedberg (1981, pp. 7–8): 'Theories of action (...) are for organizations what cognitive structures are for individuals. They filter and interpret signals from the environment and tie stimuli to responses. They are metalevel systems that supervise the identification of stimuli and the assembling of responses.' The substance of these theories of action consists of cause maps. Hedberg (1981, p. 7): 'To identify stimuli properly and to select adequate responses, organizations map their environments and infer what causal relationships operate in their environment. These maps constitute theories of action which organisations elaborate and refine as new situations are encountered.'

As a system develops more insight, it has an increasingly sophisticated reservoir from which to develop hypotheses. The theories of action help the operational units to understand the unfamiliar from the perspective of the familiar. In other words, the theories help units to develop a workable level of certainty, which is the object of organizing. In that way, theories of action can be compared to the theories about the cells from Bavelas. They help the operators to rise beyond the guessing stage and therefore beyond the stage of random action. Thus they help units to act meaningfully. The interesting characteristic of the theories of action is their pattern. They do not consist of unequivocal elements that can be distinguished on the basis of clear definitions. Rather, one can say that these theories of action consist of an indeterminate body of hypotheses that even displays contradictory elements, actually quite like the theories about the cells in Bavelas' experiment. To recapitulate Ashby's law of requisite variety (1969), the contents of the system (the theories of action) mirror the complexity in the environment. So a contradictory environment provides a contradictory content of the theories. A contradictory body of theories in a contradictory environment provides units with better adaptability. One can object that at least a certain measure

---

[54] According to Snook (2000), organizations can become incompetent as a result of too much training. If situations that organizations engage in differ from the situations that have been trained, units can display thoroughly trained but hugely inadequate responses. This is also called "trained incapacity".

of systemization is necessary in the operations of units. After all, rules can be helpful to create a workable level of certainty. The interesting part of the theories of action is their *lack* of systemization. One could consider this to be a weakness of the theories. However, this study claims that the nature of dynamic complexity is such that one cannot deal with dynamic complexity using a closed system of rules. This inevitably means that theories will lack systemization; the non-systematic ideas are considered helpful to make sense of a non-systematic environment.

5.3 Positioning Weick

According to the discussion in chapter three, the problem of openness is the essential issue for self-referential systems theory in the modeling of the problem of dealing with dynamic complexity. However, Weick could never have explicitly located himself within this current of thinking as the first edition of *The Social Psychology of Organizing* was published in 1969, before the self-referential paradigm was developed. According to Clark (2000, p. 233): 'Weick's intention is to deliver a theoretically significant perspective on organizing based on socio-evolutionary theory (...) and open, loosely coupled, systems thinking.' It is therefore important to analyze to what degree Weick's thinking on organizing is on par with the general formula of self referential systems thinking. In this section, Weick's theoretical position is analyzed. First, Weick's position in relation to the self-referential paradigm is discussed. Secondly, a critique of Weick's theoretical position is formulated by comparing his theoretical position with Giddens' structuration theory. Thirdly, the consequence of these discussions for this study are discussed.

Traces of self-referential thinking

Although Weick could never have intended his organizing model as a self-referential model, there are traces of the self-referential model in his work and I want to claim that Weick's organizing model differs significantly from the assumptions of open systems theory. In a way, therefore, one could argue that Weick's model is a self-referential model *avant la lettre*. There are various clues, more or less explicitly brought forward by Weick, that can support this claim:

- Weick's model simultaneously emphasizes the importance of sense-making, sense-discrediting and acting, so it can be interpreted as a model that is orientated to the problem of openness. The organizational system is not portrayed by Weick as an entity that adapts to environmental dynamics in a simple and straightforward way[55]. The organizational system is portrayed by Weick as an entity that wrestles to understand (making sense of) its actionss ('enactments') that are reactions to environmental contingencies;

- The elements of the organizational system in Weick's organizing model are 'ideas', or 'mental models' that provide the system with a perspective on the environment (they are the contingency the system exploits). Furthermore, according to Weick, a system is necessarily orientated to reduction of complexity (finding a 'workable level of certainty'), while at the same time this reduction of complexity becomes problematic;

- The normative element in Weick's model points to the necessity for systems to break through the 'chains' of their existing ideas. In other words, in order to achieve 'openness', a system needs to challenge or 'discredit' its existing world-view. Furthermore, Weick's theoretical logic suggests that the system's actions and reactions to environmental contingencies constitute an 'indispensable source of data from outside';

- Considering the previous points, Weick's model can be understood as a description of how *order* (structure) develops out of *chaos*. A system learns to act meaningfully first by acting (Bavelas' experiment: making random guesses) and then by developing theories about the nature of a situation and the actions of a system (i.e. meaning is retrospective). Furthermore, Weick's model gives indications about how *intelligence* should deal with order (the normative element) and emphasizes the importance of chaos to break through rigid world views ('chaotic action is preferable to orderly inaction' Weick, 1979, p. 245). At the same time, as pointed out by Stacey (1992, p. 123), Weick underlined the internal complexity of organizations, which is – in its entirety – incomprehensible for the individual. It is questionable whether Weick has deliberately developed his model to be on a par with recent trends in systems theory. It can, however, be interpreted as a model that achieves such an outcome.

Structuration in Weick

Also Clark (2000, p. 63) notes that there are important parallels between the thinking of Weick and autopoetic thinking, as does Morgan (1997). However, Clark also emphasizes that there are important differences. The finesse of Weick's position, more particularly the differences between Weick and antipoetic thinking, can be made clearer by discussing its relation to the structuration theory of Giddens. Again, Weick did not formulate his

---

[55] Weick explicitly mentioned a flaw in open systems theory: organizations can remain unaware of changes in their environment, i.e. they can develop an internal focus which closes them off from the environment.

organizing model with structuration theory in mind. Given the time structuration theory was formulated by Giddens (1984), this is impossible. As a matter of fact, the influence could well have been directed the other way: Clark (2000, p. 269) suggests that structuration thinking was given a degree of impetus from Weick's ideas on enactment. If one compares Weick and Giddens, at a first glance, they seem remarkably on par. At a second glance, however, there is a quite a fundamental difference. Exactly this difference is important for this study and will be the stepping stone for further conceptual explorations in the next chapter.

In a sense, the account of Giddens' structuration theory which was provided in chapter three seem to be a highly abstract formulation of the essence of the organizing model and Weick's views on organizing. In the first place, also Weick's views on structure compare to Giddens'. Weick (1979, pp. 3–4): 'Organizing is like a grammar in the sense that it is a systematic account of some rules and conventions by which sets of interlocked behaviors are assembled to form social processes that are intelligible to actors. It is also a grammar in the sense that it consists of rules for forming variables and causal linkages into meaningful structures (later called cause maps) that summarize the recent experience of the people who are organized. The grammar consists of recipes for getting things done when one person alone can't do them and recipes for interpreting what has been done.' The 'grammar' Weick describes in this quote can be compared to 'structures' in Giddens accounts. In the second place, the dynamic of the organizing model describes how structure develops as a result of actions, and how existing structures subsequently influence action. In other words, in Weick's model structures are produced and reproduced in interaction. Essentially, therefore, the organizing model describes a process of structuration. 'Structure' in Weick's organizing model is therefore a structure of ideas, influenced by action and subsequently influencing action.

Although Weick and Giddens seem to be essentially on par, I want to claim that there really is quite a substantial difference, which has to do with the role of what Giddens calls 'systems'. The acknowledgement of the role of 'the system' in which an individual is active seems to be strangely absent in Weick's work. Giddens (1984, p. 83) emphasizes the importance of the 'situated' nature of individual action. An individual agent is 'positioned' Giddens (1984, p. 84): 'The position of agents in circumstances of co-presence is an elemental feature of the structuration of encounters. Positioning here involves many subtle modalities of bodily movement and gesture, as well as the more general motion of the body through the regional sectors of daily routines.' In other words, agents are influenced by the characteristics of the system they are part of. Giddens certainly does not emphasize a one-way influence of 'the system' in a primitive sense as 'the system' itself is created. Nevertheless, structuration does not occur in a vacuum. However, such a vacuum does seem to be implicated by Weick's organizing model.

The 'systems' dimension seems absent in Weick's organizing model. The recognition of the reciprocal influence of systems characteristics on agents' functioning seems, furthermore, to be an underdeveloped theme in his work in general. What's more, his views on organizing seem to be formulated in a reaction on portrayals of organizational systems as 'designer-goods'. For example, in his 1993 article *Organizational redesign as improvisation*, he explicitly criticizes existing philosophies of design. He states that the phrase *organizational design* contains a trap. Weick (2001, p. 58)[56]: 'The trap is that the word design can be used as a noun as well as a verb. When people in organizations talk about the design of an organization, they tend to equate it with things like organization charts, written procedures, and job specifications. Features of organizations that are less thing-like and more continuous, fleeting and emergent, are easily overlooked. As a result, organizational design tend to focus on structures rather than processes and to contain few provisions for self-correction.' The phrase *organizational design*, in other words, carries connotations of 'blueprints', 'architecture' and 'stable order', which create blind spots to other important features of organizations. Instead, he argues the importance of structures that result from everyday action and interaction at the shop floor (emergence). He seems to emphasize the importance of *emergence* while criticizing the role of top-down design. This explains why Weick & Roberts (1993) discuss the way a crew at a flight deck work together to deal with everyday problems *without discussing the formal way in which tasks are divided and without addressing the topic of how the task structure influences dealing with the everyday problems*. It also explains why Weick & Roberts (1993) do underline the importance of the metaphor of the connectionist networks for organization theory, without making mentioning the phenomenon of 'patterns', or the influence of 'patterns' within the connectionist network on its subsequent functioning. More carefully phrased perhaps, they do not mention the way the design of the organization influences the subsequent process of patterning. In other words, the role of design on the organizing process (i.e. the process of dealing with dynamic complexity) is not discussed by Weick in this particular article, nor in any other article I could find.

The consequences for this study

Weick's thinking on organizing could perhaps be located in the realms of what Danziger (1997) calls the 'light' constructionists. Danziger. These 'light' constructionists are opposed by 'dark constructionists'. Danziger defines

---

[56] I refer to the version of this 1993 article that is reprinted in *Making Sense of the Organization* (Weick, 2001).

this opposition as following (1997, p. 410): 'Where 'light' social constructionists emphasize the ongoing construction of meaning in present dialogue,
these authors emphasize the dependence of current patterns of interaction
on rigid power structures established in the past and protected from change
by countless institutionalized practices and textual conventions'. Of course,
Weick is quite right in his critique of 'classic' organization theory and their
reliance on simple system's analogies, their ideas on design as blueprints,
the prioritizing of structure over process, etc. (Clark, 2000, pp. 37–39).
However, according to my analysis he is stretching matters too far. System
characteristics, such as the design of the organizational structure, do play
an important role in 'positioning' the agent. Ironically, these characteristics
have an important role in the organizing processes Weick is most interested
in. Nevertheless, Weick's organizing model is appreciated in this study as a
sophisticated model that clarifies important aspects of the process of dealing
with dynamic complexity.

Because this study aims to answer the question 'How can a system deal
with dynamic complexity in the best possible way?', I will aim to draw normative conclusions. My argument will be that there are normative elements
available in the organizing model, although Weick himself did not discuss
these as such (i.e. as a normative implication). Essentially I will claim that
the process of 'doubt' fulfills this normative function. Because my research
question implies a 'design-issue' which is not available in Weick's thinking,
I aim to extent Weick's thinking on the topic of doubt, in order to establish
an account on 'organizing doubt'.

Chapter 6

Normative aspect of the organizing model

The previous chapter presented the organizing model as a description of the process of dealing with dynamic complexity. The function of this model within this study is that normative elements are identified in order to answer the research question: How can a system deal with dynamic complexity in the best possible way? This chapter will focus on the normative aspect of the organizing model. It will be argued that the process 'doubt' is can be considered this normative aspect. The organizing model is not beyond critique, as the final section of the previous section showed. At the end of this the critique of this model is used to move beyond the organizing model and to put the topic of 'organizing doubt' on the agenda.

6.1 Normative elements in the organizing model

The description of Weick's model provided some indications regarding its normative element. It was, for example, stated that the contrary nature of the system's knowledge is advantageous in a 'contrary' environment. Moreover, it was stated that a system should find a way to be open. As such the organizing model fits the recent trends in system's theory. It was, furthermore, stated that if a system comes under the spell of its previous insights it becomes closed off from the environment. In that respect, the meaning of the plusses and minuses was underlined. Here, the normative element will be systematically identified, by first distinguishing between the descriptive and normative parts of the model.

The elements of the model (enactment, selection, retention) describe how things work and not how they should work. It does not indicate that organizations *should* select or *should* possess a memory. Instead, the different functions of the model describe an organizing process in a situation that is assumed to be dynamically complex[57]. As a result of the nature of dynamic complexity, operational units are confronted with problems for which no standards exist, or at least to which no existing standards can be applied automatically without thinking. A process of organizing is started out of necessity. Within the logic of Weick's organizing model this means that the dealings of operational units necessarily incorporate the various functions of the organizing model. I say 'necessarily' because Weick's model implies that organizations that are active in an equivocal environment necessarily display the various processes of the organizing model. One could also say that these processes of the organizing model are Weick's tools to describe the organizing process. An organizational system inevitably:

- is in contact with ecological change;
- enacts a certain environment (this is also an assumption, the nature of dynamic complexity is thought to be such that there is a need to act without the ability to analyze every detail of the action in advance);
- selects (it interprets what is going on);
- remembers (it remembers its actions and its interpretations thereof);
- applies experiences to new situations.

The importance of doubt

The normative element of Weick's organizing model is located in its plusses and minuses. These indicate that previous schemata used for interpretation and the organization's memory, on the one hand, help to understand new situations, or to see the common in the unique. On the other hand, focusing on the common in the unique might obscure the unique in the unique, which means that crucial information might get lost. Hence Weick's concept of doubt: one should simultaneously trust and distrust one's previous insights. One could also say that distrusting one's existing insights overcomes the risks of a positive feedback loop: ever-stronger confirmation of what one already knows.

A cornerstone of Weick's model is that organizations should be structurally critical of their past experience. It is claimed here that this 'structural criticism' is the normative element in Weick's theory. The concept of 'doubt' is used by Weick in order to capture this structural criticism, or in Weick's words, to capture the process of discrediting. As the title of this study indicates, doubt is considered to be a crucial process that organizations need to

---

[57] If the different elements of the model were the "crucial qualities" then, for example, the function of retention should be optimized. If "retention" would become optimized, organizations would be better able to remember their experiences and their past knowledge. However, within the dynamic the model describes, this is not an unequivocal advantage. A too dominant memory can close the system off from the realities it is involved in. A perfect memory can be a disadvantage in a complex environment (Van der Vlist, 1996).

organize in order to deal with dynamic complexity in the best possible way. Organizing refers to the point that organizations should structurally see to it that the chance that existing insights are doubted is enlarged. With 'structurally', I here refer to the point that organizations should ensure that it is more than mere coincidence if existing knowledge is discredited.

It should be emphasized that Weick did not present the organizing model as a normative model. Nor did he emphasizes the importance of doubt in the way that I am doing here now. He does spend a paragraph on 'the importance of doubt' (pp. 224–228) and emphasize its desirability. However, doubt returns only once in the index of *The Social Psychology of Organizing*, which is a 'circumstantial' indication that Weick did not interpret it as the crucial element of the model. Weick does stress the importance of *ambivalence* for dealing with dynamic complexity. One can, however, argue that doubt is central to ambivalence.

6.2 The concept of doubt and its intricacies

'Doubt' is a central concept in this study. It is considered to be the foundation of the capability of self-organization. In this section I want to specify what is meant by 'doubt'. Also, the topic of 'organizing doubt' will be touched upon. Although organizing doubt is an issue of implementation (implementing a process within an organizational system) and therefore a topic that belongs to part three of this study, some general remarks are made on the topic here.

Doubt as the foundation of self-organization

Doubt, as it is conceptualized in this study, is the essence of self-organization. Doubt is crucial for self-organization because it represents the ability of the system to deal with its knowledge of the environment. It captures the ability to develop meaningful ideas about the environment, while staying critical of these ideas. Doubt prevents that the system becomes closed. It seems perhaps strange to underline that organizations engaged in difficult circumstances should doubt. After all, doubt seems to be leading to passivity and apathy. Organizations can doubt too much, they can doubt about the wrong things, they can doubt about the right things, but leave it at that. Also, the unequivocal importance of doubt does not seem to follow logically from Weick's organizing model. After all, a fundamental notion of the organizing model is that thought follows action. Rather than emphasizing doubt, it seems more sensible to claim that organizations engaged in a dynamically complex environment need the ability to act.

Underlining the subtle meaning of doubt in the organizing model can solve this problem. Weick claims that doubt is 'symmetrical': 'It is not simply that an organization should doubt what it knows for certain. It should also treat as certain the very things it doubts. If to doubt is to discredit clear information, then to act decisively is to discredit ambiguous information. Therefore, if you want to act on the point that ambivalence is the optimal compromise, when things are clear, you should doubt those things; when they are unclear you should treat them as if they're clear. That's the meaning of discrediting' (2001, p. 415). This may seem to be a rather mysterious quotation that perhaps even contradicts the things claimed above. As I understand it, however, neither is the case. Dynamic complexity confronts operators with the necessity to act without being able to thoroughly analyze the situations from all possible angles. Acting on the basis of hypotheses implies that one acts in the face of doubt (*when they are unclear you should treat them as if they're clear*'; i.e. one doubts one's certainty about uncertainty). However, if one wants to retain one's adaptability, one should be able to discredit one's existing insights (*when things are clear, you should doubt those things*')[58]. Weick (1993, p. 641): 'Extreme confidence and extreme caution both can destroy what organizations most need in changing times, namely, curiosity, openness and complex sensing.'

6.3 Organizing doubt

Because the concept of doubt constitutes the normative element of Weick's organizing model, it is the basis for the analytical framework of this study. Meaningful action is beyond regulation and this is what makes self-organization essential for units. It is, however, the assumption of this study that the basis for meaningful action is not beyond regulation. **The assumption is that the process of building up knowledge and criticizing it can be structured in better and worse ways.** This means that although meaningful action is a central concept of this study, the attention is not focused on meaningful action itself but on the basis for meaningful action, i.e. on structures (in a broad sense) that influence the capabilities to doubt. The implementation of this process of doubt will be the topic of part three of this study.

---

[58] This complicated nature of the concept of doubt follows from the complicated nature of hypotheses (which implies both certainty and uncertainty). One could perhaps say that doubt represents the "opposite face" or "mirror image" of hypotheses. Dynamic complexity is necessarily dealt with by using hypotheses; doubt reminds the system of the inherent risks of hypotheses. One can see why doubt represents the normative element in dealing with complexity: necessarily one deals with dynamic complexity by using hypotheses, doubt should deal with the essential uncertainty of hypotheses. One can conclude that doubt has a subtle meaning that follows from its place in the organizing model. The ability to doubt implies the ability to choose. If organizational units have a choice, they are not forced to act according to predetermined rules or orders, but it also means that the environment leaves them more than one option.

The fact that this study is interested in organizing doubt implies that – in part three – the emphasis will be on organizational factors rather than individual factors. It will not be attempted to find ways to develop individual skills of doubt. Instead, attention will be focused on the way the process of doubt is implemented in the organizational system. Weick himself has scarcely raised the issue of organizing doubt, but this is not surprising giving his macrotheoretical positioning discussed previously. His theoretical efforts regarding this issue accumulate to diverse advice to *individuals* to become wiser[59]. The focus on organizational factors has consequences for the way organizational reality is perceived. The shouting drill-sergeant certainly can be said to influence the system's ability to doubt. He is not likely to tolerate contradiction and he is certainly not likely to evaluate the achievements of his soldiers openly on the basis of mutual reflection. This individual drill-sergeant is not of interest to this study as an individual. There are organizational arrangements lying behind this shouting individual that are of interest to this study. The organization grants this sergeant his authority and it formulates a policy that dictates how recruits ought to be trained. Furthermore, it has designed the tasks of the recruits such that it is not necessary to take them very serious as a partner in debate.

To state that doubt is important for an organizational system means that one states that it is important at systems level. A system should be able to doubt its existing knowledge. This implies, for example, that if an individual within that system can be said to truly doubt his existing knowledge not necessarily 'the system' can be said to doubt. After all, individual deliberations can fail to influence the organizational system. This underlines the idea that doubt should be organized. Given the nature of the position of operational units in crisis organizations, doubt is a process that should be *organized* within the operational units. After all, operational units possess natural autonomy.

6.4 The influence of design on operational units

The conclusion of the theoretical exploration is that the ability of operational units to doubt should be something that is organized, a conclusion drawn after an analysis of the normative element in Weick's organizing model: if organizational systems aim to deal with dynamic complexity in the best possible way, they should organize their ability to doubt. All in all, 'organiz-

---

[59] This approach is, for example, recognizable in the following quotation (Weick, 2001, p. 367): 'The idea that wisdom may be an attitude rather than a body of thought also has a certain appeal because it implies that people can improve their capability for wise action. Furthermore, once wisdom is decoupled from specific knowledge, we expect it to find it expressed by more people, more often, in more diverse settings.'

ing doubt' can be considered as an abstract normative principle (level A, according to the distinction made by Van Strien, (1986)) that can be used (1) to think about the design of organizations; (2) to analyse the ability of existing organizations to deal with dynamic complexity. In this study, the emphasis is obviously on the second of the two possibilities.

There is one particularly important issue that has not been dealt with, although in a way it has been dealt with in different words. One can ask how the design of organizations, or more generally, in what way 'structures' or 'mechanisms' can be said to influence the dealings at the operational level. This is of course a well known and intensely discussed topic in sociological theory. Most importantly, any work on 'design' should try to avoid simplified accounts on the way design can 'program' behavior in a totalitarian sense. Such straightforward causal effects are only available in closed systems. Classical theory on organization design is often criticized for providing such simplified accounts. Clark (2000, pp. 37–38): 'Design rules as a metaphor declares a tendency towards an architectural view of the role of the organization theorist. Design rules also refers to the desire to construct clusters of rules to control organizations. There is a strong implication that the design rules do provide organizational blueprints. However, there is considerable scepticism about the capacity of organization design to succeed in its modernist formation.' As was discussed in the previous chapter, Weick also rejects architectural metaphors.

I agree with both theorists with their criticism that organizational design does not dominate organizational reality in a way that the architectural metaphor might suggest. However, I do want to claim that the organizational structure influences agents in important ways, as structuration theory suggests. Weick seems to reject the topic of design, more specifically, he seems to develop his approach by contrasting it with 'design' perspectives. In my mind this can be traced back to his difference with structuration theory discussed earlier. While Giddens' structuration theory explicitly mentions the importance of 'institutions' as a category of structures that influence agency, Weick's definition of structure seems to exclude institutions. Instead, Weick focuses on 'structure in the process of projects'. My position on the way organizational design influences actors is in line with the (realist) view on causation that was discussed in Chapter Two.

This was presented as a critical realists view on causation. Clark (2000, p. 77) summarizes this realist view on the influence of structure as following: 'Pre-existing structures and causal mechanisms carry the weight of the past into the present, yet the question of whether they are reproduced or transformed depends on their interplay with agents and actors.' Clark (2000) emphasizes that there are differences between a realist's position and the position traditionally held by structuration theory. In their emphasis on multiple ontologies critical realists such as Archer (1995) criticize the way in which structuration theory conceptualizes the influence of the past on the present as a type of conflation. The finesses of these discussions are not directly relevant here. What is important to note is that this study does not claim that agents are held captive by an all-dominating organizational design. Instead, this study emphasizes the importance of meaningful action at the level of operational units. Doubt is an essential prerequisite for meaningful action and the organization should think about ways in which the process of doubt is influenced in a positive way, i.e. about ways to 'organize doubt'. This implies that there are better and worse ways in which operators can doubt. This issue is taken up in Chapter Eight.

6.5 Weick and 'naturalistic decision-making'

Those who are familiar with Gary Klein's concept of naturalistic decision-making will have noticed some agreements between this concept and Weick's approach. There is, however, quite a substantial difference between the approaches. Klein's approach shares an emphasis on the importance of hypotheses, but it differs in the normative implications it draws. As Klein's approach is becoming increasingly popular (perhaps some would consider it a logical choice for this study), I consider it to be useful to contrast it with Weick's view. The concept of naturalistic decision-making offers a description of the way in which experienced decision-makers succeed in making good decisions in difficult situations. This is what Klein meant by naturalistic: it aims to understand and describe how things go. From his descriptive observations he drew some normative conclusions. Klein was particularly interested in decision-making in situations that have characteristics such as (2001, pp. 4–6): time pressure, high stakes, uncertainty due to inadequate information, unclear goals, poorly defined procedures, dynamic conditions, and team work. In other words, Klein was interested in the same kinds of situations that are of interest to this study.

Klein emphasized that rational decision-making constitutes quite a poor model for decision-making under difficult conditions and he observed that it is not accidental that people do not use this procedure in everyday practice. In dynamic conditions, the boundary conditions, so to speak, are not met to apply rigorous analytical methods (2001, p. 269). Klein emphasized the importance of hypotheses. That is to say, he emphasized the importance of recognizing the common in the unique. More in particular he emphasized that experienced decision-makers recognize patterns in new crisis-like situations enabling them to come up with decisions quickly. In order to emphasize this point he describes his Recognition-Primed Decision-Model. He summarized the key-points of this RPD-model (2001, p. 30) as follows: 'The RPD-model claims that with experienced decision-makers:

- The focus is on the way they assess the situation and judge it familiar, not on comparing options.
- Courses of action can be quickly evaluated by imagining how they will be carried out, not by formal analysis and comparison.
- Decision makers usually look for the first workable option they can find, not the best option.
- Since the first option they consider is usually workable, they do not have to generate a large set of options to be sure they get a good one.
- They generate and evaluate options one at a time and do not bother comparing the advantages and disadvantages of alternatives.
- By imagining the option being carried out, they can spot weaknesses and find ways to avoid these, thereby making the option stronger. Conventional models just select the best, without seeing how it can be improved.
- The emphasis is on being poised to act rather than being paralyzed until all the evaluations have been completed.'

Naturalistic decision-making emphasizes that different sources of experiential knowledge are helpful to recognize patterns in new situations. Subsequently, one can base one's actions upon that. This is reminiscent of the assumptions of abduction and the function of theories of action of Hedberg. One could say that Klein provided a detailed description of the process of abduction. The existing theories help to judge new situations in a more specific way. The kind of patterns helping experienced decision-makers that Klein mentioned were, for example, metaphors, analogies, and stories. Klein (2001, p. 197): 'People use analogies and metaphors to perform a variety of difficult tasks: understanding situations, generating predictions, solving problems, anticipating events, designing equipment, and making plans. (...). Each experience we have, whether it is our own or we have heard about from someone else, can serve as an analogue or a metaphor. Each time we take on a task, we can draw on this vast knowledge base, this bank of experiences and stories and images. We may overlook an analogue, select a misleading one, or fail to interpret one correctly. Usually our experience bank works smoothly, providing us with structure and interpretation even for tasks we have not been faced with before.' In the many interesting examples he described, he showed the subtle workings of this experiential knowledge. From this descriptive part of his theory, Klein drew normative conclusions: he wanted to cultivate these assets of experienced operators. Experiential knowledge helps people to quickly recognize patterns in very difficult situations and to make sometimes surprisingly good decisions. Not incidentally, Klein called this experiential knowledge a *source of power* that decision-makers need to cultivate.

The difference with the model of Weick is that the idea of doubt is absent. The idea that previous knowledge is both helpful and risky is not a structural part of Klein's theory. One particular problem he recognized with the use of mental simulations was that people tend to get too confident in their own constructions (exactly the criticism that one would formulate when using Weick's model). The reaction of Klein to this possible criticism was that: 'that particular shortcoming, however, does not call for any other approach. If you want to deduce every inference logically, you will still run into time barriers' (2001, p. 69). This reply shows that he was aware of a particular limitation of his model but he did not try to solve it in a structural way. There is another crucial difference. Weick seemed to use the concept of experiential knowledge in a different manner compared to Klein. The attitude of wisdom, as Weick called it, refers to the awareness of experienced operators that they *cannot know everything*. This is a value of experience that was absent in Klein's thinking[60]. According to Klein, experience is a source of power *to know* in complex situations, rather than a reason to be modest about the things one can know in such situations.

6.6 Final remarks

This chapter has established doubt as a crucial capability for organizations to be able to deal with dynamic complexity. Doubt should lead to a system possessing an ambivalent attitude towards its present knowledge. Functional analyses are useful to identify the relevance of processes given a certain aim of a system. They are, however, not orientated to the content of processes. This study considers insight into the content of the process necessary as well. As it is the thing to be organized, insight into the nature of the process is an important source of information when the issue of the organization of doubt is taken up. This will be the topic of the next chapter and it is considered to be the last of the abstract elements of the analytical framework.

---

[60] One could say that in this particular sense Weick's model is closer to Janis's theory than to Klein's. Although Janis cherished an ideal of rational decision-making, he emphasized the importance of "vigilance" (Janis, 1990). One could interpret this as an advice to decision-makers to "be aware" of what is happening around them.

Chapter 7

Doubt and argumentation

The previous chapter has identified doubt as a crucial meta-process to be organized. Because Weick's model is a functional model it gives no insight into the content of the process. This chapter will explore the human capabilities that are essential for the process of doubt. The central question of this chapter is: which specific human capabilities enable a system to be doubtful? The crucial capabilities this chapter aims to find must describe the essential dynamic of doubt: creating rules, breaking rules and changing rules. In this chapter it will be argued that rhetorical psychology, as it was formulated by Michael Billig (1991, 1996, 1999), can give an account of the nature of doubt. This chapter will explore rhetorical psychology and will try to establish a link between rhetorical psychology and Weick's organizing model. More specifically, it will be argued that rhetorical psychology explicates the specific qualities of human beings that are presupposed by the 'thinking part' of Weick's organizing model.

7.1 The concept of 'argumentation'

In the previous chapters meaningful action has been defined as lying between the extremes of perfect rules and no rules at all[61]. Only on this 'edge of chaos' is meaningful action essential. In situations of absolute chaos any attempt is as good as the next. Literally, in situations of chaos anything goes. In the opposite situation of absolute order, meaningful action is equally unnecessary. The best way to deal with situations can be prescribed by rules. In that case, thinking is unnecessary; one should just follow the rules. In the intermediate situation, on the edge of chaos, it is at the same time important to construct rules (in order to develop a body of hypothetical knowledge) and to break rules (in order to deal with change and unknown situations). It is exactly on this edge of chaos where thinking is necessary. Thinking is

---

[61] Indeed, one can consider the total chaos and total order options to be theoretical possibilities only (0 % and 100 % situations in Bavelas' experiment). This implies that doubt, argumentation, and self-organization are, to a certain degree, always necessary in practice.

therefore portrayed as a dynamic process. The dynamic of human thinking is exactly what rhetorical psychology tries to capture.

The central concept of rhetorical psychology is argumentation. It will be argued that argumentation can serve as a description of the content of the function of doubt. Billig underlined the importance of argumentation for human thinking by quoting a piece of wisdom of the Greek sophist Protagoras. Billig formulated this wisdom as follows: 'In every question, there are two sides to the argument, exactly opposite to each other' (1991, p. 46). According to Billig, the implication of this wisdom is that humans are capable of formulating contrary opinions about the same issue, both equally reasonable. This capability to argue is, according to Billig, the basic characteristic of the thinking of human beings; it is even the thing that gives human thinking its dynamic quality. Billig (1996) emphasized furthermore the importance of the 'argumentative context' for the process of argumentation.

In Billig's opinion, the ability to formulate contrary opinions is based on a reservoir of arguments. Common sense provides members of a community with a variety of arguments that can be used in different situations. According to him (1996), common sense is not a neatly structured body of knowledge, but consists of contrary wisdoms. He illustrated this by referring to proverbs[62] (1988, p. 16). In his view, the contrary nature of common sense is not a weakness to be replaced by the unequivocal wisdoms of science. In fact it provides thinking the necessary flexibility[63]. (1996, p. 240). It is argued here that the concept of argumentation as it is described by rhetorical psychology can be used to describe the nature of the process of doubt. The capacity to argue contrary opinions is crucial in bending, sabotaging, and creating rules. The next sections will deal with the following issues:

- The first section aims to draw a clearer picture of some essential similarities between rhetorical psychology and Weick's organizing model.
- The second section aims to draw a picture of the extra value of Billig's concept of argumentation.

---

[62] Billig mentioned, for example, the contradictory proverbs 'out of sight, out of mind' and 'absence makes the heart grow fonder'.

[63] Billig (1996, p. 240): 'Vilfredo Pareto had an interesting argument to explain why societies possess multiplicities of values and why these values should conflict with each other. He suggested that principles tend to be expressed in simple, unqualified ways. However, these simple formulations are too extreme for guiding practical conduct, because, if they were followed with consistent literality, they would fail to achieve the desired result. (...) Therefore there need to be exceptions and qualifications to the simple principle. (...) Because every absolute principle has the character of overstepping the bounds of reality, each principle needs to be held in check by the countervailing force of contrary principles.'

7.2 Similarities between Billig and Weick

Although Weick and Billig have different perspectives (the nature of the organizing process vs. the nature of human thinking), it will be argued that rhetorical psychology shares important theoretical premises with Weick's organizing model. There are further similarities beyond this level of fundamental premises. It will be claimed that Billig's concept of argumentation describes what Weick would call discrediting. The similarities are considered to be important because they show that there is a basis for applying Billig's theoretical concepts to clarify parts of Weick's model.

Premises of rhetorical psychology

Essential in Billig's characterization of thinking is that it has an open and social character. Billig (1996) described the thinker as someone who **does not** resemble Rodin's statue, silently pondering, but as someone who takes part in the arena of debate. Billig was critical of approaches in psychology that characterize thinking as an isolated, intra-individual and mathematical process. Such approaches appear to characterize thinking as performing logical operations taking place in the enclosed parts of the cognitive system (Billig, 1996). According to Billig, however, the everyday problems the human thinker is confronted with, are of such a nature that they cannot be solved by merely using abstract logic. In order to describe the differences between rhetoric (i.e. everyday thinking) and logic Billig used an analogy of Zeno. According to Zeno, rhetoric is like an open palm and logic is like a closed fist. The looseness of rhetoric (open palm) compared to the strictness of logic (closed fist) must not be interpreted as a sign of superiority of logic over rhetoric. Billig remarked that (1996, p. 126): 'The context of rhetoric and logic can be distinguished. As has been suggested, the context of rhetoric is marked by justification and criticism. It is a social context in which the different points of view clash, or threaten to clash, and there is potential infinity to these clashes'. Argumentation is therefore situated in a context in which the nature of reality is problematic. The maxim of Protagoras suggests that an 'unarguable rightness and wrongness' (Billig's words) cannot be established because critical challenges are always possible. Logic demands a level of certainty that is not to be found in everyday affairs. Due to the lack of certainty in everyday affairs there is difference of opinion. As has been argued at the beginning of this chapter, an important feature of Weick's organizing model is that it describes a dynamic between acting and thinking. Important for this study is that Billig's rhetorical psychology does not isolate the process of thinking from action (as is implied by Rodin's statue). The problematic nature of reality does not merely present an intellectual challenge. Argumentation, as Billig described it, is rooted in practical involvement (Billig, 1991). Translated into the words used in previous chapters, a necessity to act is assumed.

The above shows that rhetorical psychology is also based upon an idea about the elementary nature of dynamic complexity. Billig referred to this as the uncertainty principle. He described this principle in this particular way (1996, pp. 92–93): 'We can call these arguments against the possibility of definite rules Quintilian's Principle of Uncertainty. The principle asserts that we can never capture the infinite variety of human affairs in a finite system of psychological laws. At any moment, the finite laws are likely to be embarrassed by unforeseen and unforeseeable events. It is only because of the possibility of such embarrassment, that the rhetorician can learn from experience. Experience gained from each novel situation contributes to this learning, as the rhetorician builds up more sagacious hunches and guidelines. However, this process of learning can never be finished. There is an infinity of possible situations, and therefore an infinity of things to be learnt.' This quotation illustrates an important point of agreement between the ideas of Billig and Weick: rules are only provisional. They are useful to develop a workable level of certainty, but an eternal type of certainty is considered to be unattainable in principle.

The structuring and de-structuring effects of argumentation

Billig (1996) characterized the argumentative momentum by describing two dimensions: criticism and justification (p. 117). If someone makes a claim or advocates a certain point of view, he is expected to find arguments for his position. Protagoras' wisdom shows that contrary ways of arguing are always possible, so someone always puts himself in a vulnerable position when making claims. However, also criticism has to be justified, which means that the critic has to find arguments. Criticism and justification are the dimensions that capture the argumentative momentum.

One could consider justification a structuring process. After all, by means of a process of justification particular arguments are sought to defend certain points of view regarding elements in the environment of units. In the logic of Weick's model one could say that the process of justification discovers reasons behind enactments. Weick also noticed the structuring effect of justifications: 'Justifications are socially acceptable reasons people give themselves for choosing something in public that is irrevocable. As these reasons accumulate into patterns of affirmation, restriction, and permission, they guide people and enable them to judge others and justify themselves to those others. Sets of justifications should form coherent and workable systems of interpretation that create a culture' (2001, p. 78). However, as the discussion on the normative element in Weick's model revealed, structuring alone is not enough to deal with dynamic complexity in the best possible way. In Weick's model the importance of discrediting is emphasized.

Billig's 'criticism' dimension describes the same opposite force. One could consider the process of criticism a force of discrediting, or indeed, de-structuring. After all, existing structures/justifications are, for whatever reason, criticized. The processes of criticism and justification can be said to presuppose each other. Justifications are formulated in order to deal with imagined criticisms. As such, they incorporate the criticism, so to speak. Justifications are usually sought when there is a real or imagined criticism on actions or thoughts (Billig 1996, p. 117). Again, this is in line with Weick's claim that organizing activities only start when practical circumstances give reason to do so.

One can see that this dynamic of justification and criticism, considered as an organizing process, involves elements of doubt. A group or unit that argues is dealing with existing structures in opposite ways. The argumentative process is concerned with simultaneously believing and disregarding existing knowledge. Therefore, this study considers argumentation the content of the abstract function of doubt. One can see that argumentation is especially important at points where previous thoughts or structures are confronted with new, dynamic, and complex situations. This is the main reason that this study considers operational units – being the ones that are most directly confronted with dynamic complexity – to be the ones that need the ability to argue.

7.3 Argumentation and its subtleties

The previous sections have made clear that there are distinct similarities between Weick's model and that of Billig's account on human thinking. There would, however, be little use in describing Billig's ideas on rhetorical psychology if they did not contain some extra value. This extra value is the description of the process of argumentation, which is interpreted here as a description of the abstract function of doubt.

The process of argumentation can be clarified by describing the tension between two fundamental operations of human thinking: the processes of categorization and particularization. Many psychologists have accepted the fact that categorization is a basic operation of the human information-processing apparatus[64]. The function of categorization, according to Billig, who referred to Eleanor Rosch, is that categorization helps to make sense out of the complex and messy world outside. Categorization therefore helps with

---

[64] Lakoff (1987, pp. 5–6) put it as follows: 'Categorization is not a matter taken lightly. There is nothing more basic than categorization to our thought, perception, action and speech. Every time we see something as a *kind* of thing, for example a tree, we are categorizing. Whenever we reason about *kinds* of things – chairs, nations, illnesses, emotions, any kind of thing at all – we are employing categories' (italics in original).

dealing with dynamic complexity; it is a process that helps to simplify the world[65]. Billig pointed out two distortions of a simplistic portrayal of the process of categorization. In the first place, a simplistic portrayal may display human beings as victims of their own system of categories, unable to perceive the world in its entire variety and complexity. In such instances, a structural ability of criticizing one's own categories is denied. Inevitably the world gets simplified by means of the system of categories that is applied by the cognitive system[66]. In the second place, a simplistic portrayal of categorization may draw a bureaucratic picture of thinking. The thinker is then portrayed as someone who is following the procedures of thought[67], or in other words, as a rule-follower: 'The thinker to emerge from this psychology, who, rather like a timid bureaucrat follows office procedures' (Billig, 1991, pp. 37–38). When a human being deals with complexity in ways that are described here, the goal seems to keep complexity, or features irrelevant according to present insight (system of official forms), out of the system.

In order to counterbalance a simple process of categorization, Billig postulated a second fundamental process of thinking: particularization. This is, in the spirit of Protagoras, the opposite of the process of categorization. The process of particularization entails that one treats a stimulus not on the basis of its similarity to other stimuli (thereby putting it in a category), but on the basis of its uniqueness. The ability to deal with stimuli from the outside

---

[65] Categorization is, according to Gardner (1987), essential to the more classical cognitive approach, which views thinking as the disembodied manipulation of abstract symbols (Lakoff, 1987, p. 8). This portrayal of thinking that is quite a literal translation from computer to human cognitive apparatus. According to Gardner (1987), however, categorization is also important to more recent formulations within cognitive science. Gardner stated this as follows: "In one sense, this classical view of categorization (members of a category share common properties, ehk) was consonant with the aura of cognitive science – a science built on the unambiguity of the computer. But just as the general view of the computer as a single all-purpose logical machine eventually gave way to a plurality of computational stances, this general view of classification was also not able to withstand the force of arguments and empirical data from several quarters." (Gardner, 1987, p. 342). According to Lakoff (1987), more recent cognitive psychologists such as Eleanor Rosch try to draw a more *embodied* (as it is often referred to) picture of thinking, using a different characterization of the process of categorization.

[66] There have been psychologists who argued that human beings are fundamentally prejudiced.

[67] As Billig stated (1996, p. 158): 'The bureaucrat cannot treat each individual case as if it were unique, but each case must be placed into bureaucratically suitable pigeon-holes. Members of the public fill out the appropriate forms, which extract the information of interest to the bureaucracy. In this way the messy features of the general public's lives can become suitably regularized. Irrelevant information, for which there is no appropriate question on the official form, will be weeded out, and need never come to the attention of the bureaucratic system. Similarly, categories or schemata, like official forms, serve to weed out the irrelevant stimuli and to organize the relevant features into ways which can be easily processed by the higher authorities of the system.'

world in opposing ways characterizes human thinking, according to Billig. The implication of this is that man is neither inevitably prejudiced nor is he a simple bureaucrat. The bureaucrat himself is not a simple bureaucrat. It is a well-known fact that bureaucrats can be very inventive in sabotaging the official procedures, for example, by dealing with a friend's case differently from usual. The most convincing argument for the contrary nature of the human cognitive system is perhaps that categorization and particularization depend on each other. An act of categorization depends upon an act of particularization[68].

All in all, this implies that dealing with information is not a matter of simple rule following (putting it in the appropriate category) but a matter of potential controversy. Billig went into detail of describing the various ways in which a categorization or a particularization can become an object of controversy (Billig, 1996, pp. 148–185). The essential point is that human thinking is fundamentally a dynamic and infinite process[69] (the final, good solution is not available in open palmed situations) because of the ever-present tension between categorization and particularization[70].

---

[68] Billig affirmed that (1996, p. 163): 'If we have a choice of ways of categorizing the stimulus arrays with which we are faced, then selection is involved in arriving at the appropriate categorization. This sort of selection is akin to what we have called particularization. Out of all possible categories, one is treated as uniquely appropriate, and must be fished out of the general pool of categories. Thus in order to categorize something by putting it in an appropriate category, we must have particularized that category. In this way, categorization depends upon the opposing process of particularization.'

[69] Van der Vlist (2000) took a comparable stance when evaluating the attempts of scientists to simulate intelligent behavior with the help of tricky computer designs. Characteristic of human beings is that they are capable of innovating on the norms they previously used to interact with their environment.

[70] Contradiction can be interpreted in more or less fundamental ways. Contradiction can be (1) interpreted as a phenomenon that exists in the overall network of categories. Contradiction can be interpreted as macro-level phenomena. In some situations a military unit should fight, in some situations it should flee. A military unit should therefore possess both capabilities. This represents a limited form of contradiction. Contradiction exists in the overall network of categories of skills (fighting and fleeing), but in single situations it may be perfectly clear what one should do. Contradiction can (2) be interpreted as being a "surface phenomenon". It may be granted that currently contradiction is the best a unit can come up with. But it can be suggested that contradiction only represents a current state of affairs. One could believe that a unit should strive for order beyond the surface of things. Contradiction can be interpreted as being "fundamental". Essential in this interpretation of contradiction is that in all situations contrary opinions can be defended. A detailed analysis of the subtle nuances of the knowledge of units will not reveal categories in which all contrary opinions are neatly distinguished on the basis of unequivocal criteria. There is no order to be found behind the appearance of things, nor is there order to be found at the level of the different categories. In rhetorical psychology, contradiction is fundamental: contrary opinions can be formulated in every situation. This is implied by Protagoras' maxim: in **every** situation contrary opinions can be defended, both equally reasonably. This is in line with Weick's emphasis on equivocality and

7.4 Consequences of the previous discussions

The goal of this chapter was to explicate the human capabilities essential for dealing with dynamic complexity. It was furthermore claimed that these capabilities are implicit in the organizing model of Weick. It was claimed that argumentation offers a description of the dynamics of doubt. There are, however, still some loose ends in the discussion that are taken up in this section.

In the previous chapter it was claimed that this study will concern itself with 'the organization of doubt'. This chapter has shown that this can be perceived as 'the organization of argumentation'. One can immediately sense that this quality is not self-evident in a military organization. Military commanders frequently claim that their organization is not a debating club. Furthermore, doubt is often considered a dangerous weakness when confronted with difficult circumstances[71]. The military organization is, according to many an organization in which action is at center stage. Systems of discipline and hierarchy support this action-orientated side of the organization. A crisis-organization should be able to act quickly, rather than to think endlessly. Furthermore, quick decision-making under stressful conditions is considered to be an essential trait of commanders. It is often thought that officers should possess traits of character that match this action side. He should be obedient, disciplined, orderly, etc. The willingness to question orders or to support an argumentative process is certainly no part of these valued traits.

This study appreciates matters a little differently. In the first place, one can question the value of above mentioned traits, or at least the kinds of persons that are often the bearers of these traits. Dixon (1976, p. 280) states that: 'At first sight the traits of orderliness, tough mindedness, obedience to authority, punitiveness and the rest may well have been seemed the very embodiment of hard hitting masculinity – ideally suited to the job of being a soldier. Unfortunately, as represented in the authoritarian personality they are only skin deep – a brittle crust of defenses against feelings of weakness and inadequacy. The authoritarian keeps up his spirits by whistling in the dark. He is a frightened child who wears the armour of a giant. His mind is a door locked and bolted against that which he fears most: himself.' In other words, not every orderly or obedient person is pathological, but a distinct

---

ambiguity (an organization should establish workable certainty instead of eternal certainty). Furthermore, the concept of hypothesis implies uncertainty and therefore the possibility of different hypotheses.

[71] Weathers, c.s. (1995, p. 110) even conclude that open discussion is a worse threat to military units than lack of cohesion: 'Strong attachments to fellow soldiers provide a good buffer against fear, whereas a lack of cohesion, or worse, open discussion, can be a significant source of distress.' This signifies that Weathers, c.s. have little appreciation for argumentation.

group, labeled the authoritarian personality, is. Much of Dixon's study is devoted to underline the claim that (a) military organizations are attractive for authoritarian personalities and (b) the military organizations provide contexts in which authoritarian personalities can thrive[72].

In the second place, argumentation and doubt are considered important not to change an organization of action into an organization of abstract deliberation. Instead, argumentation and doubt are considered important *exactly because* the military organization is an organization in which action is at center stage. A military organization that is confronted with dynamic complexity can be expected to act rather than to think endlessly about available alternatives. Such enactments provide the organization with a stream of 'raw input' that is meaningless before an organizing process weighs them against the background of existing structures. In other words, because the military organization is an organization of action, and because military units need to act meaningfully, doubt and argumentation are of crucial importance. The challenges that dynamic complexity poses on the military organization is that it needs to be action-orientated as well as argumentation orientated. They need to be self-confident and to be hesitant at the same time.

7.5 Conclusions from part two

Part two was orientated to developing an abstract answer to the question of how to deal with dynamic complexity in the best possible way. The line of reasoning that has emerged from part two can be summarized as follows:

- Organizational systems cannot deal with dynamic complexity using a closed system of rules. Inevitably an organizational system has to engage in organizing activities, i.e. in finding a workable level of certainty.
- Dealing with dynamic complexity can be characterized by the logic of abduction: actions are based on hypotheses. Hypotheses operate by recognizing the common in the unique and help the system to raise itself beyond the level of random action.
- Weick's organizing model can be understood as an abduction-model with a normative element added.
- This normative element is the capability of doubting. A system should have the ability to discredit its current insights. A system should therefore organize doubt.

Doubt is seen as a specific human capability. Billig's concept of argumentation can be used to describe the content of the abstract process of doubt.

---

[72] According to Van der Vlist (2003) traits of authoritarianism are common, not merely in military organizations, but in bureaucratic organizations in general.

PART III

Analytical framework: Organizing doubt in an organizational system

The first part of the analytical framework has identified doubt as the essential process to be organized. The second part of the analytical framework deals with the issue of organizing doubt. Eventually this should result in a tool that enables one to discern whether the operational units in the cases had the ability to doubt, i.e. whether they had adequately organized their argumentative process. Such a normative tool should be the yardstick to analyze experiences in the cases. The central question of part three is therefore:

How can the organization of doubt be observed in the cases?

It should be mentioned that previously self-organization was perceived as being **inevitable** given the circumstances. In part three, self-organization is considered to be a **normative ideal** to be established through organizational design. The assumption is that organizations can deal with the inevitable nature of self-organization in better and worse ways. The better way is one in which the inevitable nature of self-organization is taken as a point of departure in the design of the units and in which a process of argumentation is organized in a particular way. It should be repeated that Weick's concept of self-organization is based on a conception of survival. Self-organizing potential as a normative ideal is established when the organizational context provides the units the means for doubt. If self-organization, i.e. doubt, is promoted, it is claimed that an organizational system has a better chance of survival. This means that organizing doubt does not guarantee survival, but rather the chances of survival become better.

The history of military operations has shown that atrocities have frequently been justified as necessary for survival. Also, military history has shown that operational units survived by lying to higher commanders. The convoys of Logtbat sometimes came across roads they judged as too dangerous to continue on. In order to turn back they needed permission of a higher commander and they knew that one particular higher commander was not easily persuaded of the danger of routes. Knowing this, units exaggerated the danger present in the situation. The troops of Dutchbat have been accused of sending little local boys through minefields because they were aware of the location of the mines. Although this is certainly more staggeringly wicked than clever, it certainly is *a* way to deal with practical problems. This is *a* form of self-organization, but obviously not of the sort that this study aims to promote. When units display wicked forms of self-organization it can be a sign that something is wrong with the ambitions of the organizational system. If an operational unit lies to a higher commander, it is probably unable to perform its job within normal standards. If things get really bad, units can even cross ethical boundaries. Acting against the interest of the organizational system can be a sign that the organizational system is not designed correctly.

There is considerable theory available on the design of self-organizing units, and the analytical framework is built up of elements of existing theory. This part will start by selecting particular organizational perspectives on organizing doubt (Chapter Eight). Given the content of Part Two, this choice will depend on the relation between this perspective and argumentation. Chapters Nine and Ten are orientated to the way in which the organization of argumentation can be observed in the cases.

Chapter 8

Organizing doubt

The result of this chapter should be the selection of useful conceptual tools that can be used to observe the process of argumentation. Before useful conceptual tools to analyze the cases can be specified, it is important to explore how the process of argumentation can be influenced. To this end, chapter starts by discussing the nature of the argumentative process in order to distinguish between better and worse argumentative processes. An important issue will be whether it is possible to even distinguish between the two. To start with, I shall attempt to draw a picture of 'well-organized argumentation'. Next, the selection of theoretical perspectives will be explicated. The choice of a theoretical perspective depends on its explanatory power. The choice of perspectives is therefore theory-informed.

8.1 What is well-organized argumentation?

The previous chapter should have made clear that Billig's concept of argumentation can be interpreted as a description of the content of the process of doubt. It is therefore claimed that the organization of doubt can be equaled with he organization of argumentation. It is furthermore claimed here that all organizations organize their argumentative process. The design of organizations has inevitable consequences for argumentation. Organizations cannot avoid influencing their argumentative process, if only by making argumentation impossible. However, not all organizations organize their argumentative process in a way that this study would consider fruitful. Therefore this section aims to establish what this study considers to be a fruitful argumentative process. On the basis of this it will be discussed what this means for the organization of argumentation.

It should be noted that the issue of organizing argumentation is absent from Billig's thinking. Perhaps this issue ran against his theoretical temperament. Perhaps he considered it humiliating towards the argumentative powers of people to claim that argumentation in certain organizational settings is in some way 'better' than in others. In fact, he discussed several examples that showed that the argumentative powers of common people can humble those in powerful positions. The concept of argumentation is often used by Billig as a description of a messy world of communication that is too complex to be easily subjected to a system of communication rules. 'The image is one of chatter and discussion' is a typical portrayal of Billig himself. This image of argumentation is used by Billig to criticize theorists, such as Habermass, Gadamer, but also Socrates who aim to regulate dialogue. Furthermore, Billig criticized a theorist like Foucault for exaggerating the way monologue can silence argumentation. No logos can ever dominate anti-logos in an absolute way (Billig, 1996). It seems that an idea like organizing argumentation, which inevitably means a kind of regulation, is at odds with Billig's conception of argumentation. In this conception, after all, regulation is perceived as being opposed to the essence of thinking. The only rule in Billig's conception of argumentation seems to be the abolishment of all rules, so that contradiction and argumentation are not disturbed and can proceed uninterrupted. The view I want to present in this study is that although it may be impossible in principle to make argumentation impossible, certain design characteristics can certainly have a significant influence on the argumentative process. In other words, I do not disagree with Billig *in principle* (no rules can humble the argumentative process), but I do want to claim that design characteristics can make an important practical difference.

It is claimed here that Billig's ideas regarding argumentation can be translated into a characterization of well-organized argumentation. Well-organized argumentation is argumentation that is structured in such a way that its messy and open character is preserved also in organizational settings (which are, by definition, structured and not open). In order to develop such a characterization, characteristics of the argumentative process are translated into characteristics of well-organized argumentation in organizational settings. The remainder of Part Three will be devoted to how organizational factors should be designed in order to create (or approach) this ideal of well-organized argumentation.

Organizing and argumentation

In the following it will be explored what well-organized argumentation involves. This will be translated into demands on the organization of argumentation. To start with, not all talk is argument. Small talk is hardly the thing that Billig had in mind when he aimed to characterize argumentation. Also polite conversation, which appears to really discuss an interesting topic while the truly sensitive sides of the matter are skillfully avoided (Billig 1996), is not truly argumentation. Argumentation implies that in a given situation the force of arguments is of central importance, not difference in formal status (Billig, 1996). A last distinctive characteristic of argumentation is that it is the counterpart of practical action. Billig (1996) did not aim to characterize an airy process of abstract reasoning (i.e. Rodin's statue) but an everyday process of dealing with dilemmas of the real world. These characteristics have consequences for the design of the organizational setting in which argumentation is to take place.

- If the force of arguments counts, well-organized argumentation presupposes *equality*. One can imagine that this is a difficult requirement in formal organizations, especially in organizations that are focused on hierarchy;
- If argumentation is not small talk then well-organized argumentation is orientated to the *crucial issues* in hand. The crucial issues in hand can be sensitive topics because they involve questions regarding status, responsibilities, and individual talents. Janis & Mann (1977) have shown that decision-making groups can lapse into polite conversation out of fear of addressing sensitive topics. One can therefore imagine that the quality of the actual argumentative process matters in this respect;
- If argumentation should be relevant then well-organized argumentation should be *influential*. Even when the arguers are well-informed and are directly focused on the most crucial developments in hand, their debates will still be pointless if they are in principle not allowed to act on the basis of their insights;
- If argumentation implies that the arguers should have practical involvement, then well-organized argumentation implies that the arguers are *actors* as well. Within organizational settings this requirement has two sides. Everyone is familiar with the stories of generals (e.g. in World War I) who endlessly discussed complex issues of strategy without being aware of the actual situation. The opposites of the 'thinkers that do not act' are 'the doers who cannot think'. Everyone is equally aware of the fate of many soldiers (again in World War I) who were required to follow orders without thinking. The 'thinkers that do not act' are alienated from reality, which has disastrous consequences for the relevance of their arguments. The 'actors that cannot think' are deprived from behavioral control, which implies that their arguments are not influential. The implication of this issue is that because operational units are confronted with dynamic complexity they should be arguers as well as actors;
- If argumentation is different from small talk then well-organized argumentation is *relevant*. This implies that the arguers should possess the ability to identify the relevant topics. Imagine a small group of soldiers whose sole job it is to observe a house that is being rebuilt. One can imagine that such a group, while observing, kills time by arguing about the important topics in the area as a whole. However, one can equally imagine that such a group has a rather limited view on the proceedings in the area. The observers of the house are in direct contact with the environment, so they are the first witnesses of certain important develop-

ments. However, they need insight into the nature of the organization's intentions in order to recognize the important developments.

Note that these demands are not orientated to the abilities of individual arguers, but are instead orientated to the context in which argumentation should take place. Together they draw quite a complicated picture of well-organized argumentation. This issue will be tackled in the next section. Based on the previous line of thinking, the following section will distinguish between two dimensions of doubt. The first dimension could be called the external structure of doubt (the prerequisites that the organizational context provides), the second one the internal structure of doubt (the debate itself).

8.2 Perspectives on organizing argumentation

The internal structure of argumentation refers to the debate itself. This is what probably most people imagine when thinking of argumentation. This dimension refers to an *open spirit of contradiction*. The nature of this open spirit of contradiction will be worked out in later chapters of this study. The external structure of argumentation refers to the prerequisites of meaningful debate provided by the organizational context. On the basis of the foregoing it can be inferred that this refers to *insight* and *control*, that is to say, insight into the relevant matters in hand, and control to apply one's insights[73].

The internal and external structures are linked. If the prerequisites of a meaningful debate are not met, the debate itself cannot be meaningful. Although the external structure of argumentation is not conspicuous when observing debates, it is of particular importance according to this study. This line of thinking can be represented in a matrix:

Control/**Insight**	Yes	No
Yes	A. Meaningful argumentation	C. Desperate argumentation
No	B. Powerless argumentation	D. Meaningless argumentation

A. According to this study, this is the ideal situation. In this situation, arguers are well-informed. They have a good insight into the local conditions they are involved in, which enables them to implement their insights on the nature of the situation. As such the arguers are self-organizing. If they are confronted with surprises or change, they are able to discuss the nature of the situation and implement the fruits from their discussions.
B. In this situation the arguers are well-informed, but are restricted in acting on the basis of their insights. This would be a situation in which the

---

[73] The sociotechnical tradition also considers insight and control to be crucial task-dimensions (De Sitter, 2000).

arguers have insight into the nature of a situation, but in which a central controller dictates their activities. They are literally made powerless by the organizational context.

C. In this situation the arguers are confronted with practical problems and lack the insight. That is why it is called desperate argumentation. In a dynamically complex environment, operators are frequently confronted with situations that defy existing insights. The situations that I am referring to here are situations in which operational units are structurally withdrawn from developing insight **by the organizational context.**

D. In this situation the arguers lack both insight and control. To argue in such a situation is meaningless because the arguers are not able to ask the relevant questions and are not required to act on the basis of their (irrelevant) insights.

With regard to the issue of organizing argumentation, the following note is crucial. Organizing argumentation, as it is interpreted in this study, is not orientated to individual processes of argumentation. Instead, it is focused on creating the right circumstances for argumentation, by influencing both the external structure and the internal structure of argumentation. Therefore, this study agrees with De Sitter (2000), who claimed that human resources cannot be *managed*, but should be *mobilized*.

Meaningful argumentation as a complicated concept

Notwithstanding the straightforwardness of the idea of organizing argumentation, a rather complicated picture of the idealized debate within organizations is drawn. A number of complications are discussed here.

- Argumentation that, *on the surface of things*, appears to be true debate can evolve into something totally the opposite of what this study aims to capture. It can be argumentation about irrelevant matters and it can be argumentation about matters beyond the arguers' control. It can also be both. The meaningfulness of argumentation is considered to partly influenced by the context of argumentation;

- The relation between the arguers and the organizational context determines whether the arguers have insight and control. It should be emphasized that this relation between the arguers and the organizational context is in principle problematic. Operational units are defined here as a part of a larger organization, which means that they are semi-autonomous. It also means that they are designed to perform a particular job, which means that they have only limited grip on their level of ambition, and have only limited insight into the intricacies of a larger operation. However, the nature of this link to the rest of the organization does make a crucial difference, as will become clear in later parts of this chapter;

- The situation in which the debates take place can stimulate or prohibit open dialogue. It is conceivable that the arguers lack equality to address matters openly, it is also conceivable that the arguers avoid sensitive topics. Furthermore, in a hierarchically orientated organization it is conceivable that the required open climate to critically discuss sensitive matters is not available;
- In important ways the crisis organization depends on the insights at the operational level because it is directly in touch with the dynamically complex environment. The experiences of the operational units are the basis for discrediting the existing insights within the crisis organization as a whole. One can imagine that argumentation is not only important within operational units. Insights from operational units should also be involved in discussions at the strategic and tactical levels of the organization.

8.3 Analyzing the organization of doubt in the cases

There are different organizational factors that can be said to have an influence on the process of argumentation. Perhaps even, it is more difficult to find organizational factors that have no influence on the argumentative process whatsoever. One can imagine, for example, that certain critical individuals within an organization are systematically kept out of the essential discussions. One can equally imagine that certain groups of employees are strategically misinformed, or that key decision-makers lack any clear insight on the phenomena on which they should decide. The design of the debate can be influenced by various organizational factors. One could think of theory on organizational culture, organizational structure, leadership, decision-making procedures, quality management, and rules for communication between organizational parts. Since this area is too all-embracing, the perspectives need to be selected thoughtfully. To use the phrasing of Chapter Two, this study does not aim to make an atlas constituted of all thinkable maps of a particular area. Such a topic should be tackled by a study that is specifically devoted to the topic of organizing argumentation in organizations.

In the analysis of the cases, I want to focus on one category of organizational factors for the external structure of argumentation and one type for the internal structure of argumentation. In order to analyze the external structure of argumentation, I want to focus on the **organizational structure** of the crisis-organization and the particular position the operational units occupy in this organizational structure. In order to analyze the internal structure of argumentation, I want to focus on the nature of **leadership** within in the crisis organization. The choice for these organizational factors is 'theory informed', that is to say, the influence of both factors on argumentative processes is recognized in literature as being an important influence. The nature of this influence will be discussed in the forthcoming chapters. Chapter Nine will focus on the influence of the organizational structure on argumentative processes, Chapter Ten on the influence of leadership and argumentative processes. Both chapters will also discuss how these organizational perspectives will be used to analyze the cases.

8.4 Organizing argumentation: Billig and Habermass

Many researchers will probably claim that the idea of 'organizing a debate' is not original. The idea that human intelligence can be mobilized through dialogue and that this can be used to the advance of a community has been explored before. This very idea is central to the philosophy of Juergen Habermass. In effect, Habermass intended to abolish constraints on open communication (that is, constraints of power) through the development of rules that should guide debate. The rules of Habermass should establish communities in which open dialogue is not undermined.

Habermass is a sociologist who is interested in society at large. However, many researchers have been quick to recognize his ideas in the area of organizational studies. The parallels with the interpretations and intentions of Habermass and this study are strikingly obvious. This study claims that matters should be openly discussed to the advance of the organization. Therefore this study aims to organize the debate in the organization in such a way that the argumentative potential is indeed mobilized (this also has implications for status and power within organizations: argumentation implies equality).

Although the similarities between this study and the one from Habermass are obvious, there really is one crucial difference. The focal point of this difference is the way in which argumentation is conceptualized in this study which uses Michael Billig's conceptualization of argumentation. Myerson (1994) and Billig (1996) himself discussed the difference between the concept of dialogue of Habermass and the concept of argumentation of Billig. The essence of Myerson and Billig's argumentations will be outlined here. The essentials of Habermass' philosophy will be discussed at greater detail using *Rhetoric, Reason and Society. Rationality as Dialogue* by George Myerson (1994). Myerson portrayed Habermass as a thinker who is part of a larger stream of thinkers that he called 'dialogic rationalism' (p. 7). According to Myerson, this is not a neatly defined category of thinkers, but a category made up of a diversity of thinkers who have comparable orientations on one particular issue, i.e. conceiving reason as dialogue. 'His conception develops through a complex of terms; and the basic term, foundation of this enlightenment is argument, twinned with consensus. They appear to be incompatible, but for Habermass *argument* and *consensus* are united in the vision of rationality because people argue rationally only when they seek consensus' (p. 23, italics in original).

Myerson summarized the cornerstones of Habermass' philosophy (p. 9):

- Argumentative speech is central to rationality;
- Argument is interactive, it has a dialogic structure;
- The interaction leads to agreement when it is understood;
- The achieved agreement is the foundation of a good society;
- These requirements are compatible with science, but not reducible to the methods or conclusions of science.

Both Myerson and Billig were critical of Habermass' portrayal of communicative rationality. The focal point of disagreement between Habermass and Billig is the issue of consensus and the rules of argumentation that should establish this. Habermass' dialogues are subjected to rules in order to give rational dialogue a chance of deciding on a given matter. Billig's dialogues are fundamentally disorderly. Infinity of argumentation and contradiction are two catchphrases that can be used to characterize Billig's approach. Billig (1996): "Rhetorical theorists, who have attempted to operationalize Habermass' idea of 'unconstrained communication' into strategies for conversation have tended to produce heuristics for agreement" (p. 17). Myerson argued that Habermass' approach has a tendency of becoming monologic. "For Habermass, it seems that one thing that is not arguable is the definition of being rational. To be rational is to argue properly, according to his criteria, or to be ready to argue properly when challenged. But anyone who rejects this definition of rationality is automatically barred from arguing about it because we have to accept his principle in order 'to participate properly', to enter the discussion. (…). If anyone refuses to accept that argument is the proper test of rationality, Habermass can label them 'irrational' and disqualify their contributions to the subject" (p. 43).

Why Billig's account on argumentation is preferred

A critical reader might agree that Habermass' and Billig's concepts of dialogue differ, but might not be convinced of the reasons to prefer Billig over Habermass: on the contrary, intuitively an orderly dialogue seems more preferable than a disorderly dialogue, especially if one aims to 'organize' argumentation. Also this critical reader might point to the fact that, although Habermass' philosophy is orientated to consensus, the dialogue does not 'forbid' contradiction. Furthermore, this study considers argumentation to be not a goal in itself, but something that helps organizations to deal with dynamic complexity. As such it seems perhaps that, because action is the goal of argumentation, this study is implicitly orientated to consensus. The critical reader might, furthermore, argue that agreement is of paramount importance in operational units because they need to act, and they generally need to act in a coordinated way. Moreover, this study aims to be normative, and Habermass is truly normative. These points seem to force us into the Habermass camp.

The reason why this study prefers Billig's concept over that of Habermass' has to do with the importance of contradiction in dynamically complex environments. Billig (1996) defended his position against orderly debate by discussing the Socratic dialogue[74], which can be perceived as a model of ideal communication. The essence of this dialogue is a game of questions and answers. Billig (1996, p. 54): 'By questioning, he gets the debaters to agree to certain propositions, and then, by further questioning he examines the implications of this agreement. The method aims to give the debate a fixed starting point: there must be a proposition which is accepted, in order for the implications to be discovered. (…). The process will continue until the participants find a proposition which withstands the test of cross-examination.' Billig emphasized that this ideal is rarely achieved in everyday reality. The hope of giving debate a firm starting point is often not realized. Often disagreement already begins when trying to pin down the meaning of the propositions. Billig (1996, p. 55): 'What we see here is something that occurs commonly in arguments: the point of disagreement shifts and points of agreement can quickly turn in into points of disagreement. Therefore it is too simple to say that it is a pre-condition that the participants must agree on the rules of language. Arguments frequently turn into disputes about language and the meaning of words.'

This essential difference between Billig and Habermass makes two points clear. First, the Socratic dialogue showed that agreement can only be achieved by accepting certainties. In conditions that are dynamically complex it is dangerous to try to pin down the meaning of things. That is the reason Weick underlined the importance of doubt and contradiction. Here lies the crucial difference between Habermass and Billig. Habermass, in the end, remained an enlightenment philosopher and therefore remained focused on the concept of 'unity of truth', i.e. consensus. Billig, on the other hand, dismissed this idea of unity of truth and instead argued the reasonableness of contrary statements. Secondly, units that need to end argumentation in order to act, temporarily put discussions aside out of practical need. That does not imply that there is nothing left to discuss. After the actions will be finished, the same issues can be taken up again. Temporary agreements

---

[74] Not incidentally Billig (1996) pointed to the similarities of the Socratic dialogue and Habermass' concept of communicative reason (p. 16).

do not finish argumentation. It is a fundamental premise of the organizing model that the rational parts (selection, retention) cannot solve all problems before units are able to act.

'Organizing argumentation' from Habermass' perspective means improving the argumentative ability by purifying it. Choosing Billig's depiction of argumentation implies that 'organizing argumentation' means something differently. It means 'preserving' the messy character of argumentation, which involves 'protecting the messy character of argumentation from monologue'. In a way, therefore, 'organizing argumentation' in this study means 'protecting argumentation from organization'.

8.5 Final Remarks

This study focuses on argumentation; one could say on the thinking parts of Weick's organizing model. However, the thinking parts only constitute part of the phenomenon of dealing with dynamic complexity. The nature of dynamic complexity is such that units cannot discuss every problem they are confronted with before they act. It is a truism to claim that the organization of doubt, or organizing argumentation, is not the only worry for crisis organizations. Acting is at center stage. It is the difficulty of acting in a dynamically complex environment that makes argumentation important (Van der Vlist, 1981). This problem has been addressed before in different guises. However, it is essential enough to address it yet again.

No analyses or superior abstractions can provide the final answers to the problems units are confronted with. The paradox is that units on the one hand should think about their problems. At the same time, however, the nature of dynamic complexity makes that arguing and thinking are inherently limited. Units should therefore be prepared to think, but they should be prepared to be surprised as well. Acting in environments that are dynamically complex implies that units should be prepared to act while knowing that their knowledge of the environment is limited (Van der Vlist, 1981). This is a fundamental insight according to this study. This *state of mind* is perhaps the most difficult part of dealing with dynamically complex environments.

Argumentation is not a goal in itself; argumentation should support dealing with dynamic complexity. The fact that it is not a goal in itself means that it is not a sacred process within organizations that always unquestionably holds a prominent place. Instead, units should know when to argue, but also know when to stop arguing. That means that units should know when (temporary) agreement is necessary in order to act in a coordinated way. This will be an important aspect of 'organizing argumentation'. Notwithstanding the possibility of further argument, the reality of the situation the units are involved in makes that they need to act. Argumentation is, on the one hand, an infinite process because after new situations discussions on strategies can be re-opened. On the other hand, if there was no end to argumentation and it would never have any effect on actions, it would become a senseless process. The limitations are crucial if one aims to organize argumentation by using organizational arrangements. This means that they continually return to the discussions of the next chapters.

Chapter 9

Doubt and the organizational structure

This chapter has the aim to describe the prerequisites in the design of the organizational structure for meaningful argumentation at the level of operational units. This is a normative aim, which will be constructed out of two basic ingredients. It is the objective (1) to explicate how characteristics of the organizational structure influence argumentation at the level of the operational unit, and (2) to explicate how the organizational structure of the units in the case can be analyzed.

There is much literature available on the topic of designing self-organizing units, particularly in the sociotechnical tradition. Kuipers & Van Amelsvoort (1990) specifically connected the topic of self-organization to the topic of doubt. They furthermore discussed the topic of the design of self-organizing units, using the concept of 'control cycle'. Doubt is important, according to Kuipers & Van Amelsvoort (1990, pp. 157–158), in the various parts of the control cycle (perceiving, evaluating, intervening). Integration of these parts of the control cycle is essential, according to them, because it enables doubt[75]. After the discussion on the link between organizational structure and meaningful argumentation, I will discuss how the influence of organizational structuring is observed in the cases.

9.1 The influence of organizational structure on argumentation

The influence of organizational structure on argumentation is often clarified by referring to the negative sides of this influence. Organizational structure,

---

[75] One can see that these ideas are close to the ideas that are discussed in this study, but for one crucial difference. This study starts from the importance of doubt and asks how doubt can be organized. Kuipers & Van Amelsvoort started from the topic of organizational structuring and asked themselves how a process of doubt could be facilitated within the design of an organizational structure. Kuipers & Van Amelsvoort reasoned the other way around, so to speak.

it is argued within the critical realms of organizational studies, can be used to prohibit acting and thinking in an insightful way[76].

An important theorist who underlines the negative influence of system's characteristics upon the ability to act and think in an insightful manner is Charles Perrow (1999). He developed his ideas in the context of a study of accidents. He focuses on characteristics of "systems" in order to explain accidents and argues that certain types of systems are more accident prone than others, hence his idea of 'normal accidents'. Accidents can, according to Perrow, be perceived as *normal* given the nature of the systems in which they occur. Perrow's definition of systems encompasses both technical systems (the lay-out of a nuclear plant) and social systems (organizations). The central systems characteristics he is interested in are interaction and coupling. Both are actually meant as dimensions. Complexity refers to a dimension which ranges from *linear interactions* to *complex interactions* between parts of the system. What makes a system 'interactively complex' is the key question, whether or not interactions between parts are expected or not. In a complex system a failure in one part of the system influences the functioning of another part in an unexpected way (Perrow, 1999, pp. 72–73). Coupling refers to the dimension which ranges from loose coupling to tight coupling. This dimension characterizes whether the system is resilient, i.e. whether it is capable of recovering from incidents. Perrow (1999, p. 92) puts it thus: 'Loosely coupled systems, whether for good or for ill, can incorporate shocks and failures and pressures for change without destabilization. Tightly coupled systems will respond more quickly to these perturbations, but the response may be disastrous.' The system can be said to be 'tight', in a literal sense, when parts of the system influence one another in

---

[76] Based on an assumption of certainty the organization can structure its internal arrangements with mathematical precision. Morgan (1997) described how mechanical metaphors have traditionally been dominant in organizational studies. The classic organizational designer is perfectly rational and uses strict logic and perfect knowledge of the phenomenon of organizing and will design blueprints for organizations. This is also referred to as social engineering. Furthermore, mechanical metaphors also determine how many people, not necessarily familiar with organizational theory, think about organizing. If one believes to know the truth, there is no need for critical discussion of crucial assumptions and there is also no need for dialogue with the rest of the organization. The top-down voice considers the rest of the organization not well informed enough, not familiar enough with the methods of top management, or not smart enough to be a serious opponent in debate. This could be considered the modernist side of the spectrum. Alvesson & Deetz (1995, p. 194): 'In the organizational context, we use the term 'modernist' to draw attention to the instrumentalization of people and nature through the use of scientific-technical knowledge (modeled after positivism and other 'rational' ways of developing safe, robust knowledge) (...)'. Both organizational structure and leadership have been used to establish such a monologue. For example, Foucault (1975) emphasized that organizational structure can be used as a tool with which the powerful discipline the powerless. Organizational structuring, according to these classical principles, inevitably seems to lead to organizations in which the truth is determined top-down.

a direct way, without there being much slack, or buffers, or other ways of isolating processes.

Part of the problems of certain systems characteristics is that they can prohibit the insightful acting and thinking of operators. Perrow (1999, p. 10) suggests: 'High risk systems have a double penalty: because normal accidents stem from the mysterious interaction of failures, those closest to the system, the operators, have to be able to take independent and sometimes quite creative action. But because these systems are so tightly coupled, control of operators must be centralized because there is little time to check everything out and be aware of what another part of the system is doing.' Perrow does not go into discussion of to what degree design can resolve tight coupling. He merely accepts coupling and interaction as givens, perhaps because in the study of an accident the perspective of the researcher is retrospective: in that case they are a given.

Snook (2000) has taken up the essentials of Perrow's normal accidents theory up in order to explain a case of friendly fire. Snook combines Perrow's idea of complexity with an idea of 'division of labor' such as it is found in classic organizational literature (Bergson, 1986). More particular, Snook uses the twin concepts of differentiation and integration ('everything that you divide, you have to put together again') in order to show the way organizations built up complexity. Snook (2000, p. 143): 'As analytic tools the twin concepts of differentiation and integration are extremely powerful. Part of what makes them so conceptually appealing is their elegance. The logic is quite simple: Whatever you divide, you have to put together again; the more divided, the more effort to rejoin. How social systems do this is what organizing is all about.' Complexity, in Perrow, refers to 'structural complexity' in the sense that De Sitter (2000) means it. An organizational structure describes the way tasks ('labor') are divided in an organization. When tasks are divided, subsystems are created ('grouping') as well as a network of relations between those subsystems ('coupling'). Structural complexity is a consequence of division of labor and the resulting problem of control, i.e. of creating mechanisms to integrate the separated parts[77]. The

---

[77] 'Structural complexity' is slightly different from 'complexity' as Perrow has meant it. A complex system *can* be considered linear according to Perrow if it functions in the way it is intended. With Snook, Lawrence & Lorsch and De Sitter complexity itself generates non-linear functioning. De Sitter (2000) has shown that a machine-like operating of complex social systems is a mere theoretical possibility that cannot occur in actual reality. Nevertheless, complexity is sometimes used by Perrow in the sense of structural complexity. As such his

topic of division of labor is classic within organizing studies. Classic writers such as Fayol, Gulick and Urwick emphasized the importance of division of labor for efficiency, etc. (Bergson, 1986). The insight which theorists like Perrow, Snook and De Sitter point to is that division of labor leads to structural complexity, making both *insight* and *control* for operators, i.e. their ability to act and to think meaningfully, more problematic. As such structural characteristics of organizational systems influence the crucial dimensions of meaningful argumentation discussed earlier in this study.

The crisis organization divides tasks between different operational units; it therefore 'groups and couples' the different operational units. In the first place, organizational structure influences insight of operators. Once operators have to function in a complex organizational network in which they perform a narrowly defined job, it becomes increasingly more difficult for them to understand the contribution of their job and the other functioning parts of the network. A complex organizational network undermines insight. In that case, it becomes increasingly more difficult for them to act and to think in insightful ways. In the second place, an organizational structure influences the control operators have over the actual work they are doing. If a job is divided into smaller parts and if every part is attributed to a specific department (subsystem) within an organization, dependencies are created between parts of the organization ('tight coupling'). In that case, the more a job is divided into smaller parts, the more dependencies are created, the more rigid the organizational network becomes and the more subsystems are bound by rules. Such an organization increasingly relies on the stability of the environment (Kuipers & Van Amelsvoort, 1990). When an organization that is built up in this particular way is confronted with non-routine events, the central part of the organization will suffer an information overload (Simon, 1997). The classic theorist's philosophy of a maximal division of labor results in an organization that is built up of simple tasks (in order to make a task easier to standardize) and a complex structure (in order to link the different small tasks, (Kuipers & Van Amelsvoort, 1990). Or, to put the essence of this strategy differently, it is an attempt to make thinking

system characteristic 'complexity' is rather broadly defined. Probably this has to do with the way Perrow has conceptualized systems, although technical systems and social systems differ in the sense that social systems entertain a dynamic relation with their environment while technical systems are essentially closed. Also Weick (2004) has concluded that the central concepts in Perrow's normal accidents theory are rather broadly defined.

at the operational level as obsolete as possible (develop standard operating procedures) and to centralize the remaining thinking.[78]

The degree to which an entire job is divided into smaller parts influences the ability of subsystems to argue meaningfully. As such it influences the ability of subsystems to deal with dynamic complexity. Apart from the fact that the organizational structure 'shapes the world in which operators live', it also influences whether new insights can reach the higher hierarchical levels in the organization. Obviously, if operators are 'unaware' and 'unable' the 'situational awareness' of the entire organizational network involved suffers subsequently. Essential for the purpose of this chapter is that indicators are explicated that clarify in what way the organizational structure of crisis-organization influenced the ability of operators to act and to think insightful.

9.2 Analyzing self-organizing potential in the cases

The so-called 'holographic rules' are a useful tool to analyze the relevant dimensions of the design of the operational units, because they emphasize the importance of both insight and control[79]. The hologram is used as a metaphor to formulate the necessary qualities of self-organizing units. Morgan (1997, pp. 100–101): 'The metaphor of the hologram invites us to think of systems where qualities of the whole are enfolded in all the parts so that the system has an ability to self-organize and regenerate itself on a continuous basis. (...). They would, in short, be intelligent, self-organizing brains that reflect all the qualities of what we have described as a learning organiza-

---

[78] I have emphasized here the influence of structure on argumentation in a technical way. There is also a substantial literature in organizing studies that approach the subject more ideological, i.e. that emphasize that the organizational structure is a tool of the powerful to rule the powerless. Alvesson & Deetz claim for example (1995, p. 194): 'In the organizational context, we use the term 'modernist' to draw attention to the instrumentalization of people and nature through the use of scientific-technical knowledge (modeled after positivism and other 'rational' ways of developing safe, robust knowledge) (...)'. For example, Foucault (1975) emphasized that organizational structure can be used as a tool with which the powerful discipline the powerless. Organizational structuring, according to these classical principles, inevitably seems to lead to organizations in which the truth is determined top-down. Such organizations can be said to organize monologue, instead of organizing argumentation. Alvesson and Deetz (1995, p. 198) said on this subject: 'The central goal of critical theory in organizational studies has been to create societies and workplaces which are free from domination where all members have an equal opportunity to contribute to the production systems which meet human needs and lead to progressive development of all.'

[79] The holographic rules originate from the classical sociotechnical literature (e.g. Herbst, 1974). Kuipers (Kuipers, 1989a; Kuipers & Van Amelsvoort, 1990), as a representative of modern sociotechnique, used them to describe the principles of self-organization, i.e. the design principles for operational units. Morgan (1997) described the holographic rules as a means to describe the concept of self-organization. Morgan's basic description will be used below.

tion'. Five principles of holographic design are crucial here (Morgan, 1997, pp. 102–106)[80]. A peculiarity of the holographic rules that should be pointed out is that they themselves are in a sense holographic. The whole of the holographic way of thinking returns – more or less – in every principle.

The principles are connected with indicators referring to characteristics of the organizational structure. They are connected to the insight and control of operational units and with matters that can be observed in the case studies. This connection is based on my own interpretation of the principles. Because of the shortcomings of the case studies it will not always be possible to find information on the indicators in sufficient detail. Then the information has to be reconstructed from the case descriptions. This issue will be elaborated upon in the empirical parts of this study[81].

1. Create the whole in the parts

This rule refers to the way tasks are divided (the 'production structure', De Sitter, 2000). The rule implies that the production structure is designed such that a meaningful whole is created. This meaningful whole is a structural prerequisite for "insight". Morgan (p. 106): 'Under old mechanistic principles work processes were usually fragmented into narrow and highly specialized jobs, linked through some means of coordination. The whole was the sum of the parts thus designed. (...). The holographic approach to job design moves in exactly the opposite direction by defining jobs holistically. The basic unit of design is a work team that is made responsible for a complete business process (...). (...). Within the team, roles or jobs are then broadly defined with individuals being trained in multiple skills so that they are interchangeable and can function in a flexible, organic way.' This does not imply, as is often thought, that everyone should be skilled at everything. It should furthermore be emphasized that the prerequisites for creating the

---

[80] This differs from the distinction used by Kuipers & Van Amelsvoort (1990), who only described four of the five discussed here. The first principle discussed here was not described by Kuipers & Van Amelsvoort.

[81] The choice for the holographic rules to analyze how the design of the operational units influenced their ability to deal with dynamic complexity is arbitrary. One could argue that De Sitter's conceptual tools to analyze control capacity are much more refined. As such they are better suited to develop a refined picture of the self-organizing potential of workgroups. This is true; however, the case studies do not provide a sufficient level of detail to be able to analyze control capacity according to De Sitter's tight analytical tools. This has to do with the construction of the original cases. The case studies were never created to establish insight into the self-organizing potential of operational units. Instead they provide insight into the everyday problems of operational units. For example, they do not provide detailed insight into the 'domains of arrangement' of operational units, which is essential information if one aims to create a picture of the control capacity. The holographic rules, on the other hand, constitute a tool to generally reconstruct the self-organizing potential of operational units. As such they can still produce a rather good picture.

whole in the parts are established at the level of macrodesign of the organization (the level of the crisis organization).

With regard to the issue of indicators, this description of the 'whole in the parts' is comparable to what Hackman, Oldham, Janson & Purdy (1975) called task identity. They defined this as (1975, p. 59): "the degree to which the job requires completion of a 'whole' and identifiable piece of work – doing a job from beginning to end with a visible outcome." This is a rather general verdict on the nature of task design, and it can be elaborated with the distinction between preparation of activities (e.g. the planning of routes), performance in the strict sense (e.g. driving a truck), and supportive activities (e.g. maintenance of a truck) (Kuipers & Van Amelsvoort, 1990; De Sitter, 2000). In order to be optimally self-organizing, units should possess as much control as possible over these aspects as is reasonably possible.

2. Requisite variety

The first holographic principle is orientated to the design of the production structure. The principle of requisite variety is orientated to the ability of the operational unit to deal with the variety in its environment. These issues are obviously related. This principle refers to Ashby's law of requisite variety (Ashby, 1969). Morgan (1997, p. 112) '(…) the internal diversity of any self regulating system must match the variety and complexity of its environment if it is to deal with the challenges posed by that environment'. Morgan formulates implications for the design of units. Morgan (1997, p. 112): 'The principle of requisite variety thus gives clear guidelines as to how the ideas about getting the whole into the parts and redundant functions should be applied. It suggests that redundancy (variety) should always be built into a system where it is *directly* needed rather than at a distance' (italics in original). As one commander literally told us: 'The environment demands everything, so I should see to it that I take everything with me.' This holographic rule is therefore orientated to control, i.e. at having sufficient behavioral alternatives at one's disposal.

It is sometimes claimed that this rule actually is strange for an approach that emphasizes the problem of dealing with dynamic complexity. After all, how can one know what is 'requisite' in an equivocal and changing environment? Only when one operates in a closed system, one can exactly prescribe what is required. If, however, one interprets requisite variety in a looser sense, it emphasizes the importance of variety within each unit.

3. Redundancy

Morgan (1997, p. 108): 'Any system with an ability to self-organize must have a degree of redundancy: a kind of excess capacity that can create room for innovation and development to occur.' To a certain degree, this principle refs to the importance of multi-functionality (Kuipers & Van Amelsvoort, 1990). Morgan (1997, p. 108) 'Members acquire multiple skills so that they are able to perform each other's jobs and substitute as the need arises. And the team as a whole absorbs an increasing range of functions as it develops more effective ways of approaching its work. At any one time, each member possesses skills that are redundant in the sense that they are not being used for the job at hand.' One can interpret this rule also as an important prerequisite for meaningful argumentation. It influences both insight and control of the arguers. Argumentation is dependent on people being able to think outside the strict limitations of occupations. Furthermore, if one is multifunctional one has more behavioral alternatives at one's disposal. More importantly perhaps, because specialists are confronted with issues that lie outside the realm of their specialty, they are confronted with issues that groups of specialists would take for granted. As an indicator of this rule it will be studied how the operational units were composed.

4. Minimal critical specification

This rule is orientated to the way the fragmented tasks are put together again (the 'control structure', De Sitter, 2000). The principle of minimal critical specification was described by Morgan (1997, p. 114) as follows. 'The central idea here is that if a system is to have the freedom to evolve it must possess a certain degree of space or autonomy that allows appropriate innovation to occur. This seems to be stating the obvious. But the reality is that in many organizations the reverse occurs because management has a tendency to overdefine and overcontrol instead of just focusing on the *critical* variables that need to be specified, leaving others to find their own form' (Italics in original)[82]. In the analysis this general principle is worked out. It will be analyzed what parts of the job of the units are regulated and what parts not. Quite literally, this principle is orientated to the control the arguers possess.

5. Double-loop learning ('learning to learn')

This principle of self-organization was formulated by Morgan (1997, p. 115) as follows: 'As has been emphasized, there is a strong tendency in most organizations to get trapped in single-loop systems that reinforce the status quo. Continuous self-organization requires a capacity for double-loop

---

[82] It should be emphasized that this principle of design can only be applied if certain conditions are prepared in the design of the production structure. If groups are not organized around workflows, but instead are organized around functional parts then complex webs of dependencies are created between various parts of the organization. In that situation one can certainly *aspire* for "minimal critical specifications" but the dependencies that are a consequence of the design necessarily lead to many critical specifications. The dependencies between the various organizational parts mutually prohibit each other's autonomy.

learning that allows the operating norms and rules of a system to change along with transformations in the wider environment.' Double-loop learning as Morgan described it is the essence of the phenomenon of self-organization as it is presented in this study, because it emphasizes the importance of discrediting. Nevertheless, double-loop learning requires that groups can discuss matters critically, which demands argumentation in the sense that is presented here.

In the analysis of the cases it will be discussed whether units had the opportunity for double-loop learning within their group (internal double-loop learning) and whether they had the opportunity to contribute at the tactical and strategic level with their insights (external double-loop learning). This last point is crucial because (1) to be truly self-organizing, units should be able to influence their own design (it influences the amount of control they possess), and (2) due to the challenges of dynamic complexity, developments at the level of the operational units are crucial for the crisis organization (see e.g. De Sitter, 2000). By definition, (double-loop) learning is aimed at developing insight. If units possess the ability for both internal and external double-loop learning they have more control over their environment and more opportunity to experiment. The latter is a valuable source for learning.

9.3 Implications of the previous discussions

On the basis of the discussion of the holographic rules one may wonder whether the concept of argumentation is necessary. After all, if the establishment of self-organizing potential is thought to be essential in this study, the holographic rules provide a picture of the required competences of the units without once referring to the concept of argumentation. The holographic rules directly refer to meaningful action without the necessity of the concept of argumentation.

There are three reasons why the concept of argumentation is thought necessary here. In the first place, the concept of argumentation is not only useful to think about the prerequisites for self-organizing units; it is also useful to think about the process of self-organization itself. The internal structure (the debate itself) of argumentation is discussed in the next chapter. In the second place, the importance of doubt and argumentation was deduced from an abstract model, whereas the holographic rules originate from problem-orientated theory. Therefore the concept of argumentation is useful to draw a link between abstract theory and more problem-orientated theory. Both kinds of theory can benefit from this link, as it clarifies both kinds of theory. In the third place, argumentation (and doubt, for that matter) was identified as the normative element in Weick's model. Systems confronted with a dynamically complex environment need the ability to doubt in order to deal with the challenges of that environment in the best possible way. Kuipers & Van Amelsvoort (1990) emphasized that the goal of sociotechnical design is that acting and thinking, which were separated in classically designed organizations, are integrated again. Emphasizing argumentation means that one emphasizes this 'thinking' element without claiming that thinking is the only thing units need to do.

There is one particular way in which the topic of designing an organization seems to contradict the assumptions of this study. After all, operational units are supposed to deal with dynamic, uncertain, ambiguous, and equivocal environments. An organizational design is based on existing knowledge (how can it be otherwise?). An organizational system confronted with dynamic complexity knows it can be surprised. It furthermore knows that it is very difficult to design an organization in advance. In other words, how can one claim to create *enough* structural room in situations that are largely unpredictable? One can imagine that there is a difference between organizations that operate in dynamically complex environments and organizations that operate in more stable and predictable environments. The latter should be able to design an organizational structure that lasts a while; the former probably not. One can imagine that the ability to restructure is important for organizations that are engaged in dynamically complex circumstances. It is claimed here that particularly an organizational structure in which argumentation is cultivated possesses the ability to change its organizational structure. The Army should aim to create organizations in which the organizational structure itself can become object of argumentation (Kuipers & Kramer, 2002a).

All this leads to a particularly important conclusion. It has frequently been emphasized that for the external structure of argumentation it is important that operational units have both insight into and control over their actions. From this discussion one can conclude that for meaningful argumentation it is essential that arguers have the means to influence the organizational context they are part of. They need to be able to influence the way they are restructured, so they need to be able to influence the developments at the strategic and tactical level. Van der Zwaan (1999) would say that not only autonomy is important for self-organizing, but also participation. In order to be independent, arguers should be able to influence their dependencies.

Chapter 10

Leadership and the internal structure of argumentation

The previous chapter discussed the external structure of argumentation, that is to say, it was concerned with the prerequisites for a meaningful argumentative process. This chapter focuses on the internal structure of argumentation. More particularly, this chapter will discuss the relation between leadership and argumentation and will deal with the issue of how leadership can influence the argumentative process in a positive way. At the end of this chapter specific ways in which the argumentative process can be influenced will be discussed. This chapter starts, however, by placing the argumentative process in the context of the entire functioning of a group.

Often it has been claimed that there is a kind of contradiction between the concepts of self-organization and leadership (e.g. Vogelaar, 2002). Telling someone to think for himself and telling someone to take initiative seems difficult to reconcile with the essential nature of thinking and taking initiative. Leadership is a complicated concept and in developing a view on leadership one needs to take this complexity into account. An important part of this chapter is therefore concerned with how influencing the internal structure of argumentation relates to other leadership functions. Indeed, developing a process of meaningful argumentation is not the only thing units should do when confronted with a dynamically complex environment, so it is not the only process that is to be controlled. As has been claimed before, operational units confronted with dynamic complexity need to possess paradoxical qualities. Perhaps the concept of 'managing dualities' put forward by Pettigrew & Fenton (2000, p. 295) – be it in a different context – captures this need to balance paradoxical or contrary demands. This chapter will not sweep away the other leadership functions by over-emphasizing one in particular, nor will it neatly resolve the 'dualities'.

This chapter will proceed by (1) describing the functioning of groups that are confronted with dynamic complexity in order to describe the context in which argumentation is to occur; (2) defining the role of leadership within a self-organizing unit; (3) providing an account of the 'thing to be organized', i.e. argumentative processes within groups and (4) specifying the role of leaders as stimulators of argumentation. Towards the end of this chapter (5) the analysis of leadership in the cases will be discussed. At the end of this chapter, (6) the entire analytical framework will be summarized.

10.1 Dynamic complexity and self-organizing units

This section discusses the internal functioning of a self-organizing unit confronted with dynamic complexity. Weick (1993) studied the phenomenon of dealing with the unknown in extreme situations. Extreme situations are situations in which existing insights are overthrown. Weick (1993, p. 633) called this a cosmology episode: 'A cosmology episode occurs when people suddenly and deeply feel that the universe is no longer a rational, orderly system. What makes such an episode so shattering is that both the sense of what is occurring and the means to rebuild sense collapse together.' Weick (1993) asked how organizations could be made more resilient to such occasions. According to Weick, in circumstances of chaos it is crucial that **an organization continues to exist**. The phrase 'organization' means here 'structure/ relations between people' and is focused on group level. This organization can help people to make sense of the situation and find solutions for their problems. If the organization collapses, then people are on their own. Weick (1993, p. 634): 'Contextual rationality is sensitive to the fact that social actors need to create and maintain intersubjectively binding normative structures that sustain and enrich their relations. Thus, organizations become important because they can provide meaning and order in the face of environments that impose ill-defined, contradictory demands.' However, with 'an organization' Weick does not refer to the sort of relations between people that exist within a classic mechanistic organization. This is because an organization with a narrowly defined formal structure is vulnerable when the situations changes in which this structure is supposed to operate. Furthermore, such organizations have not 'invested' enough in the *relations* between people. Weick (1993) interpreted an emphasis on formal hierarchy as a threat to 'respectful interaction'[83]. Weick (1993, p. 643): 'If a role system collapses among people for whom trust, honesty, and self-respect are underdeveloped, then they are on their own.'

Subsequently, Weick aims to describe the kind of organization that is resilient to such 'cosmology episodes'. Such an organization has, also according to Weick, holographic qualities (1993, p. 640): '(...) in the manner of a holograph, each person can reconstitute the group and assume whatever role is vacated, pick up the activities, and run a credible version of the role.' Not

---

[83] Janis & Mann (1977, p. 131) indicated that directive leadership is a threat to vigilant information processing. '(...) directive leadership increases the likelihood that the leader will use his power, subtly or blatantly, to induce the member to conform to his decision'.

only formal roles, but also the relations between people should be different compared to a classic mechanistic organization. Weick (1993, pp. 642–643): 'Partnerships that endure are likely to be those that adhere to Cambell's three imperatives for social life, based on a reanalysis of Asch's (1952) conformity experiment: (1) Respect the reports of others and be willing to base beliefs and action on them (trust); (2) Report honestly so that others may use your observations in coming to valid beliefs (honesty); and (3) Respect your own perceptions and beliefs and seek to integrate them with the reports of others without depreciating them or yourselves (self-respect).' It is a widespread misunderstanding that uniformity is an essential and indispensable feature of organizations (Kuipers, Kramer & Richardson, 2002). These points, however, should not be interpreted as a one sided underlining of the importance of cohesion. There are many studies that emphasize the risk of cohesion. Janis & Mann (1977, p. 132) mentioned high cohesiveness as a danger to vigilant information processing. In the view of Janis & Mann, people can become more motivated for maintaining the cohesion than for critically discussing sensitive matters. Instead, Campbell's points should be interpreted as underlining the importance of tolerance for contradiction and deviation. A tolerance for deviance is important for maintaining a spirit of contradiction. Diversity within groups contributes to balancing a propensity for uniformity (Cox, Lobel & McLeod, 1991). Weick implied that in organizations with narrow definitions of formal responsibilities these qualities are less developed (Weick 1993, p. 643).

10.2 Leadership in a self-organizing unit

An important distinction that can be made in theories of leadership is between theories that focus on the individual leader and theories that are focus on 'group functions'. The latter theories emphasize that for a group to operate satisfactorily a number of functions need to be performed, not necessarily by the individual in the formal leadership position. One can, for example, think of *task roles*, which refer to behavior that is mainly orientated to the accomplishment of the group's tasks. A further leadership function that is frequently distinguished is the *maintenance role*, which refers to behavior that is orientated to keeping a group together as an effective instrument. This study uses an individual perspective on leadership. In military organizations the leadership function is placed in the hands of an individual (an officer). However, the things a leader should do will be determined by using a functional approach. Hemphill and Coons (1957, p. 7), defined leadership as 'the behavior of an individual when he is directing the activities of a group toward a shared goal'. This definition was also used by Van der Vlist (1991). It was emphasized by Van der Vlist that it was his intention to refer to the behavior of an individual that is in the formal leadership position (1991, p. 13). Van der Vlist furthermore emphasized that the definition implies that there are a number of group functions to be performed. More particularly, Van der Vlist mentioned a 'goal achievement function', a 'group maintenance function', and a 'future effectiveness function' (1991, p. 13).

Van der Vlist's definition emphasized the position of the individual, whereas the definition can, at the same time, be considered functional as well. Just as hierarchy can be functional in certain circumstances because it is a coordinating mechanism of larger social systems, leadership is defined functionally as well. A functional definition of leadership should emphasize the control aspects of the functioning of a self-organizing unit without which it cannot function. Metsemakers, Van Amelsvoort & Van Jaarsveld (2002) indicated what this means for the behavior of a formal leader in self-organizing units. They defined the role of formal leaders as 'adding the deficiency' and I want to adopt this definition. **Adding the deficiency is adding that element in the control of a self-organizing unit without which it cannot function.**

A comparable position was taken by Kuipers & Vogelaar (1995). Just as hierarchy only comes into existence because the nature of the organization's job makes it necessary, leadership becomes important when there is no other way to deal with matters. This indicates that the position of the formal leader is comparable to that of a guardian. He should guard whether all necessary functions are fulfilled in order to be able to function. This can range from relatively minor practical details in the everyday functioning of a unit (are the necessary budgets formally applied for?) to more important aspects of the functioning of units (indeed, are the difficulties of our unit discussed from all sides?). That is not to say that the leader should perform those functions himself (e.g. applying for budgets), but he should guard that it is taken care of[84].

Deficiencies in group functioning

'Deficiency in group functioning' can refer to a wide array of aspects. It can be expert knowledge on organizing processes, it can be the coordinating activities with the organizational context, or it can be taking a decision if circumstances indicate that a process of argumentation is not leading to

---

[84] Quite deliberately the foregoing discussed leadership in a self-organizing unit. Only when a group is designed as a self-organizing unit, are the preconditions available for leaders to function as the ones that add the deficient. That is to say, in other sorts of groups the leader should add so much deficient that indeed the behavior of the leader can be interpreted as the other side of a shortcoming.

a decision. *Not surprisingly, it can also refer to organizing argumentation within a unit*[85].

The deficiency that leaders should add can originate from a shortcoming in the design of the organization, for instance a shortcoming in the design of the organizational structure (the design of the organization makes self-organization impossible), in the design of a group (some necessary function is not available within the group), or in the education of operators, etc. It should be emphasized that a perfect group is a theoretical concept and not an empirical reality.

The deficiency that leaders should add could also originate from the nature of the situation in which a certain task needs to be performed. Certain decisions are difficult to make group-wise. Officers frequently use this point to defend that the military organization is generally orientated on hierarchy. There are situations conceivable, certainly in moments of acute crisis, in which decisions have to be made and argumentation would lead to passivity. This point refers to the fact that – although argumentation is in principle infinite – it is necessarily finite in the everyday reality of organizations. Organizing argumentation, therefore, also includes knowing when to stop arguing. As has been claimed before, crisis organizations need to possess paradoxical qualities: they need to be able to act without thinking and they need to be able to critically review their insights[86].

10.3 The spirit of contradiction

The previous has shown that the whole of the group's knowledge and awareness should be available in every member of the group in order to be able to enact the unthinkable in the best possible way. This has the following important consequences: Argumentation is *not merely* useful to discredit existing insights; it is a vehicle to develop holographic qualities within a group. It has also been mentioned in the previous chapter: in a debate, people are confronted with different points of view and a diversity of in-

---

[85] Defining leadership in self-organizing units as adding the deficiency has an interesting implication, namely that, if all goes well, a leader should not engage in leadership activities. Instead, a self-organizing unit is supposed to progress without the controlling influence of a leader. That is to say, a unit should be designed in such a way (both internally and externally) that it can progress without the necessity of leadership.

[86] Weick's model already indicated that equivocality presents systems with the need to act at moments when knowledge is hypothetical. Doubt and argumentation are important characteristics of systems to facilitate learning from experience and to discredit existing insights. As such, doubt and argumentation counterbalance the necessity of acting on the basis of hypothesis. This shows that a one-sided emphasis on the ability to act or a one-sided emphasis on argumentation both overstep the reality of the problem of dealing with dynamic complexity.

formation, and are demanded to defend their points of view (requisite variety). Consequently, operators become better aware of their environment (whole in the parts), and more broadly skilled (redundancy of functions). Furthermore, these different matters prepare the preconditions for minimal critical specification. The consequence of this line of reasoning is that to a certain degree argumentation is a goal in itself, regardless of the concrete results of the debates.

This section attempts to explicate the nature of the argumentative process that is to be organized. Billig emphasized the importance of a 'spirit of contradiction'. He described this spirit of contradiction by contrasting it with a 'spirit of accord' (1996, pp. 260–263). When involved in a spirit of accord, the arguers are motivated to present a favorable image of themselves. This can be achieved by 'impression management' or by drawing upon existing 'commonplaces', which is a well-known strategy from ancient rhetoric. Another such strategy is using the tactics of 'polite conversation' in which the sensitive topics are deliberately avoided. Such a 'spirit of accord' might help participants 'to identify warmly with each other' (Billig, 1996, p. 262), but it is not the atmosphere in which existing truths are rigorously discussed without avoidance of the more sensitive topics. When there is a spirit of contradiction, matters of controversy are deliberately sought and discussed.

Hosking & Morely (1991, pp. 254–255) refer to the importance of leaders for establishing such a spirit of contradiction. They base their suggestions on a recognition of the importance of contradiction: 'If a group is to perform skillfully it is important that there is constructive competition between different points of view.' The assumption of this chapter is that leaders should aim for conditions in which the chance for productive debate is enlarged. In other words, groups should be designed and led in a way that the potential for productive argumentation is enlarged. Not incidentally this formulation speaks of conditions that can be interpreted as an indirect way of influencing debate. This indicates that the actual thinking can only be influenced indirectly by leaders. Establishing and maintaining such a spirit of contradiction is considered to be a leadership-function in this study.

10.4 Specific influence of leaders on argumentation

After the general role of leaders within self-organizing units has been discussed, this section focuses on the topic of leadership and argumentation. This section will describe what stimulating a spirit of contradiction may involve. As will be seen, the essence of the points is that leaders should not conduct the activities in principle; they should only perform them when they are deficient in a group. The most popular leadership literature provides comprehensive lists of 'how to do'. It could be thought that also this chapter provides something of the sort. That would, however, seriously underestimate the complexity of the phenomenon of leadership. Therefore the following merely formulates points of attention, not a finite set of technical rules of how to establish a spirit of contradiction.

Selecting topics for debate

One can ask what matters units should argue about, i.e. what should be the topics for debate. It could be thought that selecting the topics for argumentation is one of the things the formal leader should add to a self-organizing group. Not surprisingly, this study does not consider this to be a part of the leadership in principle role. Topics for debate should originate from the everyday experience of operational units. One can imagine that not only the leader is able to raise these matters. As a matter of fact, other members of an operational unit may be in a better position to notice problems, to discern their underlying nature, or to come up with intelligent solutions. If a leader does raise a certain problem, he does not raise it as the leader but as a member of an operational unit who is perhaps more experienced than others or who simply gathered a useful insight. Units should debate about the problems they experience in conducting their everyday tasks and should argue about how they should deal with them. Two main questions should therefore be central in the debates of operational units:

- What are the problems that we are experiencing?
- How should we deal with these problems?

Some of the answers to these questions will be quite straightforward. In dynamically complex circumstances, however, there will be questions to which there are no straightforward answers. It may be that there is constant confusion over what the nature of a certain problem is, and that different interpretations are equally reasonable. Perhaps it is the case that, notwithstanding the possibility of contradiction, unequivocal answers are needed. The topics for debate that are displayed here do not imply that operational units should always blindly follow the issues of the day. It can be quite fruitful to question more general or abstract problems of indirect relevance to the issues of the day. Again, it is not in principle the role of the leader to address such matters, but one can imagine that these 'not everyday subjects' are a deficiency a leader could add.

Providing expert knowledge

I consider expert knowledge to be one of the main deficiencies leaders should add to the self-organizing group. I will discuss various forms of expert knowledge. In important ways task design determines whether a spirit of contradiction can prosper or not. As has been discussed earlier, if tasks are too narrowly defined people develop a limited orientation. It will be argued that the principles of organizational structuring that were discussed are not only useful to design the external structure of argumentation. They are also useful to provide the prerequisites of a spirit of contradiction. In other words, leaders should apply the principles of holographic structuring also within the boundaries of operational units.

Leaders should be aware of signs of one-sidedness and should be willing to provide contradictory arguments. Perhaps the phenomenon of groupthink as it is described by Janis & Mann can best underline the importance of knowledge on argumentation (Janis & Mann, 1977). According to Weick (1979) a system, when displaying the symptoms of groupthink, comes to perceive the environment on the basis of a dominant schema. Billig (1996, p. 146) discussed the link between this phenomenon of groupthink and argumentation (on the basis of one of Janis & Mann's case descriptions): 'An atmosphere had been created in which everyone shared the same opinion and all defensively avoided any counter-views. Anyone within the decision-making group who voiced criticisms of the prevailing view was strongly discouraged. In this way, full debate was avoided, and all 'spirit of contradiction' was suppressed. Under such conditions, according to the arguments of Janis and Mann, the quality of decision-making suffers.' Or, more in general: 'In a group which is avoiding all discussion, no-one takes the role of the other. Just as an individual lacking Cicero's mental discipline might be unable, or psychologically unwilling, to entertain opposing contradictions, so in 'groupthink' no anti-logoi are proposed to test the prevailing logoi.'[87]

Previously, argumentation was displayed as a means to develop holographic qualities in operational units. During the debates it is not necessary

---

[87] Not accidentally an everyday wisdom within organizations states that people that agree are more likely to make career than people that disagree. This is certainly a well-known characteristic of many military organizations (Dixon, 1976). Whatever the case may be, one can interpret Janis & Mann as underlining the importance of contradiction. Janis mentioned a number of structural faults in the organization that can provide an 'antecedent condition' for groupthink. Two are of particular interest here, namely isolation of a group and homogeneity of social background (Janis, 1990). An isolated group is more likely to develop a single-minded orientation on matters. This underlines the importance of debate between groups. This was already considered to be important for reasons of information sharing; now it can also be considered important for reasons of capturing a spirit of contradiction. Furthermore, also a group with homogeneity in social background is more likely to be single-minded (Janis & Mann, 1977). A group that consists of people that are, one way or the other, the same are less likely to discuss the fundaments and the implications of their sameness.

to reach unequivocal conclusions. After all, cherishing contradictory ideas can sometimes be more functional than having unequivocal ideas, as the discussion on Hedberg's theories of action indicated. Nevertheless, one can imagine that there are matters in the experiences of operational units that do ask for explicit decisions. More importantly, it is possible that there are questions for which no straightforward answer exists, but which still need quite unequivocal decisions. For example, units may experience huge difficulties in performing certain tasks. Discussions about this may lead to the conclusion that tasks need to be divided in a different way. A particular way of dividing tasks asks for an unequivocal decision, whereas it is often difficult to determine in advance what will function best. Furthermore, there may be occasions where an operational unit needs to operate in a planned and coherent way, but where the best way of operating is not so straightforward. In other words, there may be situations where there is a potential of contradiction and discussion on the one hand, but on the other hand a need to come up with a decision. In other words, the problems operational units face are frequently unstructured. Units need to act, although they do not have perfect insight into the nature of things. In other words, they need to act (or, they need to have the willingness to act) although there remains the possibility of contradiction. So although argumentation is important for units to develop holographic qualities, they cannot wait until all contradiction is resolved.

Argumentation is considered necessary in order to enable a process of self-organization. As has been stated before, argumentation may be infinite in principle; it is finite in the everyday reality of organizations. Therefore, postponing or ending argumentation is certainly an important function in groups. The question is whether decision-making is something deficient that a formal leader should add. The literature on participation has shown that this all depends on the situation (Van der Vlist & Van Breukelen, 2002). Participation refers to the influence members of a group have in the process of decision-making. Participation is quite generally considered to be essential in self-organizing units (Metsemakers, Van Amelsvoort & Van Jaarsveld, 2002). Van der Vlist stated that: 'Participation in decision-making can influence the quality of decisions. This influence will be positive if the decision incorporates an element of problem-solving and when subordinates possess information for the problem in hand' (Van der Vlist, 1991, p. 108; my translation). Generally, theories on participation distinguish various styles of leadership that differ in the degree of participation they allow members of a group in the decision-making process. Generally speaking, contingency theories describe styles that range from autocratic decision-making to pure delegation. Typically, contingency theories emphasize that the different situations suit different styles of leadership[88]. A leader has therefore different styles at his disposal. The various styles are summarized in the well-known flow chart of Vroom & Yetton (see for a discussion of this theory: Van der Vlist, 1991). One can wonder how far participation should go. One can imagine that group discussion cannot achieve unequivocal results. Given the nature of argumentation and dynamic complexity there is every reason to believe that discussion cannot produce agreement necessary for a decision.

On the other hand, given the nature of dynamic complexity one can imagine that situations necessitate action and an unequivocal decision. According to this study, this is indeed a true dilemma: a situation in which there are two opposing alternatives. The implication of considering this to be a true dilemma is that there is no neat theoretical solution to this problem (see Billig c.s., 1988). In other words, no sophisticated procedure can evade this principal problem and no sophisticated procedure can pinpoint exactly how far participation should go[89]. The consequence of this is that self-organizing groups in crisis operations can always encounter a situation in which leaders need to make decisions[90].

Attending the process of debate

Another deficiency that many may believe a formal leader should add is that of attending the process of debate. Previously it was discussed that group

---

[88] A number of limitations of Vroom & Yetton's model are discussed by Van der Vlist (1991, p. 113, based on a critical evaluation of Yukl), and one limitation is of importance here. The model presupposes that leaders are able to interpret a situation, can "effortlessly" judge matters like the importance of acceptance and the fact whether a problem is structured is not. On the basis of this study one can conclude that the model has monologic traits. The degree of participation functions within the boundaries of the leaders' interpretation of the world. Another criticism that can be formulated on the basis of the insights that are voiced in this study is the difference between "information" and "decision". The phrase "information" has an objectivist connotation and seems to imply that decision-making is a sort of mathematical procedure of studying all relevant information. The problem of equivocality of "information" is explicitly not raised by the model. Nevertheless, the model of Vroom & Yetton is considered useful because it discusses decision-making when a group is confronted with one particular problem: dealing with situations in which a top-down interpretation of a leader is not possible.

[89] A consequence of this dilemma is that the argumentative processes within groups are never guaranteed. Argumentation can become token argumentation. Argumentation becomes a ritual if a leader makes a decision that he already anticipated before anything was discussed. At such occasions argumentation is a game the results of which are settled in advance. One can imagine that there are numerous forces that put pressure on the argumentative process.

[90] Note that open discussion and argumentation can be a malicious tactic for a manipulative autocratic leader. After all, if groups meet equivocality and the need to make unequivocal decisions, the manipulative leader can always claim that "he was forced to make a decision", without even listening to arguments. In other words, group discussion is only consequential if there is the possibility that it results in decisions that a leader would never have made individually.

maintenance roles are important for group functioning and one can imagine that they are important for the process of argumentation as well. The previously discussed topic of respectful interaction also points in that direction. Again, this is not considered to be a specific role for formal leaders. Anyone in a group can perform these maintenance roles. That does not mean, of course, that maintenance behavior is taboo for leaders. However, the fact that formal leaders do aim to influence the process of debate does not mean that this role is a leaders' role in principle (although it may be a leadership role in a functional approach).

Influencing the external structure of debate

A crucial distinction in this study is that between the external and internal structure of argumentation. This link is presented as being determined by the organizational structure. The design of the organizational structure determines the tasks of an operational unit (a narrowly defined task limits the view of an operational unit on the environment and enlarges the unit's dependency on other units) and the level of autonomy it possesses for implementing its insights. Debates can be pointless if the external structure does not provide insight and control. The external structure therefore influences the validity of the discussions. This means that the external structure is conditional for the internal structure. This line of reasoning has some consequences for the position of the concept of leadership and the position of formal leaders. In the first place, although a given leader may display all the required skills of a creator of an internal spirit of contradiction, the debates may still be pointless. In the second place, the *visible* discussions and therefore also the *visible* efforts of leaders to stimulate a spirit of contradiction only tell part of the story.

This means that a unit should possess the possibilities to influence the external structure or to discuss matters with a higher hierarchical level. This may be a job for a formal leader. An organization that is not prepared to tolerate such discussions is still evasive of self-organization. Note that previously it was explained that at both the strategic and tactical level of the organization the insights at the operational level are essential. This refers to the trail of debate that has been mentioned before. Revealingly, within military organizations the operational level is often portrayed as an informer (which refers to the supply of data) rather than as a member of a discussion.

10.5 Vision and argumentation

It is frequently emphasized in literature on leadership, and not merely in classical literature, that leaders should possess a vision, i.e. should be visionary. One can ask how an emphasis on *vision* relates to an emphasis on *argu-*

mentation. According to this study it depends on the way one perceives the concept of vision. It depends on how 'vision' is conceptualized and on how one perceives the role of vision in the organizing process[91].

There is a distinct danger in emphasizing the importance of vision because it is frequently portrayed as a vision that is the possession of the leader that should be transformed to subordinates. In that case, vision and argumentation are opposites. Hosking & Morely (1991, p. 252) underlined this point as well: 'Those who argue that leaders are, or should be, managers of meanings (...) or 'interpreters' (...) also would do well to pay serious attention to the processes through which this may occur. On reading the literature it is all too easy to form the impression that leaders manage meanings through relatively simple, one-directional, causal processes in which they impose their (superior) vision and understanding.' In that case 'vision' is a top-down monologue that is forced upon the members of the organization. Hosking and Morely (1991, p. 252) contrast this with an emphasis on argumentation: 'Active open-minded dialogue is a process that is essential to skillful leadership.' Emphasizing the importance of 'vision without argumentation' to challenge dynamic complexity can be portrayed as an all too convenient way to deal with problems. If the situation is dynamically complex and the leader knows what to do, the situation is not really dynamically complex. Emphasizing that vision is important in uncertain conditions can therefore be a way of explaining away the uncertainty. Perhaps one could claim, as a way of reversing the classical truism, that being able to act *without* a vision is also important in dynamically complex environments (i.e. enactment).

Not incidentally, some theorists on transformational leadership emphasized the importance of rhetoric (Den Hartog & Verburg, 1997; Den Hartog, Koopman & Van Muijen, 1997, p. 38). An objection can be raised against theory that is concerned with the technical rules of transforming a vision.

---

[91] In this chapter I am suspicious – so to speak – of certain accounts that draw a one-dimensional picture of leadership. In this picture, a one-way traffic is portrayed with blessings from the leader to the grateful, humble, and a somewhat simple but well-meaning mass. Some publications on leadership are written in a patronizing and boy-scoutish language. The importance of leadership – both in theory and in everyday organizational reality – is often hailed because it appears to provide an easy solution to organizational problems. Is there a motivational problem? Is the environment challenging? Are the masses feeling stressful? Are the masses showing unethical tendencies? 'Leadership' is the required solution! Certain parts of leadership research are orientated at finding the magic words and attitudes in different situations. Because I am rather suspicious of such one-dimensional tendencies, it seems perhaps that I am opposed to the concept of 'leadership' and leadership research altogether. This is not the case. I am not fundamentally opposed to concepts like 'vision' and 'intellectual stimulation', and I am not blaming every theorist in this field of one-sidedness. Being suspicious when someone underlines the importance of intellectual stimulation (it often means that a leader lays out the required lines of thinking) does not mean being fundamentally opposed to such concepts. In this chapter I want to underline the fundamental complexity of the concept of leadership.

Such an approach distinguishes between the content of a message and the form in which it is presented. The rules for transforming a vision focus on the form of the message instead on what is being transformed[92]. This is not incidentally because these theorists want to develop a theory that is generally applicable. So not only a manager of a computer firm or a military leader but every leader, regardless of the nature of his work, should be able to use the rules of a transformational leader. The paradox of such theories is that they emphasize the importance of content by emphasizing the importance of vision, but at same time they merely address technical rules of transformation. The vision is considered to be essential, but at the same time the vision remains out of focus.

Opposed to the positions that perceive vision as the exclusive possession of a leader, there are positions that perceive vision as a result of an interactive-process, i.e. positions that emphasize the necessary link between vision and argumentation. Such a vision should be *developed within* a self-organizing group. Participation is essential to develop such a vision (Metsemakers, Van Amelsvoort & Van Jaarsveld, 2002). If vision is considered to be a general way of thinking about the environment that should permanently be critically discussed, this study agrees with that position. In that case, argumentation is an essential part of developing a vision.

10.6 Analyzing leadership in the cases

In this study leadership is considered to be important because it directly influences argumentation and doubt in the operational units. It directly influences whether the units focus on argumentation or a spirit of contradiction, or whether those in the formal leadership position emphasize top-down control (guidance) and adherence to rules. It could be thought that therefore the analysis of leadership will be confined to the individual operational unit. This is not the case, as it is claimed that a culture of leadership, also in the context of operational units, can have an effect on the spirit of contradiction within operational units.

The issue is, of course, how to determine whether leadership influence the spirit of contradiction within units. It is claimed here that the crucial information that should be distilled from the cases is the way leaders define their job. The definition (or description) of their job ultimately determines if leaders see themselves as the ones that should capture a spirit of contradiction

---

[92] According to Garver, one cannot distinguish between a good and a bad rhetorician on the level of technical rules. (Garver, 1994, p. 207.). One can imagine why this is the case. If there were one particular technical skill that was typical of a "good" rhetorician, the differences between "good" and "bad" would be clearly visible. In that case the "bad" rhetorician would have an exquisite opportunity for misuse: faking to possess that unique skill.

or just the opposite. One can imagine that leaders draw a desirable picture of their role. As such, one can interpret their reports as not being representative. However, I believe that if leaders draw a more desirable picture of their role, this picture is influenced by what they see as desirable or see as socially accepted standards of the leadership role. It is exactly this anticipation which reveals the leadership culture that I am looking for here. The way the leadership position is defined determines whether argumentation is supposed to be a part of that. The way the leaders defined their jobs is the mirror image of how they defined the role of the common soldiers.

10.7 Engaging the object of study: The function of the analytical framework

Although the lengthy discussion of the ingredients of the analytical framework might have given a different impression, the analytical framework is not developed for its own sake. The analytical framework as it has been presented in the previous chapters gives the impression of being a quest for adequate theoretical ingredients. The discussion of the various theoretical ingredients is far from a display of some sort of checklist of relevant ingredients. Instead, the discussion swings back and forth working through the relevant issues in developing the analytical framework. As has been discussed in Chapter Two, the analytical framework is used for *selecting data* and *interpreting patterns*. Here it will be discussed which ingredients of the analytical framework are used to select sets of data. Subsequently will be discussed how the framework is used to interpret patterns.

As has been discussed in Chapter Two, three sets of data will be selected. These are the three basic building blocks of the conceptual model of this study:

The following elements of the analytical framework will be used to select these elements.

A. *Dealing with dynamic complexity at the operational level.* The leading questions that structured the case studies were: (1) What are the problem situations junior leaders in crisis situations are confronted with? (2) How do they deal with these problems? One can say that for this reason the cases provide specific information about dynamically complex problems (problems that cannot be solved by using a closed system of rules). The descriptions of how the units dealt with their problems provide information on their 'theories of action' (Hedberg's concept). It is therefore defendable that important parts of the case descriptions are essentially about dealing with dynamic complexity . In the selection of events, practical problems are searched that can be explained according to the logic of Weick's organizing model. Weick's organizing model is a useful tool to map the way units dealt with dynamic complexity. The case material can therefore be scanned for enactments, for ways of interpreting environments (selection), for experiences that units built up (retention), for ways previous insights influenced subsequent behavior and for signs of developments in the units' body of knowledge. This involves a selection and a different interpretation of the original descriptions. The selection is that only problems that have to do with dynamic complexity will be briefly discussed (not problems with, for example, the atmosphere within groups). The difference in interpretation is that the problems are not interpreted as problems of junior leaders but as problems of operational units in general;

B. *Design of the operational units by the crisis organization.* The design of the operational units is analyzed, using information on the organizational structure and on leadership. As has been discussed in the sections on 'indicators', the organizational structure of the operational units is described, using the holographic principles. These principles provide information on the self-organizing potential of units as a result of the design of their production and control structure. As such, these principles not merely select data; they already translate the raw information on the design in an interpretation of the self-organizing potential of units. In other words, the holographic principles draw a specific normative pattern. Indications about leadership in the units are selected by searching for information about how the role of leaders was defined by various participants in the crisis organization;

C. *Design of the mother organization.* This type of data cannot be specified at this stage because the specific information on the design of the mother organization that is of interest in this study will be based on the analyses of the cases. This will be the topic of Chapter Thirteen. As a sort of preview it can be stated that information is selected on (1) the philosophy of dealing with dynamic complexity as adopted in the doctrine; (2) characteristics of the organizational structure of the mother organization; (3) leadership structures, i.e. the way the leadership function is implemented in the mother organization.

Besides selecting data, the analytical framework is used for interpreting patterns. As has been discussed in Chapter Two, the analytical framework is used here as a heuristic tool to reconstruct the relations in the conceptual model. There are two relations:

1. *A relation between the design of the operational units and the way they dealt with dynamic complexity.* As has been said, the holographic rules not merely describe the design of operational units but they allow specific normative conclusions regarding the self-organizing potential. Regarding the definition of leadership it will be analyzed whether the topic of 'creating a spirit of contradiction' is available in the way the role of leaders is defined.
2. *A relation between the design of the mother organization and the design choices made in crisis organizations.* It will be analyzed whether design characteristics of the mother organization make the design of self-organizing operational units more or less likely.

A schematic overview of both the ingredients and the function of the analytical framework is presented in Appendix I.

PART IV
Analyzing the cases

Part Four is devoted to the analysis of the cases. This part is orientated to a reflection on the case studies. Chapter Twelve, Thirteen and Fourteen will analyze the self-organizing potential of the operational units in the cases. The following central question is dealt with in this part:

How was the problem of dealing with dynamic complexity influenced by the design of the operational units?

Part Four is therefore orientated to studying the following relationship:

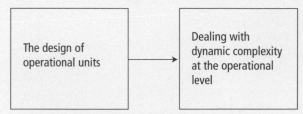

The cases will be discussed in five distinctive steps:

I.   The cases are generally introduced by providing **background information**;
II. A description of **dealing with dynamic complexity is provided**, using Weick's organizing model. This involves a description of the experiences of the operational units in the cases;
III. The **structural design** of the operational units is explicated, using the holographic rules;
IV. The way **leaders defined their role** is explicated;
V.   The relation **between the design of the units and dealing with dynamic complexity** is discussed. As was explained in Part One, due to the limitations of the case material, the analyses in these chapters have the ambition of providing hypotheses.

This distinction in five different steps will return in the discussion of each of the cases. Part Four will start, however, with a discussion of the way peace operations are defined by the Army.

Chapter 11

Peace operations according to the Army

This chapter will provide some insight into how the Dutch Armed Forces have conceptualized peace operations. The following issues will be addressed:

- It is attempted to delineate the concept of peace operation. This should provide insight into what the Army believes to be the kinds of operations it can become involved in.
- It is discussed what challenges the Army expects from these operations. More particularly, the status of dynamic complexity in the doctrine is traced.
- It will be discussed how the Army thinks it can deal with the challenges of peace operations.

11.1 Peace operations according to the doctrine

The Army has devoted a specific volume of the military doctrine to peace operations (part ADP III). The descriptions in this section will largely be based on this volume (Koninklijke Landmacht, 1999). The doctrine defines peace operations as follows: 'In peace operations, military actions focus on what the parties in the conflict do to hamper or prevent the accomplishment of the operation's objective.' The prototypical peace operation that is implicit in this definition is probably of the IFOR or SFOR type. This is an operation in which a country needs to be built up after civil war. In such operations, military units are deployed to protect a peace treaty, or in the case of IFOR and SFOR, protecting the various phases of the Dayton agreement. Furthermore it is emphasized that: 'A force deployed in a peace operation must strive for an independent position and must avoid involvement as one of the parties in the conflict' (p. 59) and 'A peace force does indeed have means of force, but will, in principle, only use them for the purpose of self-defense'. As such, peace operations as the Army defines them are different from 'war-like' operations. Such operations are directed at a specific opponent (by definition partial in nature), in which the use of force ('military means') stands in the foreground (Koninklijke Landmacht, 1999, p. 59). One could ask what different sorts of operations fall under the heading of 'peace operations'. Below, Figure 1.2 from the doctrine (p. 18) is displayed, showing the NATO categorization of peace operations:

Crisis Response Operations		
Tasks conducted in a NATO context		Tasks conducted in a national, binational or multinational context
Peace support operations		
Peacemaking · Peacekeeping · Peace enforcement · Peace-building · Conflict prevention · Humanitarian operation	Humanitarian operation · SAR operation	Military aid/support to civil authorities · Enforcement of sanctions · Non-combatant evecuations operation · Combating terrorism · Counter-drug operation · Counter insurgency operation

Figure 11.1. The various types of peace operations. (SAR refers to 'search and rescue operations') (figure 1.2, Koninklijke Landmacht (1999, p. 18).

An important distinction is made between the operations that are performed in a NATO context and those that are not. The doctrine also attempts to describe the operational tasks that are part of these operations. To start with, the following assertion is made: 'In peace operations, military personnel must not only command the basic military skills, but is also expected to perform tasks which go against the nature of the armed forces as an instrument of force. There may thus be situations in which even the controlled use of force could have an adverse effect. Social and communications skills are thus crucial at all levels in the peace force' (emphasis in original). Below, Figure 1.3 from the doctrine (p. 21) displays various operational tasks in various sorts of peace operations.

	Peace	Armed conflict/war	Post-conflict	Peace
Forms of peace operations	Conflict prevention/ preventive diplomacy			
		Peacemaking		
		Peacekeeping		
			Peace enforcement	
			Post-conflict peace-building	
		Humanitarian operations		
Operational tasks		Observation, monitoring and supervision		
	Preventive deployment			
		Enforcement of sanctions		
		Setting up and maintaining protected areas		
			Interpositioning	
		Forced separation of the parties		
			Guarantee or denial of freedom of movement	
			Demobilisation operations	
			Military aid/support to civil authorities	
		Non-combatant evacuation operations		
		Humanitarian operations		

Figure 11.2. Figure 1.3 of the doctrine displaying peace operations and operational tasks (Koninklijke Landmacht, p. 21).

Again the content of the tasks is not described in greater detail here. The finer distinctions are less relevant. In the doctrine it is emphasized that the precise operational tasks largely depend on the mandate of the operation. Although it is not explicitly stated in the doctrine it appears that a distinction is made in various degrees of violence.

11.2 'Peace operations' as a fuzzy category

If one takes a closer look at the two figures shown here, one can conclude that the category 'peace operations' is a fuzzy category. It is difficult to say in advance what type of peace operation is appropriate in what type of operational context, and it is difficult to precisely indicate what operational tasks are to be expected in a given peace operation. Most types of peace operations are expected in the 'armed conflict/war vs. post-conflict' window (only 'conflict prevention' and 'preventive deployment' are not, which goes without saying). Furthermore, in a given type of peace operation most operational tasks that are mentioned are imaginable. For example, peacekeeping extends over various operational contexts, while all eleven operational tasks are imaginable during peacekeeping operations. Moreover, the operational tasks are defined by their goal. As such, one can distinguish between 'inter-positioning' and 'preventive deployment'. However, it is far from imaginable that these different operational tasks require the same skills and the same strategies from operational units. It may be that 'interpositioning' and 'preventive deployment' are indistinguishable if one merely perceives the concrete actions of operational units.

This shows that it is difficult to precisely define the category of 'peace operations'. The difficulties of coming to grips with the category 'peace operations' has to do with the problem that all categorizations necessarily are based on previous experience, while the categorization is meant to get a grip on future operations. The exact conditions of future operations depend on many unpredictable factors, for instance on the exact nature of the conflict, the precise assignment for a unit, local conditions and political commitment of an international force. Actually, the exact conditions of a future operation are so unpredictable that one cannot even identify all the different factors on which they may depend.

For this reason one can consider the category of 'peace operations' to be a fuzzy category. It is not a category in which the various elements share a common set of properties (although this was perhaps the object of categorizing), but one in which the various elements have a family resemblance[93]. Future operations probably resemble past operations, but it is difficult to indicate the precise nature of future operations. It seems that the Army shares this conclusion. In the preface of the doctrine it is emphasized that: 'peace operations have, in practice, become highly complex operations in which, besides military actions, many other factors play a role. And this development is not at a standstill: every peace operation is different and, in each one, a peace force will face new challenges' (Koninklijke Landmacht, 1999, p. 9).

This does not mean that the categorization is not useful. On the contrary, the categorization gives insight into the kind of operations the Army can expect to be confronted with. As Weick (1979) indicated, organizations shape their environments in different ways and this strategic positioning can certainly be regarded as one of these ways. Furthermore, the categorization provides insight into the necessary competencies of crisis organizations. However, the categorization should not be considered as a strict recipe for the future. One should be careful to consider the operational tasks that are displayed in figure 2 to be a strict definition of the tasks that units should be

---

[93] The idea of categories consisting of elements with a family resemblance is originally introduced by Wittgenstein. Lakoff (1987, p. 16) explained this as follows: 'Members of a family resemble one another in various ways: they may share the build or the same facial features, the same hair colour, eye colour, or temperament and the like. But there need be no single collection of properties shared by everyone in a family.' In my opinion this is also the case with peace operations.

capable of performing. It is a general definition of the tasks units need to be able to perform. The most important lesson to be drawn from the two figures is therefore that the Army should be prepared for a diversity of operations in which a diversity of possible operational tasks can be performed. This implies that soldiers should be broadly skilled, broad-minded and able to handle a diversity of operational tasks in a complex and changing environment.

11.3 Peace operations and complexity

The issue of complexity is also underlined and worked out in the doctrine: 'The **complexity** of the tasks to be performed in combination with the circumstances under which the operation takes place can also give rise to tension. There may, for example, be a large number of groups and factions (each with their own background and objective), which must be taken into account in the execution of the tasks. This is in addition to the rules that apply to friendly actions, whether or not they relate to the use of force. The degree of complexity may be increased even further by climatologic and geographical conditions, which can transform the execution of even the simplest of tasks into a formidable challenge' (emphasis in original; 1999, p. 66)[94].

The complex nature of peace operations can, according to the doctrine, provide problems for the Army in general. It is claimed that: 'The foregoing does not alter the fact that the role that military personnel have to fill in most peace operations is at odds with the **primary role** for which the military apparatus was established. In this primary role, military means are deployed so that a decision can be forced in the short term with the use of force. The culture of the military apparatus is thus a consequence of that role. Therefore the deployment of the military apparatus in a peace operation, in which no decision can be forced immediately and which is conducted over a prolonged period, by definition gives rise to tension. This intrinsic tension may increase under the pressure of circumstances, which can be highly diverse in nature' (emphasis in original; p. 63). This quotation is interesting for a number of reasons. The doctrine acknowledges that the Army was not designed for performing peace operations and perceives this mainly

---

[94] Peace operations as they are defined by this study are complex in yet another meaning of the word. Previously a distinction was made between operational units, a crisis organization and a mother organization. This study is specifically orientated at peace operations in which this distinction is relevant. This implies that the peace operations this study is interested in involve the deployment of hundreds of soldiers performing a large number of different jobs. As will be extensively discussed in this study, this type of complexity creates a problem of coordination between different organizational parts. Needless to say, these different forms of complexity constitute a serious organizational challenge.

as a cultural problem. More recent developments within the Dutch Armed Forces have put this claim in an interesting light. As has been said, in the Army's most recent policy document, peace operations are placed at a more prominent position compared to wartime operations. The doctrine appears to sense problems of organizational change.

The topic of dealing with complexity is also dealt with in the doctrine. The importance of insight is underlined in the doctrine: 'It is, therefore, essential that all levels have insight into the **context of the operation**. The lack of such insight can lead to a feeling of hopelessness and doubt as to the sense of the peace operation and can undermine the involvement and effort of the members of the peace force' (Koninklijke Landmacht, 1999 p. 65 emphasis in original). This is a conclusion that, as will be seen, is shared by this study. However, this study does not consider insight to be merely important for motivational reasons, but necessary for insightful action at the lower levels. Insight at all levels is nevertheless considered to be important, according to the Army: 'It is clear that the environment is usually complex, while a large number of factors can pose a threat to the successful completion of the operation. It is important that all levels involved – from the political-strategic to the tactical level – are aware of their role in the decision-making and implementation of the peace operation and the way in which they can contribute to the success of the operation' (Koninklijke Landmacht, 1999, p. 67). One should be aware that what the doctrine has defined as the tactical level also refers to what this study has defined as the operational level. The following quotation shows that the Army considers the – what this study calls – inevitable autonomy of operators also as a possible threat: 'During a peace operation, the actions of an individual soldier, conducted with or without social skills, could have major repercussions in terms of the accomplishment of the operational objective. This has implications for such aspects as the specific (i.e. mission orientated) training of military personnel' (Koninklijke Landmacht, p. 60).

Mission Command

The Army has developed a philosophy of command in which autonomy at the operational level stands at the foreground. This is formulated in the Army doctrine that was published in 1996 (after the experiences of Dutchbat and Logtbat, but before SFOR). In its 1996 doctrine publication, the Dutch Army explicitly chose a system of what is generally called Mission Command (MC) (Koninklijke Landmacht, 1996). As has been discussed in the Introduction, MC is a system of decentralization. It is a system that aims to enable initiative-taking and decision-making at the lower levels. This system of command has been inspired by the system of Auftragstaktik.

According to the Dutch doctrine, one of the reasons for implementing MC is that, in the post-Cold-War era, the Army has to operate in varied circum-

154

stances and operations. This makes it very difficult to plan every operation in great detail[95] and, therefore, much should be left to the initiatives of local commanders (Egter van Wissekerke, 1996). For the implementation of MC in the Dutch Army, the same arguments were used that many authors use to explain the successes of Auftragstaktik. In the chaos of war:

- Crucial operational decisions can best be made by sub-commanders directly involved in the operations;
- Decentralization creates commitment and stimulates courage at every hierarchical level;
- Decentralization prevents an information overload up and down the hierarchy; local commanders are stimulated to act on the most recent and actual information; et cetera (Nelsen, 1989).

MC can therefore be regarded as a system of command specifically meant for dealing with dynamic complexity. According to the Dutch military doctrine, MC should be applied in all kinds of operations and in both operational and peacetime circumstances. Chapter Sixteen will analyze the doctrine, using insights from the analytical framework.

11.4 An illustration: KFOR (1999)

This section provides an illustration from a recent crisis operation of the Army. This case description is used to show that the abstract phenomena that are the center of interest in this study are recognizable in the experiences of operational units. In the following a rough description is given, which will subsequently be discussed. It is not attempted to discuss these matters into every imaginable detail because the nature of the case material does not lend itself to detailed analysis. Nevertheless, some interesting conclusions can be drawn.

The example focuses on an artillery battalion that was sent to Kosovo, not very long after the NATO air strikes. The task of this artillery unit was artillery support, their regular task. This artillery unit was sent to Kosovo just in case things would go seriously out of hand. Should that happen, the NATO forces deployed in Kosovo would be sufficiently armed to be able to defend themselves. For this routine task an artillery battalion has a strict and precisely prescribed division of labor and hierarchy. Such a battalion is a typical example of an organization that is built up on the basis of the machine metaphor (Morgan, 1997). Before a gunnery unit fires a shot, a

---

[95] This hides a subtle clue regarding the Army way of thinking. The impossibility of planning an operation into every imaginable detail is attributed to a lack of time. Apparently, the Army believes that perfect planning is *principally* possible.

complicated chain of procedures has to be strictly followed. In Kosovo artillery support was not needed during normal circumstances, so the units were used to perform other tasks. Consequently, their daily routine had little to do with the regular artillery support function. Instead, it could be characterized as a typical routine for a crisis operation, be it a crisis operation of a more complicated type. In this example, the focus will be on a particular platoon of artillery soldiers. During KFOR1, the platoon level was the actual operational level.

In the following, the range of duties of the platoon is described[96]. Typical for the new routine of the platoon was its non-routine character. During their stay, the platoon had a number of unaccustomed tasks. Furthermore, their range of duties changed as time passed on. New tasks were added and others were ended. The most central task was guarding a small village that was partly Serbian and partly Albanian. This meant that the members of the platoon were peacekeepers in the village. They controlled who went in and out of the village, monitored war criminals, and tried to prevent clashes between the Serbian and Albanian population. They performed this task by being permanently (24h) deployed in the village, by building checkpoints at strategic positions, and by patrolling the village and a nearby village. Another task of the unit was a 12-hour service in a nearby town, which meant that during that time the platoon was in charge of the city. They performed this task by manning observation posts, by building observation posts, and by patrolling the city. On top of all this, they guarded their own base-camp. Because of the chaotic situation in the area, the KFOR troops were also required to perform police and fire department tasks. In this situation the original platoon was split up into various sections and divided over the various tasks (a commander of a gunnery unit with his soldiers was then patrolling the village). During its stay in Kosovo, the platoon had been restructured three times to fit the latest demands from the environment. This simple description can be used to illustrate a number of topics that are important for this study:

- To start with, the dynamic and complex nature of the environment is illustrated by the very fact that the range of duties of the platoon changed a number of times to fit the demands of the environment;
- The case description gives an impression of the exchange between system and environment. A crucial characteristic of this exchange is the system's dispersed way of operating. One single platoon operated dispersed over more than one village, so a crisis organization as a whole interacted with the environment at different places at the same time. On the same moment a patrol spotted a war criminal in one place, a checkpoint at a

---

[96] This description is based on a description of R.J. Spruijt (2000) of his personal experiences. The interpretations and conclusions are mine.

different place might notice increasing tension between different parts of the population. This is in sharp contrast to, for example, the trench warfare of World War I, where there was a frontline that formed the firm distinction between system and environment. Gabriel & Savage (1978, p. 11) called this difference a 'circular' opposed to a 'linear' deployment. One can imagine that this fact complicates the development of insight at the various organizational levels;

- The dispersed nature of the operations illustrates the impossibility of a detailed central guidance of units. That will only be possible when there is a staff structure that follows every part of the organization in detail. If this were possible, the coordination of the staff members would become a large problem. Furthermore, developing rules for every imaginable situation is equally impossible in an unknown and dynamic environment. Therefore, at every point of interaction between system and environment, meaningful action is required. The people at the lowest hierarchical levels (those patrolling a city) are expected to be meaningful actors;

- At the same time, however, the dispersed nature of the operations complicates the organization of argumentation. After all, it is difficult to obtain insight if many things happen simultaneously. One can imagine that a debate should be organized not at one particular location (a checkpoint), but at a level where various aspects of the operation are insightful (for example a platoon). The insights at a particular location are by definition limited. The people at a location, if expected to act meaningfully, should be part of a debate involving wider issues than what is happening at the checkpoint. In other words, in order to act intelligently at a checkpoint one's 'world' should be larger than this checkpoint. One can see that the design of the task of an operational unit is important. If the task is too narrowly defined, meaningful argumentation can, by definition, almost never develop;

- Dependencies between locations do not merely exist within a single platoon. There are dependencies between the different parts of an entire battalion and even the entire international operation. Spotting a war criminal in one part of the area can have a huge impact on the other parts of the environment. Small, seemingly insignificant events at the lowest operational level (for example, at a checkpoint) can have consequences for the policy of the entire battalion. Apart from the importance of coordinated action (not the focus of this study) these dependencies show the importance of the integral development of a body of knowledge. This implies that a debate should be organized between operational units, even at the level of the crisis organization. The significance of this issue is that a large operation is always fragmented, i.e. structured, and that any system at every level is dependent upon developments in other systems. One can imagine that it is important to keep the total amount of these dependencies as low as possible. If the dependency on other units becomes too large, the autonomy of units suffers tremendously. The degree of dependency is greatly influenced by the design of the organizational structure of the crisis organization (Kuipers & Van Amelsvoort, 1990; De Sitter, 2000; Kuipers & Kramer, 2002b);

- With regard to leadership it is obvious that the dispersed way of operating and the various changes in structure have a great impact on the role of a leader. The traditional picture of a leader as the central point where authority rests is not appropriate for these situations. On the contrary, it shows the importance of the ability of people in the lower hierarchical levels to manage their own affairs;

- The units did use rules. The units manning a checkpoint, for example, used rules that specified how to build such a checkpoint effectively. The units patrolling a village used a certain role structure (which is part of basic military training). For example, every member of a patrol was situated at an exactly determined position; they used strict rules for relaying information, etc. Rules like this function, as Weick would say, as a structure that can be used to achieve a workable level of certainty. Life would become pretty impossible when in all situations even the simplest routine should be reinvented every time. The rules of craftsmanship help the craftsman to deal with a complex situation. A dangerous situation can be confronted with a workable level of certainty if one knows that building a checkpoint is a cunning way of getting a job done and if one knows a few basic rules of how to build such a checkpoint. If situations become increasingly complex (remember Bavelas' experiments), the rules of craftsmanship must be less fixed and less detailed. Maybe a checkpoint has certain disadvantages that one should be aware of, or maybe the situations in which one builds a checkpoint are so different that one cannot use a standard design. A craftsman in a very complex situation must increasingly be able to doubt his skills, or in other words, should be increasingly ambivalent towards the tricks of his trade;

- Since they were artillery units, it will be obvious that the tasks the platoon had to perform were new to them. Patrolling, building checkpoints, and making observations are all tasks the artillery specialists rarely practice. Taking over the role of the fire department is even not a military job at all. *This illustrates the difficulty of being prepared for every possible situation, but more importantly it shows the limited use of single-minded specialists.* This is a simple observation with wide implications. Artillerists are single-minded specialists. The Dutch contingent in KFOR was equipped with artillerists. It is a matter that falls outside the realm of influence of the unit that is being deployed for a crisis operation. The fact that artillerists are specialists has to do with the way the Army is structured. They are typically organized on the basis of the principle of functional concentration (Kuipers & Kramer, 2002b). As a consequence, the organization is typically composed of departments of specialists (artillerists, infantries, cavalries). *Therefore, the organization is typically not directed at educating broadly orientated soldiers, and neither at deploying mixed units.* One can therefore ask if the mother organization provides the prerequisites for organizing an ideal debate in those kinds of operations. This issue will be dealt with in the fifth part of this study;

- Argumentation is different from informing. In a stable environment the higher command can prescribe what is to be observed and how that should be rated. Literally, in stable, predictable and known environments patrolling units can be the 'eyes' that merely relay information in an unbiased way. However, the nature of facts and events in such circumstances is not that straightforward. Developments in the area are first noticed at the lower hierarchical levels. They cannot be told in advance what to observe, let alone that they can be told how to interpret it.

The case description has touched upon a number of issues that will be more elaborately discussed in this and the next chapters. It shows that operational units are dependent and independent at the same time. Relations between people and parts of organizations are typically created by the organizational structure. It is the organizational structure that designs these relations. Regarding the topic of leadership, circumstances such as in Kosovo necessitate meaningful action also at the lowest hierarchical level. This implies that also the lowest hierarchical level should be involved in a debate and this is certainly not an easy affair in an organization that is traditionally orientated to central control.

11.5 The Army and dealing with dynamic complexity

The most important conclusions of this chapter are:

- The Army considers peace operations to be complex (although it remains to be seen whether their concept of complexity is comparable with dynamic complexity).
- It recognizes the inevitability and the need for autonomy of operational units.
- It has designed and implemented a philosophy of command in order to be able to deal with the particular nature of peace operations.

The Army acknowledges the problem of dealing with complexity. Furthermore, the Army tries to find ways to deal with complexity by granting the idea of autonomy at the lower levels a central position. The Army therefore shares the essential claims of the previous chapter. However, one can state that current thinking in the Army has important shortcomings. It should be noted that it offers no deeper insight into the nature of complexity. The analysis emphasizes matters like the 'chaos of the battlefield', but what this exactly means is not analyzed, certainly no link to organizational theory is made. Also, the formulation of the Army does not offer an analysis of what dealing with complexity involves. The doctrine emphasizes that autonomy is important, but the process of dealing with complexity remains a black box. Furthermore, one can state that the concept of autonomy is broadly defined. In the formulation offered here it is still unclear whether an autonomous soldier controls the way his coffee is served or if he has the means to deal with his problems at the operational level. This criticism, however, comes at a too early stage. The doctrine will be discussed and analyzed in greater detail in Parts Five of this study.

Chapter 12

The Logistic and Transport Battalion

The first case that is discussed here is Logtbat. The case will first be generally introduced. Subsequently, the experiences at the operational level will be discussed, followed by the design features of the operational units. Finally, the relation between the design of the operational units and the way they dealt with dynamic complexity will be discussed. The case descriptions are based on the original case studies. Every claim that refers to the content of the cases is backed by a reference to the original descriptions. The references are placed behind the claims between brackets: [x]. In Appendix II the various references to the original case studies are listed.

12.1 General Description

Logtbat operated in Bosnia in the period 1992–95. Because Logtbat operated in Bosnia in the same period as Dutchbat, the political backgrounds of these operations were comparable. One could say, however, that their perspectives on the situation in Bosnia were considerably different. Originally meant as a transport battalion of humanitarian goods (later also deployed as a general provider of logistic support, hence LOGistic and Transport BATtalion), Logtbat drove through the entire region in Bosnia and was witness to the civil war that was going on there. That colored its experience.

The operational units

A logistic battalion has to transport goods from A to B and this was in generally the task the operational units had to perform. They had to distribute goods from warehouse to warehouse, from a central warehouse in the city of Split in Croatia (not in war at the time) to various smaller warehouses in Bosnia (which was engaged in a civil war at the time) [1]. A standard battalion within the Army consists of 3 companies with three platoons of about 30 soldiers and each platoon is split up into two groups of 15 soldiers. Generally speaking, a sergeant leads a group, a lieutenant leads a platoon, a captain leads a company, and the entire battalion is led by a lieu-tenant-colonel. Normally, the platoons are designed to be the operational units. The standard design of a battalion, however, is often adapted to local circumstances [2]. In the case of Logtbat, a platoon formed a convoy of 15 trucks (2 drivers per truck) that actually drove its goods through the area (the lieutenant and his deputy drove in front of the convoy in order to scan the road). The platoons were the actual operational units. During the convoys outside the camp, the lieutenant took his orders directly from the battalion-commander. In the encampment the company-commander was the commanding officer [3]. This led to a situation where the platoons were led by two bosses: the regular company-commander during the encampment and the occasional battalion-commander (that is to say, the Ops-room in his place) during the convoys. This double line of command led to a number of unclear divisions of responsibility and territorial fights between the different commanders [4]. As a general description, model 12.1 provides an overview of the organizational structure of Logtbat [5]. The battalion consisted of two Dutch companies and one Belgian company.

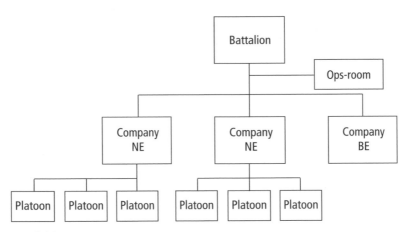

Model 12.1

The rotation policy

Of particular importance to understand the dynamics within the battalion is the rotation policy that was pursued. The rotation policy refers to the system that was used to replace soldiers who finished their (six-month) tour of duty. In principle, there are two principally different ways in which this system can operate. Logtbat used a so-called individual system of rotation. This meant that the soldiers of Logtbat originated from different parts of the mother organization, which implied that they were not deployed as part of a team that existed as a whole in the mother organization in the Netherlands.

Every two months, one third of the battalion was replaced. Consequently, at every moment the battalion consisted for one third of soldiers with 4–6 months of experience, one third of soldiers with 2–4 months of experience and one third of soldiers with 0–2 months of experience. As the battalion was 'diagonally' rotated, the platoons consisted of 3 groups with differing levels of experience.

12.2 Dealing with dynamic complexity

Before a picture of dealing with dynamic complexity at the operational level can be drawn, it should be discussed how such a picture is drawn in the first place. This is a potentially controversial matter because such a description involves selection: not all experiences are discussed, as that would involve copying the original case description. The criterion for selecting experiences should, however, be explicated. As has been discussed in Chapter One, dynamic complexity manifests itself at the operational level as everyday practical problems with a certain abstract structure. Practical problems that have to do with the problematic nature of reality and the issue of finding a way to deal with those problems constitutes this abstract structure. In the following sections the problems of the operational units will be discussed, followed by a discussion of the way the units dealt with these. As a final point it should be added that the analysis is not an 'event-analysis' in the sense that it analyses the different concrete events operational units experienced. Instead, it will be discussed what general problems units were confronted with.

Practical problems of operational units

Although riding convoys over predetermined roads, from A to B, seems to be a simple job, it is not difficult to defend that the operational units of Logtbat were indeed confronted with dynamic complexity. During the performance of their routine, units were confronted with all kinds of unexpected incidents, changing circumstances, unclear situations, etc. Transporting goods through an area engaged in a civil war proved to be far from easy. The convoys were frequently held at roadblocks, sometimes for days. Snipers occasionally shot at them, which was difficult to understand because the convoys were supposed to be neutral (their trucks were colored white) [6]. Moreover, the trucks were not armored (soft skin). This could result in extremely dangerous situations. As a result of one particular incident nine Dutch soldiers were wounded [7]. In the larger UNHCR organization some soldiers even have been killed. On 'sniper alleys' the convoys could be accompanied by a British YPR (a type of small tank) [8], but this was not the rule. The convoys sometimes also ran into mobs that tried to plunder them [9], or people that threw bricks at them [10]. Some convoys experienced attempts to bribery as they were in the possession of precious goods such as cigarettes and diesel oil [11]. Members of the battalion occasionally witnessed atrocities [12]. A major difficulty for the convoys was that confrontation lines could shift daily. A safe road one day could become a dangerous one the next day [13]. Often the convoys were the first witnesses of change, so they could only be guided centrally in a very limited way. These were problems that had to do with the more dangerous parts of their jobs. Of course they also had minor problems such as trucks breaking down, trucks skitting of the road because of icy conditions or the bad condition of the roads in general [14], and the dangers of mines. The convoys had to operate in extremely difficult circumstances, knowing that most of the food they transported would probably end up in the mouths of soldiers instead of civilians [15].

Tackling the practical problems

Logtbat platoons drove through Bosnia, far away from the compound. Units had to solve many practical problems themselves. This meant, for example, that they had to be inventive in dealing with difficult roadblocks. Due to the difficult circumstances units encountered, there are quite a number of examples of improvisation (i.e. enactments). Confronted with mobs trying to plunder their trucks [16] or confronted with a shooting, they simply had to act. When confronted with actual problems in new situations, there was little time to think about the pros and cons of various alternatives. In those situations, units had to rely on experience or intuition [17]. There are also clear signs in the cases that units developed local knowledge (selection/ retention). Especially in this case, respondents emphasized the importance of experience. Due to a specific system of rotation, new soldiers replaced one third of a platoon every two months. It took the remaining part of the platoon a while to teach the newcomers the subtle tricks of the trade, or, in other words, to pass the local knowledge on to them. This local knowledge was, unanimously, considered to be crucial [18]. The experience of units was used to deal with the problems they were confronted with. Units developed a diversity of strategies (also opposite strategies).

A standard example is that of the roadblock [19]. The operational units ran into various roadblocks and it appeared to them that there were different strategies to beat the roadblock. One particular strategy that often worked was displaying a cooperative attitude, being friendly and patient. Interestingly, also the opposite strategy worked, that is, being strict and formal. The same convoy developed these different strategies and had both of them in the back of its mind. After a brief moment of testing the water, units, mostly their commanders, could pursue one of the opposite strategies. Another simpler strategy to deal with roadblocks was supplying the people at the roadblock with cigarettes [20]. A comparable pattern can be discerned in dealing with other practical problems. One can easily recognize traces of contrary wisdom in this procedure. Units confronted a roadblock with a particular strategy, while keeping another strategy in mind. There are also signs that the process of development of experience was structured in units. Concrete actions were discussed afterwards (debriefing) [21], but also in advance [22].

Apart from these signs of self-organization that units displayed, there are also signs that units were controlled by the organizational context. For convoys there were rules about the order of the trucks, about the routes to be taken, etc. [23]. After this case, after some years of experience, an instruction book with SOPs had been compiled [24]. Furthermore, the convoys were followed via radio by their superior commanders in the Ops-room. In a number of cases these higher commanders interfered in the decisions of their subordinate commanders, who were strongly frustrated by that [25]. Differences in insight could, for example, rise regarding what was to be called 'acceptable risk'. The operations room could interpret 'risk' differently than the convoys. The operations room was in some occasions more careful than the convoys that were present in the area; in other cases they were less careful than the convoys. This difference of interpretation gave rise to conflicts between convoys and the operations room [26]. Sometimes this state of affairs led to an intelligent response of units. For example, a convoy assessed a situation as being too dangerous to proceed. They asked over the radio if they were allowed to turn back. The Ops-room, being many kilometers from the scene, ordered them to continue their route. Convoys tried to regain autonomy by pretending the radio broke down, or by drawing a far more dramatic picture than was actually realistic, so as to persuade the central command to order them to turn back [27].

Logtbat is a case in which the operational units operated on the edge of chaos. There is one example in which 9 Dutch soldiers were wounded as a result of a shooting [28]. After this shooting, UNHCR decided to stop the convoys for a while. This example also shows the vulnerability of the convoys. Suddenly the environment could become so risky that the battalion could no longer function. The case descriptions have shown that the units were confronted with many practical problems of a dynamically complex nature.

12.3 The structure of the operational units

The design of the operational units will be analyzed by considering both the organizational structure and leadership. The operational units as they were described above will be analyzed by discussing the holographic principles. As has been discussed before, the case studies have particular limitations.

Before the design of the operational units is discussed, I will briefly reflect on the nature of these limitations. It should be noted that these limitations are relevant for the other cases as well. Regarding the indicators one can state that:

- There is rather good information available on the central tasks of units and the composition of groups;
- There is general rather than specific information available on double-loop learning and the critical specifications that governed the behavior of groups;
- There are indications available on the organization of the preparation and supportive tasks within the crisis organization. It is important to note that there is little information on these matters. The cases reported on what the operational units did control, rather than on what they did not control.

The whole in the parts

The operational units performed the central tasks of the battalion. Riding convoys is – one could say – a task with a natural task identity: it is impossible to divide the task of a driver into smaller subroutines. In that sense 'the whole' necessarily returned in the parts. The orders for the transport of goods came from above, UNHCR, and the units were expected to take the official route for which they had clearances. The operations room planned the routes and gathered as much information as possible about the difficulties that were to be expected [29]. In that sense the preparation for the central tasks was performed at staff level. The operations room gathered information beforehand, and debriefed afterwards, however, the operational responsibility was in the hands of the convoy-commander [30]. This can be seen by the fact that units sometimes decided differently than the operations room advised [31]. For example, in one particular incident a lieutenant left the command of his convoy to his deputy in order to join the ambulance with the wounded [32]. With regard to the supportive tasks, the operational units performed basic maintenance jobs [33] and at scheduled intervals they guarded the compound of Logtbat [34] and performed construction and maintenance jobs on the compound. In other words, at any given time only a number of the battalion's convoys were actually en route. Others were busy with the tasks at the compound. The last supportive tasks are, of course, not directly related to their central tasks.

Requisite variety

As has been discussed in the previous section, units developed skills to beat roadblocks and plundering mobs. An experienced convoy can be said to control this type of variety, be it in some incidents with illegal means (bribing with cigarettes). There was one particular, but rather important, instance in which the units could not control the variety of the environment. They were unable to defend themselves against shootings. The short-range weapons they carried were insufficient for the defense of the units against the long-range weapons that were used in assaults [35]. On top of that, they were riding in soft-skin vehicles. Occasionally, at the most dangerous routes, they were accompanied by English YPRs, but most often this was not the case [36] (this supportive task was therefore performed by an external unit). The importance of this particular lack in requisite variety is underlined by the fact that an ambulance joined the convoy [37] (an external unit therefore performed this supportive task). The soldiers often considered this to be a relief [38]. Interestingly, soldiers did not find it a relief when they were joined by YPRs, as many reported that these 'attracted fire', while the soldiers were in soft-skin vehicles. Units were therefore not designed to control this variety in the environment. This is probably due to the fact that UNPROFOR as such had been unaware in advance of the difficulties convoys would meet riding through a war zone.

Redundancy of functions

On the surface of things, driving a truck seems to be a specialist job, so it seems odd to speak of broadly skilled workers. However, in the context of Bosnia at that time, one can discern a particular kind of redundancy. The distinction within a convoy between the inexperienced and experienced members was of particular importance. Experience in dealing with the circumstances in Bosnia was considered an important extra quality of a truck driver that convoys aimed to use [39]. For example, experienced drivers and inexperienced drivers were put together on one truck so that the experienced one could teach the inexperienced one the tricks of the trade (difficult roads, dealing with locals, problems en route, etc.). Also, tasks like negotiating at roadblocks could be performed by more than one person in the convoys, so that the inexperienced leader could be taught the tricks of that particular trade. It was certainly not only the leader that was able to do the difficult jobs [40]. It is defendable that this kind of redundancy was the consequence of intentional organizational design. After all, the mix of experience and inexperience was the consequence of using a particular rotation policy. One reason to choose this policy was indeed the building up of experience (Klep & Van Gils, 2000).

Minimal critical specifications

Due to the turbulent and unpredictable nature of the environment, a development of detailed procedures was quite impossible. Nevertheless, there were various attempts at detailed regulation, but at the time Logtbat was studied, these attempts were quite unsuccessful because of the dynamic complexity of the environment. There were various indications in the case studies that the operations room did try to get a firmer grip on the convoys [41]. The attempts to formulate decisions for convoys by the Ops-room, as it was discussed in the previous section, are the best illustration of this. Interestingly, lateral communication between convoys following each other was possible [42]. This enabled convoys to communicate suspicious looking places to the other convoys and it enabled them to inform the others when they were being shot at.

Double-loop learning

As has become clear in the previous discussions, there are different signs of internal double-loop learning (double-loop learning within operational units) in the Logtbat case: developing tricks to beat roadblocks and plundering mobs. There are few signs that members of the operational units were involved in external double-loop learning (double-loop learning of the crisis organization as a whole), which may be the consequence of shortcomings in the case material (it was not orientated to this issue). At one particular time the convoys were stopped when 9 soldiers had been wounded after a shooting. This was, however, a decision that was made at the top of the crisis organization. One particular battalion commander stimulated staff members to join convoys in order to make them aware of the difficulties en route.

12.4 Leadership

One particularly interesting aspect of the way leaders of operational units defined their job was that, at their time of arrival, they were always less experienced than two thirds of the platoon [43]. This was due to the individual system of rotation of Logtbat. It had important consequences for the way they defined their job. They simply were not the 'thinkers' and 'directors' of the units. The new commanders were dependent on the existing knowledge within the units, and they had no choice than to use this knowledge. The units were aware of that and they occasionally let commanders fail who were too stubborn (in the eyes of the rest of the operational unit). One could therefore say that this particular definition of the job of leadership was forced by the circumstances. The best leaders were considered those who were able to adapt to the inevitability of these circumstances [44]. The natural autonomy of units did give rise to certain tensions between the commanders in the Operations Room and the operators en route [45]. One problem that was mentioned in the case is that leaders frequently found it difficult to retain authority in these circumstances [46]. In this case study, soldiers and their leaders explicitly claimed to discuss the nature of the environment. Debriefing afterwards was a well-established routine in many platoons [47]. Furthermore, before convoys went en route they frequently discussed 'what if' scenarios [48]. Discussing 'what if' scenarios can be seen as a clear sign that doubt was stimulated within units. If units have various scenarios in the back of their minds they are prepared for various situations. Also, the usefulness of the mission was a topic units discussed [49]. When discussing the usefulness of the mission, some leaders indicated that they considered themselves to be a sort of 'manager of meaning'. They aimed at interpreting situations in such a way that they influenced the perspectives of soldiers. For example, if a crude fact of the situation was that 90 % of the transported humanitarian goods ended up in the possession of soldiers, leaders asked soldiers 'suppose what would happen if we were not here?' Also leaders aimed to achieve small-scale successes, like helping an individual hospital on personal initiative [50]. Other platoon-commanders indicated that they considered it to be essential that members of the platoon were aware of the kind of dangers they were going to meet beforehand [51].

12.5 The resulting hypotheses

As was explained in Part One, this study is located in the *context of discovery*. The consequence of this is that the results of the analyses in this study are considered to be hypotheses. The hypotheses resulting from the case studies are orientated to the self-organizing potential of operational units, i.e. at the nature of the relation between the design of the operational units and their ability to solve practical problems. After having selected the relevant data from the case studies, it seems reasonable to propose that:

I. *A number of characteristics in the design of the units stimulated their ability to deal with dynamic complexity.* Because convoys operated far away from the compound, the central command (ops-room) had little ability to interfere in the actions of the convoys. If they attempted to do so, the convoys could easily still follow their own line of working. As a result of the rotation-policy, the leaders of the convoys were, furthermore, not in the position of a central point of authority. They depended on the insights and the initiatives at the operational level. The choice for the policy of rotation as a means to develop experience within the convoys had a positive effect on self-organizing potential. This was probably an unintended side-effect of the rotation policy because it put leaders in a vulnerable position.

II. *It is questionable whether there was a conscious choice for self-organization as an operational concept.* Being convoys, the units had a kind of natural autonomy. The fact that, during some periods of the Logtbat operation, higher commanders deliberately joined the convoys in order to gain insight into the circumstances of Logtbat shows that the battalion as such needed bottom-up information in order to adjust higher-level policy [52]. It is an understandable policy to overcome the problem of an uninformed staff, but it is not a policy that goes in the direction of the design of self-organizing units. It is not a sign of argumentation, but a way to 'let the staff see for itself'. The staff and others higher in the hierarchy did try to find ways to restrict the autonomy of operational units, although opposite tendencies were also discernable. Actually, one can conclude therefore that the organizational context tried to deal with the inevitability of the natural autonomy of units with tendencies in the direction of more restriction and in the direction of more autonomy.

Chapter 13

SFOR

The SFOR case is discussed here in the same manner as the Logtbat case.

13.1 General description

The SFOR rotation that was studied in the original case study was operative in 1999. At the end of 1996, a Stabilization Force (SFOR) replaced IFOR, which had implemented the first steps of the Dayton agreement. The former warring factions had withdrawn to their barracks, basic peace had returned to Bosnia-Herzegovina and daily life started to take a – relatively – normal course. It was a meager peace because Bosnia was a highly segregated area with each ethnic group staying within the borders of its area, with occasional outbursts of violence between the different groups, and with rumors of small armies being built up secretly. Furthermore, the return of refugees to their homes had just started, which was a potential source of escalation. Generally it was felt that if NATO were to leave Bosnia, the fighting would start again within months. Therefore, it was reasoned that a military force had to stay in Bosnia: SFOR. The Dutch Army contributed an armored battalion to SFOR [53].

Since the situation was stabilizing, the mission of SFOR changed from a purely military mission into a more or less police mission. Although the situation was mostly quite peaceful, sometimes the situation suddenly changed and became very tense, such as when war criminals were arrested by SFOR, when SFOR was involved in (traffic) accidents, or when SFOR noticed that one of the former warring parties did not keep to the agreement. The situation also became tense when refugees, thinking they would be supported by SFOR soldiers, provoked the other party, or the other party provoked the refugees in provoking, etc. These changes made that SFOR soldiers had to be aware of the complexity of the situation they were involved in [54].

The operational units

Model 13.1 below gives an overview of the structure of the battalion. The area for which the Dutch battalion was responsible had been divided into two parts, each covered by one team: one in the Muslim-Croatian Federation and one in the Republika Srpska. The 'team level' is comparable to the 'company level' of the standard battalion. That is, a team is a company with some changes in its organizational structure. Each team consisted of three platoons, which were the actual operational units [55].

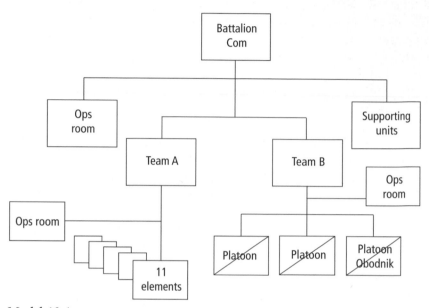

Model 13.1

Since the picture is rather complex, I shall attempt to unravel it by splitting the discussion up into several points.

- A first characteristic is that the battalion was split into two teams. These teams had their own specific area of responsibility. Within that area they had to perform all the tasks that were also the responsibility of the battalion (a kind of 'creating the whole in the parts'). Team A was located in a place called Novi Travnik, team B was located at Knesevo and at an outpost called Obodnik. The battalion staff was located at Sisava. A team was different from an original company because in a company the platoons are all the same (e.g. cavalry). In a team, one team exchanged a platoon (e.g. cavalry) with its neighboring team (e.g. infantry). Teams were therefore mixed units [56].
- A second characteristic of this picture is that the teams were organized differently [57]. The choice for creating such a structure was made by the team-commander rather than the team as a whole. The team-commander of Team A took the original platoon structure apart and created 11 so-called elements (the nature of the elements will be clarified later), which he instructed directly. In other words, the normal hierarchical structure

was not used. The team-commander of Team B retained the original platoon structure, but the platoons were mixed (indicated with the diagonal line through the platoons). The mix of teams was therefore continued at platoon level (again a kind of 'creating the whole in the parts'). An important feature of team B was that it had to man a platoon post called Obodnik. Every two months, the different platoons rotated to that post, which was special because it was located in a more or less isolated area (which was exactly the reason a platoon post was set up there). As a result of this isolation, the platoon occupying the Obodnik post had a more or less autonomous position.

- A third characteristic of the picture is the existence of the different operations rooms (Ops-room), which functioned as a sort of staff. They followed patrolling units over the radio and formulated the information need (the things the operational units had to look for) and the number of required patrols [58]. An exception was the post at Obodnik where the units were required to formulate their own 'information need' (for an explanation, see below). They were, however, not allowed to determine the number of patrols that they conducted [59].

- A fourth characteristic is that different supporting units were added to the battalion [60]. More specifically, a reconnaissance platoon, a platoon with mortars, a unit for clearing mines, one building up barracks, one for making repairs, one for medical support, one for logistic support, one for internal care, etc. A specialized unit with marines was added to play the role of a Crowd and Riot (CRC) unit. Especially the role of the reconnaissance unit will become of specific interest in the analysis. A good observer may already have discerned that because reconnaissance units gathered information for the battalion, the teams were not 'integrally responsible' for their respective areas. In the everyday experiences of the units, this fact surfaced when 'an information demand was formulated by the battalion'. This information demand was based on insights of the reconnaissance units. The logistic support for the battalion was performed by a specific battalion at an entirely different location (Support Command).

The general police task of SFOR resulted in a diversity of tasks to be performed. The teams had to patrol the area, gather information about possible hostilities between the parties, monitor elections, and protect the return of refugees to their homes. Furthermore, the operational units of the teams had to inspect sites where weapons and ammunition of the former warring factions were stored, and monitor military moves in the area. Also, they had to support all kinds of activities to restore roads, public buildings, et cetera [61]. A crucial difference between the teams was that in the area of team A two ethnic groups lived together, while in the area of team

B there was only one ethnic group. This made the task of team A more difficult. Both teams conducted patrols but there was a difference in the goals of the patrols. Within team A, the patrols were not only conducted to gather information but also to show the presence of SFOR. For that reason the patrols were conducted more frequently and at unexpected moments. This was done to give the impression that SFOR could appear at any moment [62]. In the area of team B this was not considered necessary because the area was much quieter.

The nature of the elements

Of particular interest from a point of view of organizational structure is the nature of the elements of team A. As has been stated earlier, the 'standard structure' that is used almost entirely throughout the Army is the 'platoon structure'. Platoons consist roughly of 30 soldiers and every platoon is split up into two groups of 15 soldiers. Companies or teams consist of three platoons, and battalions of 3 companies. Each part of this hierarchy has its own 'leader'. Groups are led by a sergeant, platoons by a lieutenant, companies by a captain or a major, and a battalion by a lieutenant-colonel. A team-commander has therefore 3 platoons. The team-commander of team A put this standard structure aside by creating 11 elements. He did this by putting aside the leaders of the 3 platoons. The remaining 'leaderless' groups were clustered into 11 groups that were under the direct command of the team-commander himself (sometimes the former platoon-commanders had the role of observers) [63].

The team-commander distinguished 3 types of tasks that he assigned to the elements. First, he distinguished 'long-term projects' (e.g. building a local sport facility). Such tasks were assigned to former platoon-commanders. In this type of task, the former platoon-commander was relatively autonomous. In the second place, he distinguished the short-term operational tasks. In this type of tasks (the case study does not provide examples), the platoon-commander was tightly controlled by the team-commander who acted as a 'spider in the web'. Thirdly, the team-commander distinguished the routine tasks (e.g. conducting patrols to gather information, observation tasks, manning checkpoints, etc.). These were conducted by the elements. During the performance of these tasks, the elements were tightly controlled by the team's operations room [64]. The operations room was manned by platoon-commanders and their deputies who had lost their platoon in the new structure [65]. It should be emphasized that the former platoon-commanders and their deputies did retain their administrative role and were supposed to inform the operational level of the developments taking place inside the area (in a so-called six o'clock show).

The fact that the routine tasks were called such might be slightly misleading. The elements could not decide for themselves when to conduct a patrol, in what area, what they were supposed to observe, and which soldiers should perform the patrol. This was prescribed top-down, based on an information need voiced by the battalion. One could therefore say that they were not on a fixed task and were deployed for the various 'chores' that came along. So although performing a patrol was a routine task, one could call the elements 'the pawns' of the team-commander. It should furthermore be mentioned that the battalion based its information need on reports of the reconnaissance units mentioned earlier.

The rotation policy

Again, the rotation policy of the battalion is of particular interest here. Every six months the SFOR-battalions rotated as a whole. That meant that every rotation was new in the area and was inexperienced with respect to the nature of the local circumstances. This was fundamentally different from the rotation policy observed by Logtbat. Moreover, the SFOR soldiers did not rotate individually but unit-wise. Units from the mother organization were deployed as a whole to Bosnia. That does not mean that the SFOR battalion existed as a whole in the mother organization. The backbone of the battalion was formed by a cavalry battalion. However, infantry and supporting units were added to form a functioning crisis organization. The entire SFOR battalion consisted of 57 units in the mother organization [66]. This implied that the assembly process of the SFOR rotation was particularly complex. The project group studied one particular SFOR rotation, so every time I will mention SFOR, I will be referring to this particular SFOR rotation.

13.2 Dealing with dynamic complexity

As in the previous case, it is attempted to draw a picture of the problems that the operational units experienced in the performance of their routine tasks and the way they dealt with it. This will provide an idea of the difficulty of the operation. Again, the elements of Weick's organizing model can help to trace subtleties in the way units dealt with the problems they experienced.

Practical problems for operational units

Compared to Logtbat, SFOR encountered a much safer environment. A telltale sign of the much quieter circumstances was the use of the 'escalation ladder'. The battalion as a whole developed a philosophy of dealing with threatening incidents. The 'escalation ladder' distinguished different levels of escalation and actions by SFOR to deal with those different levels [67]. The operational unit that would encounter the escalations was first required to try to avoid things getting out of hand. If matters did get out of hand, the battalion took operational control over the situation. At the worst level of escalation, the area of the incident would be closed off from the environment by creating roadblocks at crucial points. At that stage on the ladder, the Crowd and Riot Control (Quick Reaction Force) that was available to the battalion would be deployed. The philosophy behind the escalation ladder was that it was attempted to avoid incidents from escalating and spreading [68]. The worst escalation levels did not occur during the stay of the battalion that was studied [69]. This indicates that there were no situations in which the battalion experienced a serious lack of control over the situation[97].

Although the situation was less dangerous compared to Logtbat, the operational units did experience dynamic complexity. One can, however, state that the dynamic complexity was quite limited for operational units. It has already been explained that the operational units of SFOR had to perform a diversity of tasks. Due to this diversity, units experienced different problems. During the counting at the weapon depots they ran into the problem that the amount of weaponry counted did not tally with the amount that was supposed to be present at the site. Units that were active in helping to rebuild public buildings had to negotiate with the local authorities about how to tackle this project [70]. During patrols in their area of responsibility, the units occasionally had to deal with locals that were unfriendly towards SFOR, but this was, in fact, nothing special [71]. During the return of refugees to their former homes, the units experienced situations that were most explicitly dangerous [72]. They had to stand between aggressive mobs of different ethnic backgrounds. Furthermore, they had to deal with the danger of mines and with a number of traffic incidents [73].

Tackling the practical problems

There are indications of both improvisations and strategies to deal with the practical problems described above. During one particular threatening situation after a traffic incident one soldier reported that he scanned the environment in line with the guidelines he was trained for. These guidelines provided a workable level of certainty and could have been the basis for enactment. Units reported that they developed skills in negotiating with local authorities. During their stay in Bosnia, the units got more and more experienced in understanding the nature of the situation they were involved in and in approaching the local population.

Although units certainly had to deal with dynamic complexity and there-

---

[97] Actually, the escalation ladder reveals an important assumption of SFOR. The assumption is that, although an individual platoon might have been quite vulnerable, the battalion as a whole could force its will on the environment because of the superior weaponry they were equipped with (e.g. tanks).

fore had to self-organize, the opposite of self-organization is much more obvious from the case descriptions. This opposite story is that operational units were tightly controlled both by rules and by the higher hierarchical levels. In the SFOR case, the team-commanders had the autonomy to divide the tasks within their teams. The autonomy that existed at the team level resulted in teams that were organized differently, which is an interesting finding in its own right. The team commanders within both teams, however, restricted their operational units quite substantially in their autonomy. The work within the teams was mostly routine and bound by rules and regulations [74]. Each patrol was planned by the higher levels through the so-called 'intell-section' that existed at the battalion level that formulated an information need [75] together with the team. The soldiers at the operational level sometimes referred to these lists as 'imbecile lists' [76]: the questions that were formulated on the list were specified in such detail and were orientated to matters that were so obvious as if staff-level assumed that the members of the patrol were imbeciles.

There was a difference between the team-commanders with respect to the degree in which they restricted their operational units. In one particular team, patrol commanders received detailed lists specifying the required information. This team level issued the order for the patrol, and determined who should be part of the patrol as well as the route of the patrol [77]. The other team, which was located in the quieter of the two areas, transferred the information need from the Ops-room to the operational units and prescribed the frequency of the patrols to the operational level. Within these outlines the leaders of the operational units were free to organize their patrols [78]. In that sense, the soldiers in the operational units of both teams did not have autonomy. A telling sign of the lack of autonomy of operational units was the 'need-to-know' policy that was pursued by those in a leadership position [79]. Originally, this policy was introduced in order to keep certain dangerous missions secret for as long as possible. More particularly, it was used during a mission to arrest criminals of war, as it was thought that if this would become too widely known the mission could fail. However, some commanders also introduced this policy as a more general policy during the normal proceedings. The most striking example that came out of the interviews was a commander who was interested in area A. He ordered a group to observe area B, meanwhile hoping that they, unconsciously, would gather information about A. After their mission, the commander debriefed the group about B, while implicitly asking information about A. In other words, the units were literally used as 'eyes' in the area, without even being given the opportunity to be aware of the things they were supposed to see [80]. The idea behind this scheme to fool the operational level was that the irresponsibility of operational units in handling dangerous situations would endanger them. This study considers meaningful action at the operational level to be essential in order to enable the operational units to be meaningful actors. The line of reasoning that this study follows is therefore that if crucial information is denied to operational units this could endanger them as well.

The team level, on the other hand, was also limited in its autonomy. At the team level, an operations room (Ops-room) monitored the activities of a patrol. If something happened during a patrol, it was the team's Ops-room that told the patrol how to deal with the situation. As such, the team level was the first to formulate a decision ('stay put') and decided on deploying a Quick Reaction Force when things were getting out of hand. However, the work at the operational level was bound by so many SOPs (resulting from Rules of Engagement) that a second Ops-room existed at the battalion level. This second Ops-room looked up the various SOPs for handling with a problem and already formulated decisions in case things were developing a certain way [81]. This division of tasks occasionally led to frictions between the different hierarchical levels [82]. One could therefore say that the complexity of the existing rules in the area limited the autonomy at the team level. The consequence of this complexity was that not one, but two Operations Rooms were looking over the shoulder of the patrols. At the battalion level and at the team level it was acknowledged that the operations were very restricted by various rules. They pointed to the fact that these rules were forced upon them by yet another higher hierarchical level [83].

Apart from rules for conducting patrols, other activities at the operational level were also restricted by rules. There were many rules about how to perform site inspections and what should be done in a situation where shortages or surpluses of weapons and ammunition would be found, i.e. Rules of Engagement that prescribed how units ought to behave. The essence of these rules was that the operators, when counting a surplus or a shortage of weaponry should contact 'above' (the higher hierarchical levels). 'Above' would then formulate a decision within a few hours (!) [84]. Many restrictions were formulated regarding the safety of the soldiers. Team commanders felt a huge responsibility for a safe homecoming of their men. Therefore, they tried to control the behavior of their men during the patrols and other activities as much as possible. They did not want the men to become involved in situations they considered to be unnecessary risky [85]. So, they tried – for example – to prevent the patrols from taking roads that had not officially been cleared from mines [86]. An example contradicting these findings comes from the 'forward platoon base' (an observation post placed forward in an isolated area) at Obodnik. Because of its isolated nature, operational units there had more autonomy than in the rest of the team's area. Units were required to gather the information they found relevant (which meant that they had to think about the nature of their environment, which is a requirement of meaningful doubt), only they were not allowed to determine the number of patrols they found necessary for this task. Soldiers reported that they found the atmosphere at this post very refreshing indeed [87].

One can claim that the higher hierarchical levels did everything to prevent units to act on the basis of their own insights. However, again, this case showed evidence of operational units self-organizing to deal with the restrictive organizational context. At some occasions, patrols faked that the radio was breaking down so they could not report back to the central controller (mind you, the higher command suspected that the operational level was faking this [88]. More specific evidence of self-organizing against a restrictive central controller was the experience at the 'forward base' at Obodnik. At particular periods, units judged that there were no interesting developments in their area (which was part of their job) [89]. Nevertheless, they still had to conduct the required number of patrols (which was top-down demanded). Units were expected to perform a fixed number of patrols, regardless whether they saw any use for doing so. Also, some soldiers reported that they had simply disregarded rules with respect to the use of un-cleared roads [90]. Furthermore, soldiers occasionally complained that they had performed very boring jobs (deprived of basic regulatory activities) like observing a house being rebuilt [91]; they occasionally complained about the nature of the patrol forms because these specifically prescribed what units ought to ask when they were on patrol ('Is electricity working in your home?'). The men referred to these lists as the 'imbecile lists' [92]. They furthermore complained that they had performed jobs without knowing why (writing down number plates of cars [93]) and that their patrol reports had remained unread [94].

13.3 The structure of the operational units

The first question to be addressed is whether the operational units were designed on the basis of the holographic rules. Interestingly, there is a substantial difference between the ways in which Team A and Team B were structured.

The whole in the parts

The teams were each assigned a specific area of responsibility. In a way this resembles 'parallelization' as it is used in sociotechnical design (Kuipers & Van Amelsvoort, 1990). There is, however, one crucial difference. The battalion still formulated an information need, partly based on reports of specific reconnaissance units that had been added to the battalion as a supporting unit. Therefore, the teams were not integrally responsible (i.e. the whole in the parts) for the area to which they were assigned. One could also say that the different parts of the control cycle (perceiving, evaluating, and intervening) were performed by different parts of the organizational system. The reconnaissance units perceived, the battalion evaluated, and the operational units intervened. This is a classical way to divide the parts of the control cycle (De Sitter, 2000). In this description the team-commander is the commander of the interveners.

The various teams dealt differently with the issue of task design. The elements of team A have been described in detail. One could perhaps believe that the distinction between routine and non-routine tasks is a kind of segmentation as it is used in sociotechnical design (Kuipers & Van Amelsvoort, 1990). However, the distinction in different kinds of tasks was not made to give the elements control, quite the opposite actually. Team B operated differently. The team formulated assignments to the platoons (with a top-down formulated information need [95]). It was left to the operational units (a platoon-commander) to divide tasks between the members of the operational units (a more exact picture of the different tasks in team B is not available). At Obodnik the platoons operated even more autonomously, the patrol frequency was prescribed but not the information need because that required local knowledge [96]. Furthermore, the platoons of team B were mixed; they were built up of soldiers with different backgrounds (infantry, cavalry). In a literal sense, the platoons were therefore broadly skilled [97].

With regard to the distinction in preparation, performance, and supporting, one can state that particularly the routine elements of team A were occupied with performance in the strictest sense. They had little influence on the preparation of patrols: an information need was determined top-down and units did not determine which group members performed the patrols. The team commander did indicate that 'within reason' the patrols could depart from their assignment [98], which can be considered as a way to stay open to variety in the environment. However, one can question this claim by pointing to the status of the 'need-to-know' policy. Furthermore, there is no indication that they influenced supportive tasks. Because they had no control over the way they were deployed, the team-commander used his elements as a sort of pawns [99]. The platoons of team B were also confronted with an information need, but were allowed to prepare the internal matters of the patrols. At Obodnik, they even decided their own information need.

Requisite variety

A basic ability of military units during crisis operations is that they can deal with different operational scenarios. They are, on the one hand, active in the reconstruction of the country. On the other hand, they need to be able to defend themselves and others when things get out of hand. A single operational unit is vulnerable (not able to deal with a massive attack), but the battalion as a whole is less vulnerable. The fact that an escalation ladder was developed shows that the battalion did prepare for various states of the environment. In other words, the requisite variety regarding this issue existed at battalion level, not at the operational level. This is quite understandable because the serious escalations were not likely to happen and because the consequences of serious escalation would exceed the realm of influence of the operational unit.

Team B was mixed in order to gain a kind of requisite variety. According to the team-commander, because all 'types of soldiers' were present in all platoons, the platoons were always present with a diversity of means [100]. Team A had a different philosophy. The operational units were designed as small units that needed to perform a task that was top-down specified. Perhaps the team-commander of team A believed the environment to be variable. However, he apparently believed that he could judge the nature of this variability and instruct and equip units in such a way as to tailor them for this variability [101]. Although this also seems a way to design a kind of 'requisite variety', it is fundamentally different from the kind of requisite variety that is meant by the holographic principles, as it is supposed that there is a sort of top-down control over the variability.

Redundancy of functions

Being multi-functional is important in an environment that demands so many different roles. On the one hand SFOR was a military force that enforced particular demands of the Dayton agreement (return of refugees), on the other hand it was helping with the reconstruction of the country [102]. In addition to traditional soldier skills, operational units should have negotiating skills and social skills in order to gain information, and they should be alert to eventualities in the environment [103]. Frequently, soldiers and lower-level commanders have claimed that peace operations demand a different attitude from them. A soldier in a peace operation should possess a far broader range of skills than a soldier in a traditional Army. This held true for the soldiers of both teams.

Minimal critical specifications

One could say that SFOR did not strive for minimal critical specifications, but instead, for maximal critical specification. Various arguments for this hypothesis have been discussed. The staff level formulated an information demand; platoons had to perform scheduled patrols to meet these demands and had to report in a standardized format. Furthermore, the operational units were closely monitored during their operations. The general philosophy was that if a platoon would run into an unexpected situation, the staff level would look up the appropriate Standard Operating Procedure in the available manuals. An exception formed the platoon post at Obodnik (team

B), where units were allowed to formulate their own information demand, but were not allowed to determine the number of patrols they conducted. All in all, one could say that SFOR aimed to organize a perfect machine (perfectly prescribed actions) and aimed for perfect top-down control rather than the opposite (decentralization). As was concluded in the case study itself, the battalion did not strive for decentralization. They primarily tried to control top-down, unless the reality of the situation no longer made this possible [104].

Double-loop learning

The previous discussions have drawn a picture of a crisis organization that aimed to run the operation on the basis of top-down control. As such, operational units were perhaps allowed to improve existing routines (lower-level commanders were allowed to fill in the details of assignments). They were certainly not expected to challenge the basis of their routines (the operational units were not allowed to challenge an assignment as such), let alone that operational units contributed to issues at the tactical and strategic level. This was especially the case for team A, in which the operational units had little insight into the reasons behind their tasks ('why am I checking the plates of vehicles?'). The need-to-know policy that was pursued in the battalion is especially revealing in that respect. Commanders sometimes gave units certain tasks without informing them about the true nature, let alone the true intentions behind their assignments [105]. A particular conception of complexity emerges from the previous discussion. This is a conception of an environment that is perhaps uncertain (therefore information is needed, therefore units are restricted, therefore there is an escalation ladder) but is ultimately knowable and top-down controllable on the basis of top-down rules and orders. This conception appears to be a more limited conception of complexity than the military doctrine describes, but the analysis in Chapter Sixteen will reveal that this is not the case, because the doctrine is not what it appears. The SFOR design logic was certainly based on a different conception of complexity compared to the analytical framework of this study, if not an essentially contradictory conception. Double-loop learning was therefore not intended.

13.4 Leadership

There are a number of salient topics that returned in the way leaders defined their jobs. These topics will be described below. Most interviewees considered leadership to be a crucial factor in crisis operations. Most leaders that were interviewed were particularly keen to explicate their philosophy of leadership and the way in which they approached different kinds of matters.

For that reason there is relatively much information available regarding this topic, compared to the Logtbat case.

Leaders as spiders in the information web

This role specifically refers to the team-commanders. They were very keen to monitor developments in their area of responsibility. For that reason they sent out patrols to collect specific information that was relevant in their minds, not necessarily in the minds of the operational units. This information could, for example, be used to keep the local groups within the limits of the agreement. That leaders defined their roles as spiders in the information web had the by-product that they defined their role as the thinkers of units. As justification of the fact that they did the thinking, some commanders emphasized they had to deal with an intelligent opponent.

Leaders as managers of information

One particular role leaders emphasized was that of provider of information. The most salient example of this role was the 'six o'clock show', which was held everyday. During this meeting the most recent developments were conveyed to the commanders of operational units, who were required to transfer the news to their units [106]. However, there are also indications regarding the opposite: the need-to-know policy implied that only certain people were informed regarding the actual nature of a situation. One could therefore say that leaders saw the management of who should be informed about what as an important part of their job.

Leaders as clarifiers of the 'framework of meaning' surrounding the operations

This role is different from the previous one because it does not refer to operational details but to the more general matter of 'usefulness of the mission'. Actually, the battalion-commander mentioned this role as a crucial one for the officers in his battalion [107]. Because of the relatively stable circumstances during SFOR, people occasionally questioned the usefulness of tasks. Leaders saw a role for themselves in explaining the framework of meaning to the wavering souls within the operational units [108].

Leaders as protectors of those at the operational level

Generally, leaders indicated that they felt responsible for the 'safe homecoming' of their men. Some claimed that this responsibility was truly a burden [109]. This was why individual leaders went quite far in their protective attitude. As has been explained, soldiers were not allowed to take routes that were not checked for mines, although it may have been abundantly clear that there were no mines on a certain route (e.g. the local population took

183

the road). As has been explained a number of times before, units were closely monitored on the radio, which was partly done for protective reasons. Also the need-to-know policy that was described in the previous chapter was defended with protective reasons, although this might be interpreted as a fine-sounding excuse. One particular commander claimed that if soldiers would know too much about the true reasons behind certain assignments, they would take too many risks (e.g. provoking dangerous locals).

Most salient about these different roles is that doubt and argumentation in general, or promoting a spirit of contradiction in particular, is no part of it. More specifically, the roles of the leader all point to a philosophy of centralization.

13.5 The resulting hypotheses

Again, the discussion of the case is finished by proposing a number of hypotheses about the self-organizing potential of units. After having selecting relevant data from the case studies, it seems reasonable to propose that:

I. *SFOR encountered a relatively stable and predictable environment and it therefore was reasonably able to guide and control operational units.* The operational units did experience dynamic complexity but several times it was claimed that these experiences were not very important. Instead, they were confronted with straightforward tasks (counting weapons; patrolling with standardized questionnaires, observing houses, etc.) and were expected to report any anomaly. In a way, therefore, their task structure prevented them from encountering certain difficulties. The important questions regarding the way to deal with the environment (questions that belong to the preparation: what tasks need to be done?, what are crucial developments in the area?, where are the dangers?, etc.) were dealt with at the higher hierarchical levels. Therefore one can question whether, if they had encountered important information (1) they would have recognized the importance of the information, and (2) whether their insights would have been taken seriously at the higher level. An illustrative example is the story that some of the lower-level 'pawns' told. They told that locals kept large amounts of weapons hidden from SFOR. They also told that locals were able to invalidate SFOR with mines [110] Of course, there is no means to judge whether this is a realistic story or not. It shows, however, that many stories about the local circumstances existed at the lower levels, without the higher levels being aware of them (which was the reason they were told to the interviewer). Either the lower level was so badly informed that they developed stupid ideas, or the higher levels were unaware of crucial information. It is well known from theory that a tightly controlled system is extremely vulnerable when the environment puts pressure on it. But apparently it did not, which appears to underline the claim of some respondents that not the tasks SFOR performed were crucial, but the mere presence of SFOR.

II. *There is a substantial difference between team A and B.* The elements of team A were used as the unthinking pawns of the team-commander. Because they were split up into a large number of elements, they were given particular tasks and were followed closely on the radio in case something out of the ordinary would occur. Units could not doubt and argue constructively because they were mere pawns in the unknown schemes of the team-commander. Team B did allow the operational unit more autonomy (the platoon-commander was allowed to divide tasks between the members of the team). However, both the tasks themselves (the number of patrols) and the things to be done (the kind of information necessary) were prescribed by the team level. An exception was the platoon post at Obodnik. There, operational units were required to find relevant information themselves, but, on the other hand, were not allowed to determine the necessary number of patrols.

III. *The case studies convey an image of team-commanders that were overloaded with regulatory tasks (what one would expect) and were afraid of making even the slightest mistakes (what one – given the Army culture – also would expect).* Various team-commanders indicated that they found SFOR a complex and difficult operation. One particular team-commander admitted that he made the mistake of being overly afraid of catastrophe. He claimed that he was afraid that behind every tree a Serb would be hiding with a knife between his teeth [111], resulting in what he in hindsight considered as erratic control behavior. This is an interesting (and for an officer exceptionally honest) claim because it reveals something about the pressures on team-commanders. Apparently these pressures can give rise to irrational fears and erratic behavior. Some appear to react to a fundamental uncertainty (it is never *completely* unthinkable that a Serb hides behind a tree with a knife between his teeth) by aiming to exclude all possible doubt. An organization that emphasizes the importance 'no mistakes' when it is confronted with fundamental uncertainty can stimulate such fears and such behavior.

Chapter 14

Dutchbat

Dutchbat is discussed in a way comparable to the previous cases. The reflections made in this case description are occasionally supported by a reflection written by the battalion-commander of Dutchbat II: *Command and Control in stressful conditions* (Everts, 1998). The Dutchbat case is controversial because in the end the Srebrenica enclave fell into the hands of the Serbian forces. It is estimated that about 8,000 members of the Muslim population were massacred as a result of that fall. After the publication of the *Nederlands Instituut voor Oorlogsdocumentatie* (NIOD)[98]research in the spring of 2002 (...) the Dutch cabinet resigned because it had been severely criticized for its role surrounding the Dutchbat mission. There is a general consensus, confirmed by the NIOD, that Dutchbat was on a mission impossible. This judgment is based on the unclarity of the essential 'Safe Area' concept, the unclear, unrealistic, and restricting mandate for Dutchbat, and the light weapons with which Dutchbat had been equipped (Blom, 2002).

Given this controversial background, I want to make two preliminary remarks. In the first place, this case study is orientated on Dutchbat II, which was active in the area six months before Dutchbat III. Dutchbat III was the battalion that experienced the actual fall of the enclave. The fall of the enclave is therefore no part of this reflection. In the second place, although I share the general consensus that Dutchbat was on a mission impossible, I believe that it is still interesting to reflect on the functioning of Dutchbat as a crisis organization. Although 'politics' might be to blame for the eventual tragedy, there still might be valuable lessons for the Army in the Dutchbat operation. Not studying the functioning of Dutchbat as a crisis organization because of the general consensus that 'politics' made the crucial mistakes is hiding behind the mistakes of the political level. Apart from this, the case is interesting from a theoretical perspective.

14.1 General description

The political background of the UNPROFOR operation in Bosnia was an internal conflict between the Serbian community, on the one hand, and the

---

[98] Netherlands Institute for War Documentation.

Muslim and Croatian communities, on the other. This evolved in an overall civil war. As this conflict caused a large number of victims and a stream of refugees, in 1992 it was decided by the United Nations that an international military protection force (UNPROFOR) should intervene. After the establishment of so-called Safe Areas, particular areas in which the Muslim population was supposed to be safe, UN troops were needed to guard these Safe Areas. Subsequently these areas were protected by light-armed neutral (blue helmet) soldiers, whose job it was to disarm the people within the Safe Area and to monitor and patrol its borders. The Dutch Armed Forces contributed an infantry battalion that was called Dutchbat to be deployed in the Safe Area of Srebrenica as a peacekeeping unit. Dutchbat rotated 'as a whole'. That is to say, the infantry battalion that was the core of Dutchbat existed as a whole in the Netherlands in the then newly established Air Maneuver Brigade.

The operational units

What is obvious from the various case studies is that the standard design of a battalion is often adapted to local circumstances. In Dutchbat, the groups ('Gr') operated as the smallest operational units. This meant that the direct supervisor of the groups was not the platoon-commander but the group-commander [112].

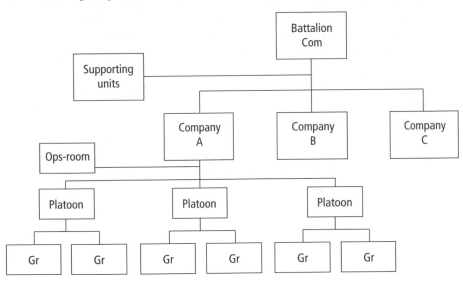

Model 14.1

The following characteristics are of particular interest:

- The organizational chart only shows company A to its full extent. The other companies are structured in the same way. The tasks of the different companies were divided geographically. Each of the companies had its own Area Of Responsibility (AOR), in which they were responsible for the whole of the battalion's activities [113]. Company A was responsible for the southern part of the enclave of Srebrenica, company C was responsible for the northern part of the enclave. Company B was somewhat of an exception as it was located in an area outside the enclave of Srebrenica. This area was called the Sapna Finger, because the form of this particular area resembled a finger. Each of the companies had its particular compound and its own Operations-room (Ops-room). Company C was located in Potocari, together with the Battalion staff. Company A was located within the city of Srebrenica and company B was located in the village of Simin Han [114].

- The geographical division of labor was continued within the companies A and C. Platoon-commanders were responsible for a sector with a number of Observation Posts (OPs). A so-called group (Gr) manned the observation posts and a group-commander was the actual commander at the OP [115]. They were in direct contact with the so-called patrol coordinator at the Ops-room. Within company B, a somewhat different division of labor was used. This company used a kind of rotation schedule in which in some period of time each of the platoons was busy with one of the tasks that were distinguished, namely manning the stationary OPs, guarding the compound, patrolling the area, and performing the role of the Quick Reaction Force [116].

- Generally, one can say that there was a difference in experience between the companies of Srebrenica (A and C) and the company in the Sapna Finger (B), because of the differences in tasks. Srebrenica was a total exclusion zone, which meant that officially there were no weapons inside the enclave [117]. Also, one can say that the companies in Srebrenica had to deal with a much more difficult situation. Most of the experiences described below were, for example, part of the experiences of the companies A and C. A limitation of the case studies is that the distinction between A/C and B is sometimes difficult to draw, because the relevance of this distinction is something that dawned on the researchers only after the case studies had been completed.

- For the duration of the deployment in Bosnia, some supportive units had been added. There were units for different kinds of construction tasks (e.g. local roads), medical units, and units for internal care-taking. At a different location (Lukavac) a so-called Support Command took care of the logistic needs of Dutchbat [118].

The Dutchbat battalion concerned itself with a number of central tasks: gathering of information about the warring parties, guarding of confrontation lines to prevent infiltration and arms smuggling, providing humanitarian support, supporting humanitarian aid provided by UNHCR, and generally demonstrating the presence of the UN. Information gathering and reporting was the primary job of the infantry platoons, together with more internal jobs like improving the compound and Observations Posts (OPs). The operational units conducted these tasks mainly by patrolling the area. They distinguished different categories of patrols:

- Border patrols. These were patrols over the confrontation lines.
- Social patrols. These were patrols in which contact was made with the local population within the Safe Area to assess the local problems and needs.
- Area patrols. These were patrols in which the area was assessed with vehicles.

14.2 Dealing with dynamic complexity

As with the previous cases, it is attempted to draw a picture of the problems that the operational level experienced and the way these were dealt with. This will give an impression of the difficulty of the operation. Again, the elements of Weick's organizing model can help to trace subtleties in the way units dealt with the problems they experienced.

Practical problems for operational units

The difficulties of Dutchbat proved to be so serious that the original intentions were unreachable. As mentioned before, it was generally felt that Dutchbat was confronted with a mission impossible [119]. The soldiers had to operate in a hostile environment without the adequate means and possibilities to perform their tasks and to defend themselves. Peacekeeping proved to be impossible because the warring parties were unwilling to observe the official terms of UNPROFOR and they far outnumbered Dutchbat both in quantities of personnel and in equipment [120]. The situation developed in such a way that units could do little more than keeping up appearances ('protecting the Safe Area from infiltration' while patrolling the borderline only once every day) [121]. Attempts to actually take the original mission seriously resulted in heavy intimidation by both the Serbian and the Muslim side (shootings, mines, etc.) [122]. A particular problem for Dutchbat was that the Serbs controlled the logistic supplies into the enclave. Towards the end of the mission of Dutchbat II this meant that units were confronted with shortages of petrol (which restricted mobility) and food. According to the battalion-commander, Dutchbat was even the 'hostage' of the Serbs (Everts, 1998, p. 21). For operational units the restrictions in mobility meant that they increasingly became isolated (because of a lack of diesel oil they could not be reached) and had to be creative in dealing with a shortage of supplies. It is obvious that this further impeded Dutchbat's ability to fulfill the original mission. Apart from the sheer danger and the shortages, events in the enclave could be equivocal. Shootings could be 'mere intimidations' or 'true shootings'. 'Shootings from the side of the Muslim population' could be 'Muslims impersonating Serbs in an attempt to provide the Serbs with difficulties at the political level', etc. One can imagine that defining one's role in such circumstances demands tolerance for ambiguity and paradox.

Tackling the practical problems

The higher command wanted to avoid great risks after the early experiences showed that the local parties were prepared to go quite far. One could say that Dutchbat as a whole learnt from the early enactments (which inevitably meant taking risks) that they should not take too many risks. Also, when units did observe something they had to deal with according to the original mission, they were prohibited from acting by 'above' (e.g. the Ops-room). For example, a patrol unit spotted a group of people dealing with weapons. While the patrol was passing, the group acted as if nothing was going on. When they had passed, the patrol unit silently observed the group for a while and the weapons reappeared. When the unit wanted to act and disarm the people, as they were supposed to, they were called back by 'above' [123]. There are many of such examples. Patrolling the confrontation line was essential, according to the higher command, because it showed to both sides that the UN was present [124]. However, at the same time the policy of Dutchbat was to 'avoid great risks' [125], which implied that if the various sides in Srebrenica really wanted to they could intimidate Dutchbat in such a way that they were quite powerless. For example, after a mine incident it was decided that a certain area was not to be patrolled again [126]. The locals from both sides appeared to be prepared to play along with the official game as long as Dutchbat was prepared not to take the original mission too seriously. Consequently, Dutchbat found itself in a schizophrenic situation: performing a mission in such a way that the mission was actually denied (patrolling borders in such a way that they disturbed the local parties as little as possible)[99].

One can hypothesize from the case descriptions that the higher command had an explicit policy of keeping operational units out of trouble. Actually, this hypothesis is supported by the reflection that was written by the battalion-commander (Everts, 1998, p. 18): '(...) both parties in the conflict could arbitrarily strike the battalion wherever they wanted, and therefore for the fulfillment of its mission, the battalion was fully dependent on the

---

[99] As such, Dutchbat is a good example of the point that one can deal with dynamic complexity by engaging in organizing activities or by reducing one's level of ambition. Dutchbat is an example of the last.

approval of the Serbs for its logistical and leave convoys, and promises of support from the UN would not quickly result in an improvement of the situation in which the battalion found itself. As for the battalion's own personnel, this situation reinforced my opinion that unnecessary risks were to be avoided: they served no purpose. From August onwards the battalion had to tread more carefully on the fine line between fulfilling the mission and the interests of all parties.' Patrols had fixed routes (although the actual situation was dynamic and demanded the opposite of fixed patrols) and had to be executed when ordered by higher commanders in the operations room (Ops-room), even if the group-commander (the patrol-commander) did not see the point of it [127]. Actually, it is not far-fetched to hypothesize that the soldiers were ordered not to take certain routes because that would produce more information. As has been made clear, the patrols of Dutchbat were closely followed by radio, and central commanders interfered in the proceedings. For instance, a group-commander, a sergeant, who had just decided to disarm a Muslim fighter was ordered by one of his superiors not to do so and to leave the place immediately [128]. The reason for this order could have been a political issue, not known to the local commander. One can also interpret the restrictions as a kind of fear that units would act out of control. The platoon-commanders and group-commanders were autonomous with respect to internal functioning in their respective units, such as how tasks were divided among their soldiers, how their soldiers' problems were dealt with, et cetera.

At the higher command there was awareness that a platoon on patrol is very autonomous indeed [129]. Units indeed developed strategies for approaching locals and found out ways to work together at observation posts. The most interesting cases of self-organization are those in which units overstepped moral boundaries. It should be added that this kind of self-organization is quite unlike the self-organization this study wants to establish as a design ideal. As has been said, the soldiers of Dutchbat had trouble with mines on their paths so they were very eager to know were exactly the mines were hidden. What they did, according to a particular rumor, was to force little local boys, of the population they were supposed to protect, into the minefields. Their reason for doing so was because these little boys were thought to be aware of the location of the mines, probably (according to the reasoning of the soldiers) because they themselves or their family or acquaintances had put them there[100].

---

[100] This claim is based upon a description of the NIOD, who subsequently based it on a newspaper report of Haerkens (1995): "The soldiers were said to have been guilty of rape and the misuse of alcohol and weapons. They were even said to have willfully enticed children into minefields by throwing candies into the fields. Thus, the soldiers could check whether or not the area was safe for them. Experts regard the last-mentioned excesses as 'very close to war crimes'."

There is something paradoxical about an organization that denies the dynamic complexity of the environment. In order to be able to deny this complexity one should be very aware of what is going on. The fake patrol is the perfect example of this: Dutchbat needed to know where *not* to look. This is, after all, implied by Everts when he stated that he did not want to put his men at risk. This can also be interpreted as a form of self-organization, but a sad form to say the least. These examples notwithstanding, one can generally conclude from the accounts that the operational units were mainly internally focused. Their attention was focused on internal matters, such as internal conflicts, work schedules, etc. (for a comparable conclusion regarding Dutchbat III, see Blom, 2002).

14.3 The structure of the operational units

This issue is dealt with in the same manner as in the previous cases.

The whole in the parts

The companies were assigned a certain area of responsibility in which the whole of the battalion's tasks returned. Such a division of labor can stimulate task identity because the whole of a battalion's tasks returns in a given area. It is questionable, however, whether this structure was deliberately chosen as a way to create self-organizing units or whether it was chosen because the situation made no other way of dividing tasks very likely. Regarding the issue of the distinction in preparation, performance and supportive tasks, one can state that units were merely focused on the performance of tasks. A unit's leader made the personal planning of the patrols but he had little control over other preparation tasks. As has been said, patrols had fixed routes that had to be executed when ordered by higher commanders in the operations room, even if the patrol-commander did not see the point of it [130]. Units were, however, responsible for one particular supportive task: they had to do the 'housekeeping' at the OPs.

Requisite variety

This demand specifies that the variety within the group must be enough to match the variety in the environment. One of the most salient features of the experience of Dutchbat was that this demand was not met by far. Dutchbat was simply unable to perform its original mission. This is a conclusion that is widely supported by other researchers. The NIOD, for example, reached comparable conclusions[101]. The local military units of both sides (although

---

[101] NIOD, 2002. The conclusion of the NIOD referred to the experiences of Dutchbat III, which was active in Srebrenica six months after Dutchbat II.

the forces on the inside were unofficial) far outnumbered Dutchbat both in quantity of material and quantity of soldiers. On top of that, the local parties were much more heavily armed. For whatever reason, these parties were unwilling to take the existing treaties seriously[102] and they did not accept Dutchbat and its role in the situation. Subsequently, both parties were powerful enough to force their will on Dutchbat. Dutchbat was eventually forced into a symbolic role in which keeping up appearances was perhaps the only reasonable line of action (e.g. Vogelaar & Kramer, 2004). Dutchbat was an organization confronted with an environment that necessitated – if it wanted to take the original mission seriously – dramatic change (more soldiers, different mandates, more weaponry, etc.). This issue was never seriously addressed both by the political level and the higher military command [131]. The battalion-commander also raised this issue in his reflection (Everts, 1998, p. 20): 'I indicated earlier that only a limited number of officials in the chain of command were aware of the precise situation in the enclave. I also indicated that the perception of the situation in the enclave differed from reality. This made communication regarding the situation extremely difficult. I felt that there was often a case of being at cross purposes as far a communication was concerned, particularly because the messages coming from my battalion in the enclave were not always hopeful. For me, this meant that the possibilities I had for explaining the situation were severely limited by the false conceptions that existed at other levels. (…). A special lesson I have learned from this is that the local commander (also within the battalion) has the best knowledge of the situation, and that it sometimes takes a great deal of personal courage to trust him to take the right decision.' This last sentence is particularly interesting because earlier it was shown that the battalion-commanders restricted the lower levels because of their freedom. Apparently he himself also did not possess this 'personal courage'. According to my interpretation, Dutchbat was aware that change was necessary. This awareness was crucial; the local parties did not accept that Dutchbat would take its original mission seriously. Being aware of this part of everyday reality was therefore crucial to survive in the environment. Dutchbat needs therefore be understood as a crisis organization that was no longer truly a crisis organization.

Redundancy of functions

In everyday practice, the operational units of companies A and C were expected to perform all the various tasks that had to be performed by Dutchbat. They were expected to patrol the borders of the enclave, to patrol

---

[102] This has been the topic of quite a lot of political speculation. The nature of the different interpretations does not matter for this analysis, so I want to stick to the obvious fact that the parties did not attend to the treaty.

the villages ('social patrols'), and to observe the proceedings from the operation posts. In other words, the battalion did attempt to create 'multi-skilled crisis soldiers' (although, they originally had been trained as infantry, which is a specialist job in the context of the regular operations). An interesting detail regarding the issue of requisite variety was that after earlier incidents 'an assault engineer' (a specialist on explosives) and a medical orderly joined the patrols (Everts, 1998, p. 17). This increased the multi-functionality of the patrol as a group (but not as individuals as this was a case of adding specialists: i.e. redundancy of parts).

Minimal critical specification

Also, this principle of design was not practiced when forming the operational units. The operations-room interfered in the proceedings of the patrols at crucial moments. It can be claimed that central control tried to avoid that units were confronted with risky situations. One could therefore say that they expected that units 'did not see', rather than that they explored the environment and gathered important new information. Interestingly, the decision to stay unaware was in that situation based on a keen analysis of the situation: the environment provided Dutchbat the luxury of that option. This contributed to the interpretation of Dutchbat as a crisis organization that was no longer really occupied with its central task. Some will perhaps argue that the large number of Rules of Engagement also contributed to the critical specifications. This was, according to the present analysis, not the case. The Rules of Engagement (ROE) were part of the demands that came from outside the organization. They were not created by the organization itself. Perhaps these ROE were overly restrictive or perhaps it was just impossible to apply them in everyday practice. This is, however, not a discussion that belongs to this analysis. In his reflection on this issue the battalion-commander clearly voiced his tendency to restrict the operational level (Everts, 1998, p. 20): 'Actions by individuals were regarded as the responsibility of the battalion as a whole, which meant that decisions at the low levels had to be taken into account within the battalion. With the passage of time, and the increasing complexity of the circumstances in the former Yugoslavia, the involvement of political and senior military authorities increased. The impact of decisions taken at the lower levels on higher levels therefore grew at the same rate. Obviously, this limited the possibilities of the local commander to exercise freedom in his decision-making. (…). In my opinion it was therefore necessary to issue stringent guidelines with regard to the action of the various elements of the battalion, and to restrict the freedom of the sub-commanders.' The basic message of Everts is that – in the context in which Dutchbat was operating– the natural autonomy of operational units 'obviously' led to attempts to restrict this autonomy.

Double-loop learning

The question is whether the operational units were allowed to innovate internally and externally. As regards the issue of external double-loop learning, one of the most interesting aspects of the Dutchbat experience was that throughout the organization it was felt that change was inevitable. The soldiers were very aware of their limited possibilities and the higher command indicated that they also knew about the reality of the situation. However, the organization was not allowed to change. The operational units learned to survive by keeping up appearances. One could consider this a particular kind of double-loop learning. However, this learning to avoid trouble can hardly be considered to be a kind of double-loop learning that is in line with the spirit of the concept. The ability to learn in line with the original mission was not consciously designed into the groups. One could even say that the higher command did its utmost to avoid that groups learned (not letting them patrol certain dangerous areas). Regarding the issue of internal double-loop learning one can state that this was also very restricted. The battalion-commander indicated that patrol schedules were adapted to the circumstances (Everts, 1998, p. 22), but this is not internal double-loop learning because the adaptation was issued top-down. There are indications that units learnt to deal with a life of shortages (food, diesel oil), which certainly can be interpreted as a form of internal double-loop learning.

14.4 Leadership

This topic is discussed the same way as in the previous cases.

Leaders as managers of the internal affairs of units

In the interviews especially qualities of leaders that had to do with internal group functioning were stressed. A good leader was considered to be someone who knew how to deal with internal conflicts, with soldiers with symptoms of stress, etc. Most particularly, a good leader was considered to be someone who knew how to make work schedules a week in advance [132]. Also a good leader knew when to get his hands dirty and when to stick to his position of authority. It was also emphasized that a good leader is a guard of discipline. One could interpret this as a sign of an internal focus of Dutchbat [133], because these are all matters that relate to the internal functioning of units. This internal focus can be explained as being the consequence of the nature of the circumstances Dutchbat was involved in. A means of survival of Dutchbat was not looking outside of their unit but only inside [134].

Leaders as arguers about the usefulness of the mission

This point refers to a particular conflict the leaders experienced in the definition of their role. Dutchbat started with intentions that gradually appeared to be less realistic. The conflict leaders had in defining their role was: should they stick to the original intentions and try to motivate soldiers in line with these original intentions or should they accept the nature of reality and make the best of a bad situation? Generally, leaders made few attempts to transform the vision of the mission and focused on making the best of the situation [135].

14.5 The resulting hypotheses

After having selecting the relevant data from the case studies, it seems reasonable to propose that:

I. *Dutchbat dealt with dynamic complexity by turning down its level of ambition.* As has been stated a number of times before, dealing with dynamic complexity inevitably means taking risks. One of the most obvious elements of the experience of Dutchbat is that they avoided taking risks, which differs from 'being careful'. Furthermore, the leaders of the operational units did not cultivate a spirit of contradiction but chose to make the best of a bad situation and told soldiers to do likewise. Making the best of a bad situation can be interpreted as 'do not think, do your job'[103]. In a way, this turning down of the level of ambitions is an escape from an impossible reality. One can add to this that Dutchbat had the luxury that it could escape reality.

II. *The crisis organization tried to restrict the operational level.* The case descriptions allow quite an unequivocal conclusion. The intention of the crisis organization (see the claims of the battalion-commander) was to create the opposite of self-organizing units. It is interesting to note that the rationale behind this intention was the extreme turbulence of the environment. In other words, central command did not try to control the behavior of operational units because it did not believe the environment to be dynamically complex and self-organization to be unnecessary; it did instead exactly so because it believed the environment to be extremely turbulent. Centralization prevented units from becoming too smart. Patrols were sent out to gather information, but in the case of Dutchbat, the higher command aimed to limit the amount of informa-

---

[103] Bootsma (2002, p. 178), a member of the NIOD research group concluded that: 'The informal goal of Dutchbat III, and already of Dutchbat II, increasingly shifted in the direction of getting the entire battalion home safely' (my translation).

tion that was gathered. Central command was very aware that the nature of the environment increased the risk of units acting out of control. Not only were units supposed to perform a complex job in a difficult environment, the units also operated widely dispersed and the shortages within the battalion led to their increasing isolation. Central command indicated that it was afraid of this autonomy. Throughout this study it has been emphasized that dealing with dynamic complexity necessitates self-organization. Dutchbat is an example of an organization that dealt with its environment by avoiding self-organization.

III. *Dutchbat developed an internal focus.* It was observed that Dutchbat developed an internal focus ('a good leader is someone who provides good planning')[104]. They developed a culture of passivity, of not being vigilant and not questioning the nature of the circumstances[105]. Many people ask themselves why Dutchbat III did not do more to prevent the eventual massacre. One explanation is that already Dutchbat II developed a routine of focusing internally rather than being focused externally. It is well known that groups under certain conditions can display very dangerous patterns of decision-making. They can deny certain crucial information; they can avoid to discuss obvious questions, etc. One can ask to what degree Dutchbat fell victim to the conditions of groupthink or learned helplessness. I believe that these conditions were certainly observable: they were (more and more) isolated and their groups were of a uniform background.

IV. *Dutchbat did not do a good job because it was confronted with a mission impossible.* In the Netherlands there has been an extensive discussion on whether Dutchbat failed or whether they were confronted with a mission impossible. This discussion is related to the experiences of Dutchbat III, which is no part of the present analysis (which focuses on Dutchbat II). However, on the basis of the present analysis it is possible to contribute to this discussion. The original case description gives every reason to believe that Dutchbat was indeed engaged in a mission impossible. The pressure from the environment was far too great to accomplish the mission with the available means. This conclusion is shared by the NIOD (2002). From the contention of a mission impossible it is frequently concluded that Dutchbat did a good job in bad circumstances. This is, however, not a conclusion that follows from the analysis in this study. As has been stated, Dutchbat sacrificed its ambition to be a crisis

---

[104] Group processes within Dutchbat have, for example, been analyzed by Roemers (2002).

[105] Blom (2002, p. 315), the chairperson of the NIOD research team, about this: 'The situation was altogether frustrating and demotivating for Dutchbat. Especially the last two battalions (Dutchbat II and III, ehk) became physically and mentally exhausted' during their deployment, (my translation).

organization for reasons of safety. This cannot possibly be called 'doing a good job in bad circumstances', although it may be understandable that Dutchbat was not able to accomplish its original mission. One could say that from this analysis one can conclude that Dutchbat did not a good job because it was confronted with a mission impossible.

14.6 Final remarks

A possible counterargument against the value of the concept of 'self-organization' can be formulated as a result of the reflections in the cases. The battalion-commander of Dutchbat made it clear that he was confronted with such Rules of Engagement that made initiative at the lower levels impossible. A comparable claim was made by SFOR representatives who claimed that the ROE were so restricting that it seriously undermined possibilities of granting autonomy. This seems a reasonable point. What if the formal demands placed on the organizational system are such that self-organization becomes impossible because every action of units is prescribed? One can imagine that it is possible to aim at formulating Rules of Engagement in such a way as to provide the appropriate solution for every imaginable situation. One can imagine that such Rules of Engagement can be very restricting indeed. In that case the organization appears to be left with little choice than designing a system of extreme control. An often heard 'off the record' criticism of Mission Command within the military organization itself is that it is impossible to implement with today's politicians.

De Sitter (2000, p. 91) made a distinction between specific task demands and non-specific task demands on an organizational system. Specific demands are demands of the organizational system's environment (flexibility, etc.); non-specific demands refer to matters such as Rules of Engagement, laws, etc. De Sitter makes clear that first a design should be made based on specific demands before it will be evaluated what parts of this design can be realized in light of the non-specific demands. This is essential because otherwise an 'ideal' design is disregarded on practical grounds before it is even seriously considered.

Suppose that the non-specific demands are such that one cannot implement an organizational system designed for meeting the specific demands. In that case one is simply stating that it is impossible to accomplish a mission. After all, if specific demands make flexibility necessary and non-specific demands make flexibility impossible, one is confronted with impossible demands. If that is the case, the designer of the organization should return to his superiors with the conclusion that he is confronted with an impossibility. Note that this is exactly what should have happened in the

Dutchbat case[106]. It should be mentioned that Rules of Engagement provide a rather good excuse for designing a system of top-down control: 'we have no choice'.

---

[106] Also note that this is exactly the reason why one should be careful to generalize "practical lessons" from Dutchbat to other operations. If initiative is impossible in an impossible situation it will not always be impossible.

PART V
The influence of the mother organization

In this part, the influence of the mother organization on the crisis organizations is explored. More specifically, this part focuses on the influence of the mother organization on the possibility of designing self-organizing units. This exploration is orientated on the constraints the mother organization generally confronts crisis organizations with. One can imagine that, apart from the operational context or other reasons, difficulties in designing self-organizing units are influenced by structural characteristics of the mother organization. A reason to study the influences of the mother organization is the issue of generalization. If one aims to build a substantive theory that has relevance beyond the explorative case studies, one should look for factors that all crisis organizations potentially share, i.e. structural influences of the mother organization. The following research question is central to Part Five:

How is the possibility of designing self-organizing units in crisis organizations influenced by characteristics of the mother organization?

The following conceptual model can represent the relation that is central in this question. It is part of the conceptual model that was introduced in Part One.

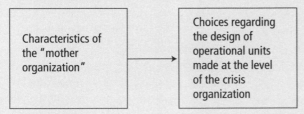

Chapter Fifteen will focus on the identification of the relevant characteristics of the mother organization. Chapters Sixteen, Seventeen and Eighteen will each analyze a relevant characteristic.

The influence of the mother organization

That the mother organization influences crisis organizations is a statement that can hardly be denied in this general sense. Therefore the central question of Part Five needs some specification. The relation that is indicated by the conceptual model is much too general to study in its entirety; it is even too general to explore in its entirety. There are countless characteristics that may influence crisis organizations in many different ways. A choice needs to be made of characteristics that are considered to be the most relevant in this study. Furthermore, one can ask what is specifically meant by the statement that characteristics of the mother organization influence all crisis organizations. This chapter is meant to make the required preparations to study the influence of the mother organization. In the following sections, the ambitions of the reflections will be discussed and the choice for certain characteristics will be made. First, however, it is defended that there are similarities between the cases.

15.1 Indications of the influences of the mother organization

To state that the mother organization has an influence on crisis organizations is to state that there are similarities between the various operations. More specifically, it is to state that there are similarities notwithstanding certain differences. The most eye-catching differences between the cases will be discussed. Subsequently, the most essential similarity is identified. The differences and similarities discussed here, are, of course, all related to the topic of self-organization.

Differences between the cases
- *The environments of the crisis organizations in the cases differed significantly.* It seems that they differed on a continuum ranging from 'order' (SFOR) to 'chaos' (Dutchbat) and an environment on 'the edge of chaos'

203

(Logtbat). Circumstances in the Dutchbat case could be called chaotic because Dutchbat's mission was impossible. No clever insights and solutions (in other words, meaningful doubt) at any level seemed to matter. On the other hand, SFOR was organized in a way that attempted to make clever insights and solutions at the operational level superfluous. Indeed, it was attempted to let operational units know what they needed to know (interestingly, boredom was a major problem these units had to deal with). Logtbat is an example of a battalion in which clever insights and solutions made a tremendous difference in the performance of the battalion's central tasks.

- *The solutions that the different crisis organizations developed to deal with the environment were quite different.* The Logtbat case provided examples of convoys with considerable elbowroom for self-organization. This can be explained as being the consequence of the kinds of tasks that had to be performed in that particular environment. SFOR provided an example of higher commanders that went pretty far in restricting such elbowroom. The 'need-to-know' policy, as it was put in practice by some, is significant in that respect. One is tempted to conclude that the limits of restriction were the limits of the creativity to find restrictions. Dutchbat also restricted elbowroom, but for a different reason. Where in the SFOR-case higher commanders appeared to restrict it because they believed to be able to centrally control the operation, higher command of Dutchbat restricted it because it knew the operational units had considerable natural autonomy.

- *Different commanders that were part of the same crisis organization developed different organizational solutions.* This meant that two neighboring teams operated quite differently. The SFOR case provided evidence of this. An important conclusion following this observation is that, apparently, at the team level (company level) commanders have a particular autonomy to organize their teams according to their liking, although this autonomy should not be overstated (consider the role of the reconnaissance units). Although one can appreciate the autonomy the team commanders had in designing the operational units, one should also note that this autonomy is a sort of 'unguided freedom'. They appeared to possess, in other words, the autonomy to develop rather strange solutions. The implementation of the 'need-to-know' policy – in some instances – is witness to that claim. Another interesting finding in that regard is that the team-commanders occupied themselves with problems of the division of labor. While the military doctrine emphasizes the importance of autonomy at the operational level, some team-commanders designed structures that ran diametrically against such ambitions.

- *The units from the cases were assembled from the mother organization in different ways.* Logtbat used an individual system of rotation and provided examples of operational units being built up of soldiers and leaders with different levels of experience. SFOR and Dutchbat rotated unitwise. Particularly SFOR showed that – notwithstanding such a system of rotation – the assembly process can still be considerably complex.
- *There were individual differences between commanders in dealing with the issues of 'natural autonomy of operational units'.* Some commanders were quite generous with granting 'elbowroom'. The Logtbat case provided evidence for this claim. There are two tentative hypotheses that one can formulate from this observation. In complex environments, units have a kind of natural autonomy. Some commanders find it hard to deal with this natural autonomy and desperately try to entangle the operational units in a web of regulations. Other individual commanders are more inclined to accept this autonomy as a *fait accompli* and adjust their entire policy to this.

Similarity

- *The crisis organizations were similar in the sense that self-organization proved to be a problematic concept.* With 'problematic' I refer to the point that none of the crisis organizations that were studied straightforwardly designed units according to the holographic principles. Of course, the concept of self-organization was problematic in various ways. In circumstances of relatively little turbulence and equivocality (SFOR), the operational units had a limited amount of autonomy compared to circumstances of significant turbulence and equivocality (Logtbat). On the one hand, this is quite understandable. In the circumstances of Logtbat, the units had a kind of 'natural autonomy': no matter how badly the central command may have wanted to control units, circumstances were not suited for control. In the far more stable circumstances of SFOR, central command had far more possibilities for prescription and control, which it subsequently used. As Weick (1979) noted, in circumstances of little equivocality one is able to use far more rules to assemble a process, e.g. one has a better opportunity for detailed control. However, circumstances with a lot of equivocality are far more challenging than circumstances with little equivocality. The contradictory element in this is that the easy jobs are centrally steered and controlled while the difficult jobs are not. If an organization grants units autonomy in performing difficult jobs, why should they control the easy jobs?

The logic underlying the problem stated above could be that the Army is an organization that as a rule aims for 'maximal critical specification' except in the cases where this is completely impossible (e.g. not 'decentralization unless' but 'centralization unless')[107]. This would imply that this is a general influence of the mother organization.

15.2 The influence of structural characteristics of the mother organization

If the Army wants to develop itself as a crisis organization, a crucial question is whether structural characteristics (in the sense of 'stable characteristics') of the mother organization influence the ability of crisis organizations to design self-organizing operational units. As was stated above, the cases provided some indications regarding such an influence of the mother organization. These indications are a point of departure for exploring the influence of specific characteristics of the mother organization. Here, a choice for three such structural characteristics is defended. Of course there may be influences from numerous other characteristics. As such, a choice is always a limitation. However, if the general influence of a particular structural characteristic can be defended, this can be tremendously informative for the Army, without denying that there are other influences. Here, the choice for three characteristics that fit this study are defended.

- The Army has developed a philosophy of command that is particularly meant for complex situations. Autonomy for the operational level occupies a central place in this doctrine. However, the cases provided little evidence that this doctrine is wholeheartedly used. On the contrary even, particularly in the SFOR case (the only case that was studied after the implementation of Mission Command) centralization of command was the philosophy of command as it was actually put into practice. Particularly in the SFOR case, however, commanders did claim that the doctrine was applied. This indicates that there might be misunderstandings regarding the doctrine. In Chapter Fourteen **the doctrine** will be analyzed by making a comparison with the analytical framework of this study.

---

[107] Regarding self-organization there is one interesting topic that was not described in the original case descriptions, but which returned time and time again in the interviews. The men only stayed in Bosnia for six months. After such a period, they were replaced by another battalion (Dutchbat, IFOR, SFOR) or by another individual (Logtbat). Some times "the old" cooperated with "the new" for a week or so to teach them the details of the local situation. This was something "the old" generally found an extremely difficult job. They simply could not bear the sight of a successor organizing things differently. Within six months the new had become the old and they reported the same experience with "their new". One can interpret this as a clear sign of the importance of self-organization. Over time the old built a very personal way of organizing their affairs. This cumulated in a style of working in which insignificant details for outsiders were significant for insiders. The insiders almost unanimously reported that they found it difficult that their carefully built-up style of working was disregarded.

- A second indication that is interesting to explore is that particularly in the Logtbat and the SFOR case people had to work together who did not know each other on a personal level, or were even unfamiliar with each other's way of working. In the Logtbat case this was due to the system of individual rotation. In the SFOR case it was due to the fact that the battalion was assembled from a number of different units from the mother organization and units were mixed by team-commanders. In both teams in the SFOR case these units from different parts of the organization were mixed in order to form operational units. This shows that the mother organization is not structured in such a way that it can deploy units as a whole. A process of assembly appears to be necessary, and one can imagine that this process of assembly influences self-organization. In Chapter Fifteen the influence of the **organizational structure** of the mother organization will be analyzed.
- When one considers the way in which leaders defined their role, it is interesting to note that ideas that are related to argumentation, doubt, and self-organization are never mentioned. Instead, leaders appear to define their role in rather classical way. This was not the case in the Logtbat case, but there circumstances (the rotation policy) made it very difficult for leaders to adopt a classical role. Chapter Sixteen will explore the way the leadership function is implemented in the mother organization. In this study the different ways in which the leadership-function is implemented are called **leadership structures**.

15.3 The ambitions of the reflection

With respect to the ambition of the reflection, three issues are of particular importance. These are issues that are related to the nature of the claims being made:

- The cases provided examples of units that originated from different parts of the organization. Logtbat was composed of different parts of the Army's logistic organization, which is a supporting unit in the mother organization. Dutchbat originated from the (at that time) newly established Air Maneuver Brigade. SFOR originated from the First Division which consists of various brigades composed of Cavalry, Infantry, and Artillery. In other words, the organizational context of the crisis organizations in the cases differed significantly. This seems to complicate the drawing of general conclusions, that is to say, the establishment of links between characteristics of 'the' mother organization and choices made at the level of the crisis organization. It is, however, intended to draw links between a general description of the mother organization and the crisis organization. The crucial step to make such an analysis possible is to establish a 'loose coupling' between the characteristics of the mother organization and the crisis organizations that were deployed. I am therefore interested in 'principles' that characterize the mother organization, rather than a precise account of a particular unit. There are two advantages in using such an analysis. The first advantage is that although the crisis organizations in the cases originated from different parts of the organization, it is quite defendable that they were built up on the basis of comparable principles, although there might always be differences between organizational parts. The second advantage is that the basic principles remain relatively stable. An implication of this is that the analysis is not limited to the particulars of a concrete case.

- The foregoing claimed that the exploration focuses on characteristics of the mother organization that structurally influence crisis organizations. This formulation might give the impression that it is pretended that each and every crisis organization, regardless its individual circumstances, is the victim of the proposed mechanisms and is influenced in exactly the same way. This would imply a classic view on causation. Everyday reality is much too complex for the identification of such mechanisms. As has been discussed in Chapter Two, this study has a different view on causation, one in which factors are considered to possess causal potential, i.e. the capability of influence. The different relations between mother organization and crisis organization that will be identified in the next chapters are considered to be *general mechanisms* that might influence crisis organizations, and which can influence crisis organizations in different ways.

- Because the principles behind the organizational arrangements are explicated it is actually studied what general influence the mother organization has on the proceedings in the crisis organization. Therefore it is attempted to make the pressures on the crisis organization insightful. Insightful means that choices can be made understandable, while at the same time it is not claimed that they are inevitable. The unique circumstances of every operation determine whether the causal potential is effectuated and in which particular way. If the mother organization aims to develop itself as a crisis organization, it is important that it is aware of such mechanisms, although it is perhaps tempting for them to conclude that 'potential' means 'not necessarily'.

Chapter 16

The Army doctrine and dealing with dynamic complexity

Decentralization may have been the dominant 'espoused' philosophy of command; the reflection on the cases made it clear that it was certainly not the dominant philosophy of command in use[108]. Given this finding, one can pursue different lines of research. One can ask why commanders did not aim to apply a philosophy of decentralization. The next chapter will argue that because of the structure of the mother organization, crisis organizations consist of a mix of people, making it more difficult for commanders to decentralize. The analysis of the cases, furthermore, showed that the context in which the cases were performed also made a tremendous difference. Dutchbat was deployed in chaotic circumstances in which they gave up their ambitions as a crisis organization. SFOR, on the other hand, was deployed in circumstances in which the commanders had the possibility for centralized command.

The present chapter follows a different clue. Particularly in the SFOR case, commanders claimed that they had applied military doctrine while the analysis of the cases showed that units had little self-organizing potential. There is, in other words, apparently a difference between what people say and what people do. This difference is interesting in its own right, because it indicates that people perhaps understand the doctrine differently. In this chapter, the content of the doctrine will be analyzed and compared to the analytical framework. Furthermore, three issues will be discussed. In the first place, a description of the doctrine will be given and it will be attempted to expand on the description given in Chapter Eleven. In the second place, it will be discussed how the philosophy influences choices at the level of the crisis organization. In the third place, it is discussed whether the assumptions of the doctrine were recognizable in the cases.

---

[108] Argyris (1996, p. 216): 'Espoused theories are those that an individual claims to follow. Theories-in-use are those that can be inferred from action.'

16.1 A description of the doctrine

The Army doctrine (part LDP I) was published in 1996 (after the experiences of Logtbat and Dutchbat, but before SFOR). In Chapter Three it has been explicated that in its recent doctrine publication the Dutch Army has chosen for a system of what is generally called Mission Command (MC). In its essence, MC is a system of command specifically meant for dynamically complex operations. It is a system of decentralization that aims to enable initiative and decision-making at the lower levels. This system of command has been inspired by the system of Auftragstaktik. MC, as it is formulated in the Army doctrine, consists of five so-called elements (Koninklijke Landmacht, 1996, pp. 109–110):

a. A commander gives his orders in a way that ensures that his subordinates understand his view, their own mission, the objectives to be met, and the broader context of that mission in the operation of the entire unit;
b. A commander indicates to his subordinates what objectives they should meet and the reason why meeting them is necessary;
c. A commander allocates the appropriate means to his subordinate commanders to fulfill their mission;
d. A commander leaves his subordinates free in the way in which they want to accomplish the mission, except for strictly necessary preconditions, for instance because of the missions of higher or subsidiary units;
e. During the operation, a commander only gives his subordinates instructions when the success of the operation is at stake.

The Dutch doctrine of MC presumes that commanders at all hierarchical levels are able and willing to take responsibility for their decisions and actions. Therefore, commanders at each and every level should be trained and stimulated to take initiatives and risks instead of merely following orders. Furthermore, it is mentioned that – besides taking responsibility – the desired accompanying leadership behavior for MC consists of a number of aspects:

• Commanders at every hierarchical level should be prepared to set the example for their men;
• They should be self-confident and courageous;
• They should show decisiveness and not be risk-aversive.

The system of MC is not considered to be solely dependent upon the qualities of commanders; it is also considered to be dependent on the qualities of the interrelationships between commanders. In a system of decentralized command, commanders at different hierarchical levels depend on each other's initiatives. Therefore, the system should be built on a high level of 'implicit coordination' between commanders. The doctrine mentions team spirit, unity of view, cohesion, and mutual trust as important preconditions for MC to be viable. Therefore, the recent Dutch Army's leadership policy (Beleidsvisie Leidinggeven, 1998a) describes mutual trust and mutual respect together with autonomy of action as essential aspects of leadership. When mutual trust and mutual respect are absent, a system of decentralized command is thought to fail. According to the Dutch military doctrine, MC should be applied in all kinds of operations and in both operational and peacetime circumstances. The choice for a system of decentralization implies that the Army explicitly aims for autonomy at the operational level.

16.2 The military doctrine and the analytical framework of this study

Superficially the text of the doctrine bears a close resemblance to the analytical framework of this study. Both emphasize the complexity of operations and the importance of decision-making at the lower levels of the organization. More specifically:

- Both the analytical framework developed in this study and the military doctrine are based on the assumption of the complexity of crisis operations. Decentralization is thought to be important because of the turbulence of crisis-situations.
- The consequence of this outlook on crisis operations is that both this study and the military doctrine consider it to be essential that in 'crisis operations' units cannot be guided on the basis of a closed set of perfect rules, nor can they be perfectly guided on the basis of direct supervision. In order to achieve flexibility, lower-level initiative is essential. The operational level is supposed to be given enough space, autonomy, to be able to do so.

A closer reading, however, will reveal major differences.

The definition of complexity

A crucial sign that the doctrine is based on a limited conception of dynamic complexity is the fact that the concepts of doubt and double-loop learning are absent. In the view of this study both concepts are essential because the environment can surprise the organization. Sense-discrediting and double-loop learning both represent a way in which the organizational system can be open to the environment. In the account of Mission Command in the military doctrine there is no indication that bottom-up experiences or insights are to be taken seriously. Perhaps the doctrine considers bottom-up information to be important. However, one gathers information on certain specified objects *that are known in advance* (perhaps the doctrine assumes that crucial information is gathered by specialized reconnaissance units). Dynamic complexity makes it impossible to specify in advance the kind of information one needs because the environment is largely unknown. Furthermore, because of the equivocality of the environment more information will not resolve dynamic complexity. Merely gathering information is a form of single-loop learning.

If such a single-loop learning perspective is used to interpret the doctrine, a different light is shed on the formulation of the elements of the doctrine. Orders are top-down formulated (element a). Initiative and freedom at the operational level are meant for dealing with the top-down assignments (elements b to e). Autonomy and initiative should safely stay between the limits that are determined top-down, which are – apparently – unquestionable. Prerequisites are formulated to ensure this: there should be unity of view (while this study underlines the importance of contradiction) and cohesion (this study underlines that cohesion can threaten a spirit of contradiction). The idea that the experiences at the operational level can lead to *really* new insights is simply absent.

This observation could already have become clear in Chapter Eleven, which emphasized that, according to the doctrine, peace operations can be complex because 'a lot of groups and fractions are involved', because of 'climatic and geographical conditions' and because of 'complex Rules of Engagement'. The problems of uncertain meaning, confusing meaning, and multiple meaning were never explicitly mentioned. Furthermore, the observation in the SFOR case that specialized reconnaissance units were active in order to determine the 'information-need' shows that the 'evaluating' part of the control cycle is performed by a different functional component of the organization.

The concept of self-organization

Because of the limited concept of dynamic complexity, MC emphasizes a limited kind of self-organization. Although the importance of operational initiative is emphasized, a firm, top-down formulated fence is placed around the self-organizing activities that are considered to be acceptable[109]. Within the definition of this study it cannot even be called self-organization, as the operational level is not concerned with finding 'workable levels of certainty'. Certainty is supposed to be provided by the higher levels.

The matters that are decentralized have to do with 'working out the de-

---

[109] It is for this reason questionable if Mission Command is a good translation of *Auftragstaktik* as it was used by the German and later the Israeli Army. Van Creveld (1985) emphasized that bottom-up initiatives of the Israeli Army changed the nature of the 1956 campaign, probably one of the explanations for its success. Revealing is the comment of the highest Israeli military commander in those days, Dayan: "Our capacity for misadventure is limitless."

tails' of an operation. In that sense it can be perceived as a system that is meant as an attempt to reduce the workload of higher commanders rather than as a concept that is meant for dealing with dynamic complexity. This study, on the other hand, emphasizes that the nature of dynamic complexity is such that the possibilities for centralized control of an operation are limited. Experiences and insights on the operational level will have to be taken seriously at the other levels as well. The nature of dynamic complexity is therefore such that dialogue and argumentation are necessary on the operational, the tactical, and the strategic level. This is a fundamental difference between the analytical framework of this study and MC as it is formulated by the military doctrine.

'Situations' for Mission Command

MC was originally interpreted as quite a liberal concept, which is understandable because originally the Army emphasized centralized control. That the doctrine is a strategically phrased document can be read from the 'factors that influence MC' as they are formulated in the *commander's guideline* (leidraad commandovoering) (Koninklijke Landmacht, 2000, p. 51). It appears that the doctrine brings these 'factors of influence' forward as situations that complicate the granting of autonomy by the higher levels. The 'factors' are actually 'situations' in which:

- Units do not operate in their regular composition;
- Political sensitivity surround operations;
- Units have to cooperate with international organizations with different cultures;
- Differences between units in the way tasks are conducted are unwanted.

The Dutch text of the doctrine is surprisingly unclear here, if not semantically incorrect. 'With peace operations, a number of factors influence the decentralized execution' (my translation)[110]. The exact nature and consequences of this influence is difficult to determine on the basis of the text. I suspect that the passage is not incidentally unclear. The lack of clarity hides the crucial point whether or not MC should be put aside in certain situations. This would imply that if a situation becomes more complex than the top-down defined borders have anticipated, the central commander takes absolute control again.

One should appreciate the deeper conflict of the Army regarding this particular point. There is not a single operation in which these factors are absent. Every military operation is politically sensitive. Every peace operation involves the deployment of mixed units (crisis organizations are by defini-

---

[110] *"Bij vredesoperaties is een aantal factoren van invloed op de decentrale uitvoering"* (Koninklijke Landmacht, 2000, p. 51).

tion 'task forces', see Chapter Seventeen). Every peace operation by definition involves cooperation with other cultures. In every peace operation too much divergence between units in the way tasks are conducted is by definition unwanted. After all, all the units of a crisis organization are bound by the same Rules of Engagement. One can imagine why the commander's guideline is not saying that these factors mean the abolishment of MC, because that would effectively mean that it is claimed that MC cannot be used in peace operations. If it is claimed that these complications make MC impossible, it is actually stated that a system of command *particularly meant for complex situations* is abolished because of complexity. This would imply that MC could only be applied in the safest of circumstances. By remaining unclear about this crucial issue, the doctrine provides every commander in every situation the arguments to abolish MC. At the same time, however, the casual observer is led to believe that the Army is implementing modern concepts of decentralization.

I should emphasize that I do not want to claim that the factors that are mentioned are unimportant. One can easily imagine that all the different factors generally complicate operations in crisis areas. They are very likely to be matters that should be taken into account when a crisis organization is designed. Because this is not the topic of this study, I will devote no further attention to that. However, there is one remark I should make. The doctrine suggests that the factors are arguments against decentralization. That is, in my opinion, a wrong suggestion. In my interpretation the factors *generally complicate the issue of control over an operation*. The same factors would also complicate operations for organizations with a centralized system of control. As a matter of fact, military history has shown that centralized systems of command are less able to maintain control over complicated operations than decentralized systems of command (Van Creveld, 1985; Kramer & Kuipers, 2002). The fact that the doctrine interprets the factors as an argument against decentralization (according to my interpretation) to my mind is a sign that the Army is still primarily focused on a philosophy of centralization.

Implementation of initiative

MC is phrased in the language of leadership. It is phrased in terms of what leaders should and should not do. All in all, it means that officers are believed to be able to apply MC more or less regardless of the nature of the organizational context they operate in. This study emphasizes, however, that especially structural characteristics of an organization create the possibilities and limitations (control capacity, elbowroom) for self-organization. As a matter of fact, it is emphasized that an external structure of argumentation creates the prerequisites for meaningful argumentation at the operational level. The idea that leaders operate in an organizational context that can restrict the possibilities of meaningful action is no part of MC.

Because MC is predominantly a leadership concept, other organizational prerequisites receive little or no attention. When other organizational prerequisites are mentioned, they are of the soft and intangible sort, such as the emphasis on 'mutual trust'. I certainly do not want to claim that something like 'mutual trust' is unimportant, but I do want to claim that it is an attractive concept for an organization because of its non-committal nature. It does not commit the organization to fundamental – or true – change. One can easily claim the importance of 'trust' without being committed to 'hard' consequences, such as a change in structural design. In this sense, resistance to change can hide behind the emphasis on the importance of 'soft' factors.

The fact that MC is phrased in the language of leadership has one further consequence. MC seems to be meant as a game that is played between officers[111]. Also operational units are supposed to be led by officers (whereas the cases show that also NCOs can be the leaders of such units). Because leaders are emphasized in the doctrine, little or no attention is paid to subordinates. There is no sign that operators are structurally taken serious as arguers or that they are supposed to think. One can infer that MC is a system of decentralization **between officers and therefore between leaders**. Initiative is emphasized as an important character trait **of leaders**. A higher commander is not to interfere in the proceedings at the lower level **because another leader is supposed to be present at this lower level**. Reference to the importance of delegation to the non-officer levels is nowhere to be found, neither in the doctrine nor in the philosophy of leadership supporting the doctrine. This is a further indication that the doctrine appears modern (thinking at the operational level) while on a closer look it is not so modern (the common soldier is not expected to think).

Operational units that are 'out of control'

One can imagine why control is important for a crisis organization. A crisis organization is deployed for certain purposes and if the organization loses

---

[111] I had a revealing experience in a discussion with "student officers" (students with a few years of working experience) at the Military Academy. The idea that common soldiers should be a part of the philosophy of MC and should be given responsibilities appeared completely hilarious to them. These students were all convinced that a system of decentralization is crucial in crisis operations and were convinced that the traditional ways of the Army were too centralized. They can, in other words, be seen as "modern officers". Supportive of this general conviction that it is impossible for soldiers to be part of a system of decentralization is the idea (or myth?) that common soldiers are simply too stupid and morally inadequate to be given that kind of responsibility. Implicit in this idea is that leaders are a superior breed of people (this is understandable if one takes the education of leaders into account, see later in this study).

control it cannot achieve those purposes. Dutchbat was a very interesting case in that respect. Furthermore, it is obvious that no one is in favor of soldiers that cross ethical boundaries or units that chase their own goal. Some might misunderstand an emphasis on self-organization to be an argument against the importance of control. This is a fundamental misunderstanding. Instead, one should understand 'self-organization' as a way to control a difficult environment. According to the analysis in this chapter, the fear for units to act 'out of control' is the reason the Army is hesitant of (truly) choosing for a decentralized style of command. This is an important issue, but it is mystified by the discussions in the doctrine. When reading the Army doctrine one sees on the one hand an organization that recognizes that 'initiative' and 'not being risk aversive' is important in crisis operations; on the other hand one sees an organization that formulates hesitations regarding these issues.

The reply of this study is quite simple. Units are not in danger of getting 'out of control' because of a lack of discipline as a result of a liberal philosophy of command. They are in danger of getting out of control because of the nature of the environment. The real problem for the Army is therefore the acceptance that they are confronted with dynamically complex environments. According to the definitions of dynamic complexity that has been used in this study, an organization that is active in such an environment is in principle at risk of losing control. One does not avoid these risks by tightening control on units. Quite the opposite, it is well established in organizational studies that classical organizations have overwhelming difficulties when it comes to controlling their essential processes in difficult circumstances (Kuipers & Van Amelsvoort, 1990; De Sitter, 2000; Kuipers, Kramer & Richardson, 2002). The inconsequence in the doctrine regarding these issues has been interpreted as rhetorical. If one uses a more understanding line of interpretation, one can see the inconsequence as the manifestation of a latent fear of dynamically complex environments. In other words, the Army should accept that in such circumstances total control is impossible. Actually, I believe that both interpretations are true at the same time: a 'nothing is wrong, we are very modern' image is conveyed in order to ward off difficult questions regarding the nature of the operations of the Army.

16.3 The military doctrine and the SFOR case

It would be interesting to see whether the claim that the doctrine has a rhetorical function can explain what is actually happening in crisis operations. An inconsequent application of principles of decentralization can perhaps be made insightful when the unclarity of the doctrine is taken in mind. I only focus on SFOR because this is the only operation studied here that was performed after the introduction of the doctrine. I will discuss several interesting points.

- Within SFOR, an 'information demand' was top-down formulated; operational units were deployed as pawns to collect this information. Furthermore, they had to report unusual situations. The information that the units gathered was transferred to staff level where it was used for reasons unclear to the operational units. Thus, operational units were perceived as 'the eyes' that transmit objective information preferably in an unbiased way, without the necessity to know why information is needed and why some things are more interesting than others. The environment was seen as partly unknown (otherwise the information was not needed) with an occasional surprise. However, the organization was under the impression that the location of the unknown could be exactly specified. This is a way of working that is in line with the doctrine (bottom-up *insights* are unnecessary) but not with the ideal of self-organization that is promoted in this study;
- Crucial elements in the doctrine like 'not interfering in the operational proceedings' were simply not applied in the SFOR case. Vogelaar c.s. (2001) remarked that the SFOR contingent used the philosophy of 'centralization, unless…' rather than the philosophy of 'decentralization, unless…' as it is prescribed by the doctrine. But this practice is in line with the doctrine because SFOR consisted of mixed units, in an international context;
- An interesting aspect of the SFOR case was that the team-commanders adapted the structure of their platoons to the situation which they were confronted with. Thus it shows the importance of knowledge of theory about organizational structuring. Splitting up a team in 11 elements and deploy them as pawns is in contradiction with the concept of self-organization in this study. However, according to the letter of the doctrine, the team-commanders were not at fault, as principles of organizational structuring are considered to be no part of this;
- An interesting feature of the SFOR case was that commanders claimed that they did actually apply the doctrine. As Vogelaar c.s. (2001) argued, it seems that commanders interpreted Mission Command in a (yet more) limited way. The problem of MC is that it can lead to a *reductio ad absurdum*. Commanders can claim to use the doctrine when they tell people to stir their coffee but do not tell them how to do that. This is a consequence of the fact that there is no theory of task-structuring supporting the doctrine. This is what makes 'tell people what to do, instead of how' open for multiple interpretations.

16.4 Hypotheses about the influence of the doctrine

The central issue of this chapter was to explore the influence of the doctrine on the design of operational units in crisis organizations. On the basis of the discussions in this chapter, it seems reasonable to suggest the following hypotheses:

I.   *The doctrine is meant for relatively easy (not dynamically complex) circumstances even though it is meant as a doctrine for crisis operations.* The different elements of the doctrine add up to a system to facilitate single-loop learning. Insights resembling double-loop learning, which is an essential faculty for dealing with dynamic complexity, are nowhere to be found;

II. *The present formulation of the doctrine provides commanders in every operation the arguments not to apply the doctrine.* In its current form, the doctrine formulates so many 'factors that influence MC' (should be read as: situations in which MC should not be applied) that it provides commanders in every conceivable operation the arguments not to apply the doctrine;

III. *The doctrine fulfills a rhetorical role.* The doctrine gives a strong appearance of being a system of command especially developed for dynamically complex environments. As the doctrine provides (1) a limited view of dynamic complexity and (2) the arguments for centralized control in situations that are complex, one can hypothesize that the modern appearance it makes to the outside world is its true 'rationale'.

Chapter 17

The influence of the organizational structure

The crisis organizations in the cases were not deployed as a whole, but were assembled from the mother organization. In quite a literal sense the mother organization supplies the building blocks (the basic constituent parts of a crisis organization) from which the crisis organization is assembled. One can therefore suggest that the organizational structure of the mother organization influences the crisis organization. Therefore one can also suggest that the organizational structure of the mother organization influenced self-organization in the cases. The present chapter will explore this influence. The following conceptual model represents the 'traces' that are being explored in this chapter:

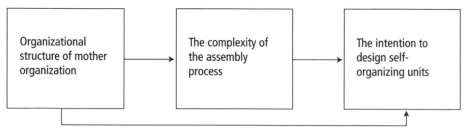

Model 17.1

The model suggests that the organizational structure of the mother organization has two types of influence on self-organization:

- There is a direct effect of the organizational structure of the mother organization on the intention of crisis organizations to design self-organizing operational units. It will be argued that this effect is negative in the present-day Army.
- There is an indirect effect of the organizational structure on the intention of crisis organizations to design self-organizing operational units. This indirect effect is effectuated through the complexity of the assembly process. It will be argued that in the present-day Army, the relation between

219

the complexity of the assembly process and the intention displayed in the conceptual model here is negative. A more complex assembly process has a negative effect on the intention to design self-organizing units.

This chapter will proceed by taking the following steps. Firstly, the organizational structure of the mother organization will be characterized. It will be attempted to identify the principles on which the organizational structure is built. Furthermore, the nature of crisis organizations according to the Army will be discussed. Secondly, it will be discussed what is particularly meant by 'the process of assembly' and what the hypothetical influence of the assembly process is on the preconditions of designing self-organizing units in crisis organizations. The direct effect of the organizational structure of the mother organization will subsequently be discussed.

17.1 The organizational structure of the mother organization

In this section the principles on which the organizational structure of the Army is built will be described. One can say that, although the actual organizational structure of the Army changes all the time, the principles on which it is based remain relatively stable. This means that the principles can be regarded as a general context for the different crisis organizations in the cases. Furthermore, this structural context is not limited to the cases described in this study, but can be considered to be largely relevant for crisis organizations that are assembled by the Army. A more detailed description is not considered to be necessary because the general description can provide the necessary information that is needed here.

As a general description of the organizational structure of the Army, two organizational charts are displayed (model 17.2 and 17.3). These charts are 'edited' pictures of the larger organizational charts which are displayed in Appendix III. They are edited to display the most relevant information for our purposes here and they display the situation in January 2003. This situation may have changed, but its underlying principles will not have changed. The first picture (1 (GE/NL) C) shows the organizational chart of the mixed German and Dutch Army corps. The picture displays the '11 Air Man Bde' (air maneuver brigade; the mother organization of Dutchbat). What is furthermore relevant for our purposes is the box '1 DIV', which refers to a division. It can be seen that a division is built up of three 'MECHBRIGS' (mechanized brigades). In these brigades 'the Army's operational capacity' comes together. The second picture focuses on one particular brigade, '13 MECHBRIG'. Important is that this brigade is composed of functional parts (see the discussion below). The brigade consists of two infantry battalions (PAINFBAT), a cavalry-battalion (TKBAT) and an artillery battalion (AFDRA). Furthermore, the different battalions are built up of three or four companies.

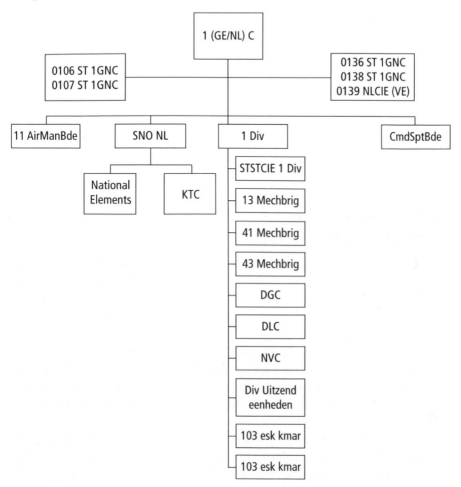

Model 17.2[112]

[112] DLC: Divisie Logistiek Commando (logistic units)
    AirManBde: Air Manoevre Brigade
    CmdSptBde: Command Support Brigade

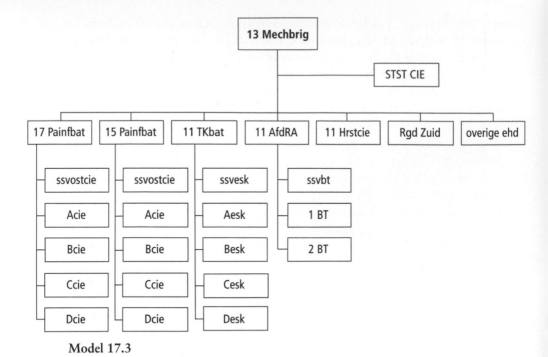

Model 17.3

It is important to establish that the organizational structure of the Army is predominantly designed for the so-called 'regular operations' (i.e. war). This is not the case for the Air Maneuver Brigade, which is built up from both Army and Air Force units. The discussion below is nevertheless relevant for this brigade as well, because Dutchbat was structured as a classical infantry battalion. Below, the organizational structure of the Army will be described on the basis of a number of defining characteristics. This means that, rather than providing a detailed organizational chart, the principles underlying the design of the organizational structure of the Army will be discussed. The reason for this is that the principles provide, what one could call, the 'logic of the organizational structure'. The following description is based on facts from the doctrine, part LDP II (Koninklijke Landmacht, 1998b). The doctrine is considered to be a suitable source because it specifies the principles of different kinds of military operation. Therefore the basic principles of the organizational structure are explicated as well.

- The configuration of the Army is divisional. The Army is split up into a number of 'smaller armies' that can, more or less, function as autonomous wholes because they integrate the different 'weapon departments' (Koninklijke Landmacht, 1998b, p. 108)[113]. The Army calls the division-

---

[113] I hesitate to use the phrase "autonomous whole" because the autonomy of the brigades is limited. It is autonomous because it integrates the different "weapon departments"; it is

al level 'brigade'[114]. A brigade consists of about 2,000–2,500 soldiers[115]. Different supportive functions are centralized at the level of the division (i.e. DLC – logistic command) or even at the level of the Army corps (Command Support Brigade) and not decentralized at the level of the brigade. This limits the autonomy of brigades.

- An important distinction within the organizational structure of the Army is between 'weapon departments' (the departments that are meant for the performance of the primary process) and 'service departments' (the departments meant for the supportive processes). This distinction inevitably means that soldiers originating from weapon departments are not considered to have control over supportive processes.

- The third important characteristic of the Army's organizational structure is that the brigades are built up on the basis of the principle of functional concentration (see also Kuipers & Kramer, 2002). The weapon departments are split up into groups of specialists. There are three major 'weapon components': the infantry, the cavalry and the artillery (Koninklijke Landmacht, 1998b, p. 109). Each of these weapon departments has its own specialist role on the battlefield. These departments are called 'battalions' and consist of about 600 soldiers. The consequence of this is that groups of soldiers with comparable specialties are clustered in the same department (this is the so-called functional concentration). Another consequence of this functional design is that there are fundamental dependencies between the various weapon departments in their regular operations. The actions of the artillery depend on the actions of the cavalry and the infantry. These dependencies are only clear on brigade level, so the brigade level has both an initializing and a coordinating function.

- A fourth characteristic is that a battalion is split up into a number of equal components, the companies (see also model 17.3). The companies are again built up of a number of equal components, the so-called platoons. One can therefore say that a battalion largely consists of groups performing comparable tasks. This task – for example, the task of the cavalry on the battlefield – is specified in detail in war doctrines.

- A fifth characteristic of the organizational structure is the distinction between performance and control activities at the level of the operational units. In military organizations this distinction is classical because of the distinction between officers and soldiers. The officer with the lowest rank is the lowest controller. The military doctrine that was discussed in the previous chapter implied this difference when it was stated that

---

limited because the staff level has a firm influence on many of the proceedings within the brigades.

[114] Confusingly, the level hierarchically above the brigades is called '1 DIV' (first division).

[115] It is important to realize that within organizational studies 2,500 soldiers is considered to be 'quite large', but for an Army it is considered to be 'relatively small'.

autonomy may be granted to the lower levels, but only to officers at these lower levels.

- A sixth characteristic of the organizational structure of the Army is that individual tasks are defined and precisely described. The tasks of a platoon are analyzed and split up into a number of constituent components. There is a definition of a standard platoon with each individual operating in a specific role. This specific role has to be trained extensively (see, for example, the KFOR case that was discussed earlier).

This is a rather superficial analysis of the characteristics of the organizational structure of the mother organization, but the general message is quite unequivocal. Functional concentration, a distinction between performance and control activities, a distinction between performance and supportive units (also called: specialization in performance activities), detailed task descriptions for individual soldiers (also called: division of performance activities) are all typical characteristics of a classical organizational structure aimed at a maximal division of labor (De Sitter, 2000). All in all, this results in an organization that can be characterized using Morgan's machine metaphor (1997, p. 18): 'If we implement these principles, we arrive at the kind of organization represented in the familiar organization chart (…): a pattern of precisely defined jobs organized in a hierarchical manner through precisely defined lines of command or communication. If we examine these principles closely, we find that the classical theorists were in fact designing the organization exactly as if they were designing a machine.' In sociotechnical literature it is considered a truism that in such organizations the prerequisites for self-organization are extremely bad.

Crisis organizations according to the Army

The Army is, of course, aware that crisis organizations are not designed for 'regular' operations and that such organizations need to be put together. This section focuses on what the Army itself says about putting units together. Crisis organizations are temporary configurations. This means that they exist only for the duration of the crisis operation. The temporary nature of their configuration makes that crisis organizations fall in the doctrine under the heading of task forces[116]. Snook (2000, p. 33) remarked: 'Task forces are designed by taking basic unit building blocks and assembling them along hierarchical lines consistent with the demands of the mission and time-honored military traditions of command and control.' There are different ways in which task forces can be assembled, depending on the

---

[116] The LDP II (Koninklijke Landmacht, 1998b, p. 104) distinguishes between:
- *"Organieke eenheden"* (regular) units; units that are deployed in their usual configuration;
- *"Taakgroepen"* (task forces) – units that are of a temporary configuration.
- *"Formaties"* (formations). A configuration of large troops.

nature of the 'basic building blocks' that are used. The LDP II (Koninklijke Landmacht, 1998b, p. 106) distinguished between:

- Reinforced units. A unit of a regular part of the organization with some additional units (e.g. logistic support) to make the organization suitable as a task force for specific purposes forms the basis of this task force;
- Mixed units. The basis is a regular part of the organization with one of the units subtracted and one unit from another organizational source added (e.g. a cavalry unit with one company subtracted and one infantry company added). The sum of units remains the same;
- Unit-'minus'. At least two parts of a regular part of an organization are subtracted to form a crisis organization.

The Army uses the first two options as a way to build crisis organizations. Dutchbat is an example of a reinforced unit with an infantry battalion as basis (also KFOR, which has not been studied systematically, is another example of a reinforced unit, with an artillery battalion as a basis). SFOR is an example of a mixed unit with a cavalry unit as a basis with an infantry unit added. Logtbat falls out of these categories. It appears to be a reinforced logistic unit. However, it is quite exceptional because one logistic company was subtracted and a Belgian company was added (the added unit, being, strictly speaking, not of a different nature) and because of the individual system rotation policy, units were not deployed as a whole.

An important question is how the mix is established within units. The doctrine gives some insight into how this mix should be accomplished in practice. This falls under the heading of '*teamoptreden*' (team operations). A team is a mix of infantry and cavalry platoons at company level. Suppose that a taskforce is built up of a cavalry company (three platoons) and an infantry company. In the team concept both companies swap one platoon. The result is one team with two cavalry platoons and one infantry platoon and one team with two infantry platoons and one cavalry platoon (Koninklijke Landmacht, 1998b, p. 109). SFOR and IFOR are both examples of team operations. The mix is – officially – not continued beyond the company level. That means that – officially – platoons are not to be mixed and therefore the actual operators are not to be confronted with other 'types' of soldiers. The cases provided examples of team-commanders that had the freedom to form units to their liking. Team B, for example, in the SFOR operation was mixed beyond the platoon level. The IFOR case, which was not worked out in this study, provided probably the best example of two neighboring teams that mixed their platoons differently. One team mixed cavalry and infantry at platoon level, another team kept cavalry and infantry strictly apart (Vogelaar c.s., 1997b).

17.2 The influence of the assembly process

The fact that crisis organizations are considered to be task forces indicates that assembly is necessary. Depending on the specifics of an operation, the nature of the assembly process can differ. It is suggested here that the process of assembly negatively influences self-organization: the more complicated the process of assembly is, the less crisis organizations will intend to design self-organizing units. After all, the more complicated the assembly process, the more the crisis organization consists of fragmented groups from different origins in the mother organization. In that case the crisis organization consists of units that do not normally operate together. There are two sources for the complexity of the assembly process:

- *Building block complexity.* In the first place the complexity of the assembly process is determined by the number of different building blocks that are necessary to form a crisis organization. If the crisis organization exists as a whole in the mother organization, no assembly will be necessary. In that case, an integral part of the mother organization can be 'picked up' and put in the crisis operation and it can function 'as usual'. In this instance of an extremely simple assembly process, the preconditions for self-organization are particularly good. After all, the crisis organization is designed to function as a whole. Nevertheless, this instance is not realistic in the present day Army. The Army should be changed fundamentally to make this possible. Opposed to the no-assembly option, one can imagine a situation of absolute assembly. In that case a crisis organization consisting of 600 soldiers could originate from 600 different units in the mother organization. In that particular case one can imagine that the preconditions of designing self-organizing units would be extremely bad. In the reality of the present-day Army, the complexity of the assembly process is likely to fall in between the extremes of no assembly and absolute assembly.
- *Complexity of the internal construction.* In the second place, the complexity of the assembly process is determined by 'the nature of the internal construction' that is necessary to create a functioning crisis organization out of raw building blocks. One can imagine that two teams that exist as a whole within the mother organization are assembled to form a crisis organization. In that case, the effects of assembly would be less negative compared to a situation in which two units from the mother organization are mixed to form two teams (e.g. cavalry and infantry). In other words, if the different building blocks can operate as self-organizing units, the effects of assembly on self-organization are less serious. If the nature of the units that are assembled is such that they make a 'modular' construction within crisis organizations possible, the prerequisites for self-organization are better compared to a situation in which units have to be mixed

extensively. Given this assumption there are two sources that complicate the internal construction: (1) if the original building blocks are mixed at the operational level, and (2) if operational units are structurally dependent on other units (for supportive processes, etc.).

The organizational structure of the mother organization influences both sources of complexity. An organizational structure 'groups' and 'couples', therefore the organizational structure determines the nature of departments and groups within the mother organization. The nature of the departments and groups determines whether they are suited to be deployed integrally into a crisis area and whether building blocks can handle a job integrally if they are dependent upon planners, supportive units, etc.

The process of assembly and the organizational structure

In this section it is discussed how the organizational structure of the mother organization influences the complexity of the assembly process. In a number of distinctive ways the existing structure of the mother organization complicates the process of assembly. With respect to the two sources of complexity one can remark the following about the present organizational structure of the mother organization.

- *Building block complexity.* Given the nature of the mother organization the chance that 'whole' units can integrally handle a certain task is not that substantial/great. The mother organization is not designed for crisis operations. Consequently 'whole crisis-units' are not available in the Army, which means that some assembly will always be necessary (that is the implication of the definition of 'task forces'). Within the existing structure one can only achieve 'broadly skilled units' by mixing various units. As the mother organization is built up of specialists and the crisis organization, as a whole, needs enough variety to deal with its environment (the principle of requisite variety applied to a crisis organization as a whole) a complex process of assembly is an inevitable consequence of functional concentration. **The assemblers need to 'shop' in the various functional groups and departments in order to find enough variety for an organization to be able to operate in crisis operations.** This has far-reaching consequences. For example, the SFOR rotation we studied was built up of soldiers that originated from 57 different departments in the mother organization. This fragmentation of a crisis organization shows why the intention to design self-organizing units is limited. It should be added that this fragmentation is not only due to functional concentration but also to the fact that – at the time we studied SFOR – different battalions in the Army were not up to their required strength and needed to 'borrow' soldiers from other battalions in the Army. The prerequisites for self-organization in *reinforced units* should be better than in mixed units. The backbone of reinforced units is formed by a part of the regular organization, with units added for the purpose of the operation. In *mixed units*, such as SFOR, even the operational units are composed from units of different origin, which implies that more building blocks are necessary.

- *Complexity of the internal construction.* If specialized units (units that need to clear mines, or need to build barracks) are deployed to perform a specialized job, construction complexity will be less because these units can indeed be deployed in a 'modular way'. Opposed to that, if units from the traditional brigades in the Army need to perform tasks such as displayed in Figure 11.2 in Chapter Eleven, the internal construction becomes more difficult. If units are mixed on operational level (i.e. in *mixed units*) the prerequisites for self-organization are obviously not very good. In that case it is possible that people have to cooperate who are unacquainted on a personal level, unfamiliar with each other's routines and in a totally new hierarchy (e.g. the 11 elements of SFOR). However, also in *reinforced* units the prerequisites are not very good. Functional concentration of the mother organization complicates the process of internal construction of the crisis organization. As a result of the principle of functional concentration, the weapon departments of the mother organization are not designed to have control over supportive processes. If supportive units are added, the structural complexity of the crisis organization increases and autonomy of operational units decreases.

One can conclude that different characteristics of the organizational structure of the mother organization complicate the assembly process. Both types of task force need a complicated process of assembly to become functioning crisis organizations. Mixed units need to be built up from different building blocks and there is a good chance that these blocks need to be mixed as well. Reinforced units are constructed out of fewer building blocks, but internally these task forces can be structurally complex. In later sections it will be argued that reinforced units suffer a second disadvantage: because the Army is not designed for crisis operations, these units need to perform tasks that are unfamiliar' to them.

The 'direction' of assembly

The mother organization is designed for large-scale operations. Within the large-scale brigade operation, a platoon is built to perform its specialist job. Crisis operations have, so far, not been that large-scaled. In operations such as IFOR, SFOR, and KFOR, the Dutch units that were deployed were not larger than a battalion (+/– 600). Crisis operations are therefore relatively small-scale operations. This inevitably means that a contingent of about 600 soldiers is taken out of a brigade. A brigade is, however, designed to operate as a whole. The different parts of the brigade have tasks that fit into the logic of an operational brigade. The identity of the parts, in other words, is determined by the larger whole they are part of. The consequence of this is that soldiers are taken out of the organization in which the definition of their task makes sense.

Because of the nature of the organizational structure of the mother organization, the process of assembly has an inevitable logic. Within the current logic of assembly of the Army, assembling a crisis organization is a process that runs in the direction from 'large' to 'small'. From a large organization parts are taken out and put together. These parts have a specialist background. Their job makes sense in a large-scale operation of a different kind. Units are cut from the context in which their tasks and routines make sense to become rather unfitting blocks for the purposes of a certain mission. One can also imagine a 'logic of assembly' that runs from small to large. In that case, small 'holographic' units are put together to form a crisis organization[117]. A large unit is in that case a collection of small-scale 'holographic' units. The process of assembly is an inevitable consequence of the organizational structure of the Army. If one aims to change 'the logic of assembly' that is being used, it is necessary to structurally change the mother organization.

17.3 The direct effect of the organizational structure

The disadvantages of the type of structural design of the mother organization are extensively analyzed and discussed in sociotechnical literature. This section discusses general disadvantages of the organizational structure of the Army without a direct link to crisis operations. Disadvantages of the principle of functional concentration are that it creates 'structural complexity' because of the difficult coordination between organizational columns, which makes an organization less efficient, less flexible, and less controllable

---

[117] The terminology that is being used here can lead to some confusion. According to the sociotechnical design logic, organizations should be designed from "large" to "small". First, tasks are divided at macro-level. Subsequently, tasks are divided at meso-level. According to Kuipers & Van Amelsvoort (1990), this design logic is necessary if one aims to implement a philosophy of minimal division of labor. This is a design logic that is orientated at the design of individual organizations. The "small" to "large" direction that I propose here refers to the assembly of complete organizational components, which is actually a different topic. Organizations that are assembled from small to large consist of units that can operate relatively independent and therefore the prerequisites for self-organization are better.

(e.g. Kuipers & Van Amelsvoort, 1990; De Sitter, 2000; Kuipers & Kramer, 2002b). The acts of one platoon of specialists are structurally dependent on other parts of the organization: the artillery, the infantry and cavalry can only act when they are aware of each other's location and movements. This awareness is created by means of complex mechanisms of coordination. The difficult dependencies between parts of the organization are not insightful at the operational level, which means that they become entangled in dense webs of regulations and orders. Such organizations need a large techno-structure in order to establish the necessary coordination. Furthermore, the emphasis on rules and procedures does not positively influence the quality of working life (De Sitter, 2000; Kuipers & Kramer, 2002b). A frequently mentioned advantage is that groups of specialists are well-skilled in their respective specialist areas and up to date regarding, for example, state of the art technology. This advantage is challenged by De Sitter (2000) who argued that true innovation necessitates synergy of different specialists, which is not stimulated by putting them in different columns of organizations.

These are, however, disadvantages of this particular type of organizational structure related to their regular operations. This is not the topic of this study. The Army is designed for a specific type of operation: all-out war, more specifically, on a concept of what 'all-out war' entails. A consequence of this is that crisis operations are, in the logic of the design, exceptional operations. This is represented in model 17.2 by the box DIV UITZEND EHDN (which could be translated as 'diverse crisis organizations'). The paradox in this state of affairs is that the operations that are performed on a regular basis are, in the logic of the design, exceptions and not the real work. One can nevertheless hypothesize that in an organization that is built upon the principle of functional concentration and that is dependent upon the precise following of orders and routines, concepts like self-organization, doubt, and argumentation remain rather underdeveloped. One can therefore reasonably hypothesize that crisis organizations inherit characteristics of 'the original'.

Not made for crisis operations

Perhaps the most eye-catching characteristic of the organizational structure of the mother organization is that it is not designed to perform crisis operations. The organizational structure of the Army is made for traditional warfare on battlefields. Not incidentally these traditional battles are called 'regular missions'. A basic brigade is essentially built up of the 'weapon departments' (infantry, cavalry, and artillery), departments that are built up of *specialists* that have a particular role on the battlefield. Infantry is the department with the 'ground forces', cavalry is the department with 'the tanks' and artillery is the department with 'the heavy guns'. It is expected that on a battlefield all three are needed. After the Army adopted crisis op-

230

erations as one of its central jobs, it did not change the orientation of their organizational structure.

There is a particular consequence for crisis organizations that is relevant. During crisis operations, units are confronted with tasks, roles, and problems they are not familiar with. Units have, for the most part, a neutral role during crisis operations, they have to perform tasks like social patrols, helping to build up local resources, and accompanying refugees to their former homes, taking over the role of the fire brigade, etc. Furthermore, they are confronted with situations in which they are provoked but not allowed to act. Also, compared to war, performing crisis operations can be considered a 'boring' occupation. Most importantly perhaps, operational units can be confronted with a diversity of tasks that are unpredictable in advance and with a whole range of problems that are equally unpredictable. The best example of this is perhaps KFOR, where operational units took over the role of the fire-brigade. The nature of crisis operations demands that operational units are broadly orientated rather than specialized.

This results in units that are not suited to the demands of the task environment. In the present-day Army it is rather likely that units are deployed whose original task has nothing to do with complexities in the environment. After all, if an environment demands that units are able to patrol, to build checkpoints at strategic locations and take over the role of the fire brigade, a mix of infantry and cavalry does not contribute to the establishment of units that are able to conduct these different tasks. It is as if one aims to create a unit of car mechanics by mixing painters and carpenters. Furthermore, a broadly skilled unit is different from a unit consisting of 'a mix of specialists'. Essential in a 'broadly skilled unit' is that members are not single-mindedly focused on one task, but *individually* have a broad orientation on the demands in the task environment. One does not create such ability by putting together two types of specialist. Such a strategy would be called 'redundancy of parts' by Morgan, which can be translated as 'adding spare parts'. This strategy is fundamentally different from the sociotechnical philosophy of 'redundancy of functions' (Morgan, 1997). Not only is a specialist's mind not very suited for crisis operations, it certainly is not very suited if the specialty is largely irrelevant for the operation in hand.

17.4 Hypotheses about the influence of the organizational structure

On the basis of this analysis, one can propose the following hypotheses about the influence of the organizational structure on the ability to design self-organizing units.

I. *There are different ways in which the current organizational structure of the Army can potentially hinder the intention to design self-organizing units.* The Army is not made for crisis operations; it is built up of specialists, and is made for large-scale operations. The organization is, furthermore, not made for assembly. Already in the simplest form of assembly (assembling a task force) the Army's ability to design self-organizing units is seriously undermined. When put together, these reasons reinforce one another.

Chapter 18

The influence of leadership structures

The analysis of the case studies showed that the leaders in the crisis organization defined their role in a classical way. There was little indication that argumentation and doubt were considered important by leaders. Perhaps it occurred only in the Logtbat case, but as a consequence of Logtbat's rotation policy the circumstances gave leaders no other choice. If they had a choice, for example in the SFOR case, leaders defined their role in a classical way. One can suggest that the way leadership is defined in the mother organization influences the way leaders defined their role. The hypothesis on which the analysis in this chapter is based is: the way the leadership role was defined in the cases is influenced by the way the leadership function is implemented in the mother organization. In the earlier parts of this study this has been called 'leadership structures'. These leadership structures refer to the way the leadership function is implemented in the Army organization. Leadership structures are considered to have both a conscious and unconscious influence on the way leaders define their role[118]. The analysis of the characteristics of the leadership structures will not claim that certain leadership structures inevitably have a bad influence on the intention to design self-organizing units. Rather, leadership structures are considered to influence the definition of leadership in the cases. Therefore it is important for the mother organization to create leadership structures that stimulate argumentation. Below, a number of characteristic leadership structures will be discussed that can provide insight into the way the role of leaders is implemented in the Army.

---

[118] A crucial note is that the mother organization is not the only force that influences the definition of leadership. The discussion of the cases in Part Four showed that this definition depended on the circumstances and on personal characteristics of a leader. In the particular circumstances of Logtbat, leaders were not able to fulfill a "centralistic" role and some characteristics of a climate in which argumentation was stimulated were recognizable. Again, this has to do with the issue of causality.

18.1 The nature of the leadership structures

The leadership structures that are discussed in this chapter are not selected on the basis of an analytical model. Instead, the discussions in this chapter can be regarded as an exploration of the leadership structures in the Army. One could consider this to be an arbitrary procedure of selection. A likely criticism would be that I have selected those structures that support the general argument in this study. In my opinion there are two arguments to contradict such a claim:

- Although one can question whether the present discussion presents a complete picture of the leadership structures in the Army, one can state that the leadership structures that are discussed are particularly important. For example, De Sitter (2000) stated that characteristics of the organizational structure are the most important predictors of the behavior of leaders.
- The discussions of the various structures present an unequivocal picture. There is little evidence that the leadership structures within the Army support leaders to stimulate argumentation and aim to create a spirit of contradiction. On the contrary, within the present leadership climate it would not be surprising that leaders do not even develop the thought that argumentation is important.

18.2 The leadership structures

In the following, various leadership structures will be explored. Their assumed effects on leadership in crisis organizations will subsequently be discussed. The picture that is drawn of the various leadership structures hides an interesting contradiction. On the one hand, leaders are not supportive of argumentation with those they lead because their officer-status elevates them to a position that makes them 'too superior to argue'. On the other hand, leaders in the Army are part of a restrictive hierarchy that makes an individual leader rather powerless. Although there is little room available here to work out an explanation for this contradiction, I tend towards a psychoanalytical account: Images of nobility and superiority serve to push a reality of powerlessness away from consciousness.

The organizational structure

Within sociotechnical theory it has been well-established, both empirically and theoretically, that leadership is strongly influenced by the structural regime of the organization (De Sitter, 1970, 2000; Kuipers, 1989b). An organizational structure can bind the operational work to strict and detailed rules. This has an important influence on the leadership role. One can therefore claim that the existing structural regime is an important leadership structure, in other words, an implementation of the leadership function that determines how leaders define their role.

In the previous chapter the existing structure of the Army has been discussed. It was concluded that the principles of the organizational structure of the Army are classical and can be characterized by Morgan's machine metaphor. This is a structural regime that binds the operational level to strict rules. As a consequence, leaders at the lower hierarchical levels have a relatively low degree of freedom themselves. They are unable to doubt and argue the existing operational rules, because these rules are a necessary consequence of the structural regime. Leadership in classical organizations is consequent with consistent the existing structural regime, which is understandable because the organizational structure shapes the tasks of leaders. It should be added that assembly breaks the chains of the existing structure. However, the previous chapter has shown that the effects of assembly are likely to have a more restricting effect.

Command and control

In order to understand the activities of individuals in a military organization, one should be familiar with the concepts of command and control (Snook, 2000). Command refers to 'communicating intent and providing direction' and control is considered necessary to set limits and provide structure (Snook, 2000, p. 31). Snook described the situation in the US Army. However, the situation of the US Army and the Dutch Armed Forces are comparable. The twin-concepts of command and control can be compared to the Dutch concept of *commandovoering* (Koninklijke Landmacht, 1998b, p. 38). It is necessary to describe these concepts because they can explain why leadership structures in the Army are built up in a particular way. Snook about this: 'The twin-concepts of command and control and those systems designed to execute these functions structure the formal flow of communication and coordination in complex military organizations. To fully understand any behavior of interest in a military organization (...) we have to first understand how such action is influenced by complex systems of command and control'.

The brief definition of command reveals that it has to do with how authority is structured in military organizations. The 'chain of command' describes how the authority of a central commander flows down to a local commander. The existing system of ranks, which is a very visible characteristic of a military organization, reveals who has authority over whom. A basic principle of command is that someone is always in charge. Snook (2000, p. 33): 'Someone is always in charge; someone is always responsible; and knowing who that is at all times is of utmost importance. Commanders are responsible for everything their units do or fail to do.' As a matter of fact, one of the first things new recruits at the Military Academy learn is that they can be punished for something that someone else did if they were formally in command. It does not matter if they were personally involved in the forbidden activities; it even does not matter if the forbidden activities were such that the one formally in charge could not reasonably have anticipated them. Another basic principle of command is 'unity of command', which means that the chain between highest and lowest commander is unbroken. No individual military wanders through an area without being an identifiable member of the pyramid of command, no individual military acts without this act being a part of the intentions of the higher commander, to which he has an explicit relation.

The control process is meant as a series of supplemental coordinating mechanisms. Snook (2000, p. 34): 'In generic terms, all actions within military organizations are guided by a broad set of doctrine, tactics, techniques and procedures'. One must think about manuals that describe how to use material, principles that describe how the doctrine should be applied, procedures that prescribe military conduct, etc.'[119]. Snook (2000, p. 37): '(...) series of local procedures not only supplement general command guidance contained in higher level orders and plans, but they also attempt to integrate such broad mission-specific direction with a whole host of existing standard technical publications. Individual service member behavior is not only guided by direct lawful instructions from their chain of command, but also by more task-orientated direction contained in volumes of technical orders, training manuals, service regulations handbooks and operator manuals'[120].

---

[119] One of the first curious things I encountered when I started to work in a military organization is that it is often made explicit that at a specific occasion, there will be no specific dress code for civilians. In other words, it is felt necessary to make **explicit** that there is **no** dress code. This subtlety reveals an important aspect of military thinking: the state of "no orders" is considered to be the abnormal state that has to be officially announced.

[120] Interestingly, Scott Snook, who analyzed a case of friendly fire, draws a parallel between this dense web of orders, rules and regulations and the concept of a total institution such as it is described by Goffman (1961): "This general insight is not new; however, a particularly unique and powerful aspect of military organizational contexts is the broad framework of command and control relationships within which all individual and collective behavior is embedded" (Snook, 2000, p. 39). He subsequently claimed that this perhaps *appears* to be overwhelming. However, because it is part of the matter-of-course world of the military, he proposed that it fades into the background, becoming context, be it important context. This seems a conclusion with a strange twist. One could also reason that especially because it is taken for granted it becomes even more important because the system implicitly influences the behavior of individuals. On top of that, Snook himself emphasized the importance of context on the behavior of individuals in an organization. It seems therefore contradictory to claim that the system is not overwhelming because it fades into the background. I want to propose an explanation with again a psychoanalytical flavor. Snook himself used to be an officer. It is my experience that officers may be rather critical of aspects of the military organization. Snook's excellent case study is an example of that. When it comes to criticize the

It should be underlined that the concepts of command and control are consequent with the classical view of organizations. 'Command and control' describe the instructions for the machine. This study has emphasized that hierarchy is a functional phenomenon. As such the coordinating mechanisms described above do not need to be dysfunctional. One can imagine that it is important in a crisis area that the organization knows where its members are; one can imagine it is important that soldiers observe the Rules of Engagement. However, the most important argument throughout this study has been that an organization cannot deal with dynamic complexity on the basis of top-down control alone. Instead, bottom-up insights and bottom-up meaningful action are of essential importance to a crisis organization. This study is therefore not opposed to a system of command and control; it is opposed to a single-minded emphasis on command and control. If this emphasis is not counterbalanced by the establishment of bottom-up structures, then a system of command and control as it is described here contributes to leaders emphasizing central control and not recognizing the importance of self-organization, doubt, argumentation, and contradiction. According to the logic of this study, this leads to organizations that essentially underestimate the complexity of the environment.

The distinction between officers and soldiers

The foregoing focused on the 'powerless part' of the leadership role. Here I want to focus on a 'superiority part'. Traditionally, in any Army, a distinction is made between officers and soldiers. This originated from the distinction between the 'nobility' and the 'commons'. In the past, the nobility occupied the positions of the 'the thinkers' and the commons the place of the 'the doers'. This distinction is, of course, a characteristic of all present-day armies. What I like to point out is that this distinction carries a specific connotation which runs counter to the idea that leaders should stimulate a spirit of contradiction.

Dixon (1976) showed that – in the English Army – it has not been uncommon for officers to feel extremely superior[121]. What is interesting about Dixon's claim is that these feelings of extreme superiority are not a queer

fundaments of the military organization, however, officers tend to go out of their way to find rationalizations.

[121] Consider the following quote of an English officer speaking about his men (Dixon, 1976, p. 229): "They are rather like pet animals", he said to me of his men one day. 'One must keep them clean and properly fed, so that they do not get diseased and are in good working order. One must teach them to react swiftly and without thought to certain external stimuli or signals. Just as you whistle for a dog, so must there be certain simple and easily recognizable forms of words for the men. (...). They must expect, and on the whole receive, justice – a lump of sugar when they have done well, a whipping when they have been disobedient (...).' The officer went on and on, but the tendency will be clear.

leftover from the past; it is a fairly recent phenomenon. In the past, the nobility felt superior, but given the fact that society at large was structured in this way, they took their superiority for granted.[122] It is known that sometimes there are cadets of the Military Academy in Breda that refer to themselves as 'Sons of God' (Kuipers, 2003). The distinction between officers and soldiers is therefore anything but neutral.

Furthermore, the way the distinction is implemented within the Army is certainly not supportive of argumentation. The officers within the Army form a closed group of rulers. One cannot reach the higher ranks without first having worked at the lowest officer-rank, but one does not need to have worked as a soldier (unlike in the German Army). The highest general has worked as a platoon-commander. The consequence of this is that the highest general has been in the Army for about thirty years. Leaders in the Army are therefore in a way isolated from influences from outside the Army. In this way, the existing culture is sustained. Furthermore, almost all officers in the Army are trained and educated at the Military Academy in Breda, certainly the ones in the higher ranks. In this respect, the Military Academy really is a 'founding institute'[123].

18.3 The education of leaders

One particular leadership structure that deserves specific attention is the Military Academy. Leaders in the Army are trained and educated at the Military Academy in Breda. Before they start at an operational function they have been educated at the Academy for a number of years. In a number of ways the Military Academy can be said to emphasize the role of leaders as 'rulers' rather than as the people that emphasize contradiction and argumentation. At the same time, the Academy demands conformity, thus creating an institute that seems almost the epitome of a classic view on leadership. I believe I can support these claims by drawing upon analyses from others. A number of typical characteristics of the Military Academy as an institute are discussed here. It should again be emphasized that these are explorations and not a systematic analysis of the topic. Therefore the results

---

[122] Dixon (1976, p. 233): 'Nowadays things are different. The social distance between officers and men is, more often than not, contrived rather than rooted in their ancestry. For officers of humble origins this might well be expected to produce sizable problems of adjustment. The first jolt to their social reinforcement standard will be one of positive discrepancy. From being nobodies they suddenly find themselves elevated on to an institutionalized pedestal of dizzying proportions.'

[123] It is, however, not the only training institute for officers. In later parts of their careers, officers that display promising talent follow a distinctive "career path" with specific "staff training" to match.

of these discussions are hypotheses that may be the starting point for further research.

A distinct goal of the Military Academy is the establishment of an 'elite' (Moelker & Richardson, 2002). Currently the education at the Military Academy is built up of three 'cornerstones': the 'officer corps' (for the process of personality development), the 'military instruction' (in order to learn the basic military skills) and the 'academic study' (in order to build up a scientific attitude). The officer corps is an informal network of leaders. An important reason for its existence is the thought that the corps consists of people that can be trusted in difficult circumstances (Klinkert, 1998). In theory the members of the officer corps are expected to be trustworthy because they are 'socialized into the values of the corps' and because of the informal bonds that exist between the members. One can therefore say that leaders within the Army are part of a strong informal network that has been established in the early phases of their careers.

The Military Academy possesses some modern educational views. These are represented by the acronym ZACVEM. The Military Academy explicitly aims to educate leaders that possess so called ZACVEM qualities (in Dutch: *Zelfstandigheid, Activiteit, Creativiteit, Verantwoordelijkheidsbewustzijn, Ethisch bewust, Milieubewust*). This can be translated as independence (Z), initiative (A), creativity (C), sense of responsibility (V) ethical awareness (E) and environmental awareness (M). One could read an argumentative spirit into this short list of qualities. The ZACVE (I will not take the M into account because it appears to have been added for purposes of political correctness) characteristics are supposed to be found in leaders. One could interpret ZACVE as a first step towards argumentation. Again, my conclusion will be that this is not the case and that ZACVE fulfils a rhetorical role. This claim is based on the thought that ZACVE cannot possibly prosper in an organizational context as currently exists at the Military Academy. The restricting influence of this organizational context is discussed in the subsequent sections.

Socialization

The values that constitute the cornerstones of this officer corps are heavily socialized into the new recruits (Moelker & Richardson, 2002). As a result of that, Kuipers (2003) concluded that the Military Academy puts strong forces on recruits to conform, a conclusion that was shared by Ramakers (2003). In order to reach these goals, the Military Academy has explicitly been formed on the basis of the principles of the total institution as described by Goffman, although the Military Academy is not a total institution in its purest form (Moelker & Richardson, 2002). This is not the place to discuss the ins and outs of Goffman's theory of the total institution; however, one particular aspect of his theory is relevant here. One of the most penetrating concepts of Goffman is mortification. According to Goffman (1965), total institutions explicitly aim to 'break down' the existing individuality of their members in order to replace it by an ego that is handed over by the institute. These rites of mortification are certainly recognizable in the Military Academy (Moelker & Richardson, 2002) as an explicit tool of socialization. One can question if argumentation and mortification are compatible. My conclusion is that they are incompatible. For example, a particular peculiarity of cadets that was noted by Vroom (2003) is that hierarchy becomes to be perceived as a panacea (a solution for all problems). Heijster claimed that the institute functions as a means to create clones with a standard outlook on reality, a standard idea of the nature of problems, and a standard idea on how to solve them (Heijster, 2003). A particularly visible aspect of socialization is the ceremony of initiation[124]. The ceremony of initiation is built up of ingredients that are essentially repressive and humiliating (Ramakers, 2003). Frequently it is defended as a way to teach the cadets the 'values of the officer corps'.

It is questionable whether such a ceremony stimulates a spirit of contradiction. In fact, Heijster (2003) claimed that one of the first things cadets learn is that a critical attitude is fiercely punished. One official justification for the initiation rites is that 'the individual' should offer private interests for group interests'. Another official justification of the initiation rite at the Academy is that it is supposed to build psychological toughness (Soeters, 2003). 'The strong survive', in other words. Ramakers (2003) remarked that it is questionable whether physical and psychological 'toughness' can be trained by means of repression. Besides, if one considers the ability to contradict a quality that necessitates psychological strength then not the strong survive, but the weak. I like to claim that the initiation is more than 'training'. Instead, I claim that it is a 'ceremony of conformity to the powers-that-be'. Furthermore, the officer corps as such can be seen as a 'formal-informal' (or 'a formally implemented informal circuit') group of people that occupy the most important functions in the Army. As such, one can interpret the officer corps to be a 'guardian' of the existing Army culture, or perhaps better phrased, a guardian of the existing 'power structures' in the organization, which one enters through conformity after humiliation.

Opponents of this view will probably claim that there is a substantial gap between total institutions such as monasteries in the Middle Ages and the Military Academy today. They are, of course, right. The regime at the

---

[124] Those who want to justify the ceremony often claim that 'new recruits understand that it is merely a game'. I also believe that – in itself – the ceremony as a tool of socialization is not as important as everyday life at the academy. However, the ceremony would merely be a silly game if it was in entire contrast with everyday reality at the Academy. The fact that the Academy cherishes the total institution as an ideal shows that it is not merely a game. As such, the ceremony becomes a suitable symbol for discussing the total institution.

Military Academy and the regime at the prototypical total institutions are worlds apart. The boarding-school system, for example, is no longer absolutely obligatory (Groen & Klinkert, 2003). What is crucial for the argument here is that the educational philosophy still is derived from Goffman's description of total institutions. Various kinds of developments make a 'pure' total institution not realistic. In the logic of educational philosophy, 'the ideal' is therefore threatened by outside forces. Not incidentally, Groen & Klinkert presented a picture of decay when they discussed the place of the officer corps at the present-day Academy (2003, pp. 546–550). They appeared to interpret deviations from 'the ideal' (i.e. a less restrictive total institution) as a threat to the (superior) values that traditionally constituted the officer corps. Against these claims I want to put forward that one can question whether repression is a way to teach values. In a way, repression goes against the essence of 'values' because it takes out the 'voluntary' part.

My conclusion on this point is on par with Sagan's (1993) remarks about 'total institutions'. Granting that *organizational control over members* can be advantageous in certain circumstances, Sagan (1993, p. 254) remarks: 'In any "total institution" (wheter it is a military command or a mental hospital) the official goal of the organization (to protect society, for example, or to serve patients) coexists with a set of more parochial, self-serving organizational objectives (to promote and to protect itself). Because this is the case, strong "organizational control over members" can be used not only to promote the official goal of the organization, but also more narrow self-interests. This can encourage excessive loyalty and secrecy, disdain for outside expertise, and in some cases even cover-ups of safety problems, in order to protect the reputation of the institution'.

Isolation

The Academy is isolated from the rest of the organization because after their recruitment the cadets start directly at the Academy[125]. After their education at the Academy they will occupy an officer position within the Dutch Armed Forces (the Military Academy also educates officers for the Air Force and the Military Police). One can wonder whether it is ideal that recruits are educated in an institute that is more or less isolated from the rest of the organization. The consequence of this is that until cadets start in an officer

---

[125] In an interview, a higher officer at the Academy has recently rejected the claim that the Military Academy is isolated. He pointed to the initiatives that are being employed to bring the outside world into the academy, for example by means of public lectures (Karels & Hager, 2003). In my view, this is beside the point. The academy is isolated from the outside world not merely because a canal surrounding the campus prevents the outside world to visit the Academy. The academy is isolated because leaders are educated outside the organization and because the particular philosophy of socialization is effectuated by means of isolation. These different ways of isolation work against an idea of developing an argumentative spirit.

position, they have not seen a soldier from close-by (so to speak). Instead, for a number of years they have been indoctrinated with ideas about elite, about loyalty (one could also say 'another word for being non-critical'), the 'values of the officer corps' (one could also say, 'conformity to traditional power structures'), and 'true comrades' (one could also say 'the social structures that replace the normal ties in the outside world')[126]. Meaningful argumentation necessitates a healthy link with the outside world. Furthermore, meaningful argumentation necessitates an open and critical interest in this outside world.

The intellectual climate at the Academy

On the basis of personal experience, I can certainly confirm that there exists a distinct culture of anti-intellectualism among cadets[127], a problem that is also observed by Dixon (1976) within the English Army. The symptoms are a chronic lack of attention to the study with the expectable meager results, chronic demotivation, chronic culture of complaint, chronic pressure on instructors to lower norms, etc. (Sagan: disdain for outside expertise). Groen & Klinkert (2003) discussed that lack of attention for the academic side is a problem that has existed in the entire history of the Academy. One can claim that an academic climate is important for an officer education because particularly in an academic climate 'argumentation' is essential. The cases that have been discussed in this study indicate that the modern operations the Army is becoming involved in demand well developed intellectual qualities. An evaluation study of the Academic study revealed that although formally the largest part of the scheduled time is reserved for the academic study, a significantly smaller proportion of this formal time is actually devoted to the study by the larger part of the cadets (Kuipers c.s., 1999).

There are various reasons why such a climate may exist at the Military Academy. One reason has already been mentioned: cadets that start at the Military Academy are orientated to their officer function and not at the intellectual challenges an academic study might offer. Furthermore, Kuipers c.s. (1999) concluded that because of the nature of an academic style of working (more free time for studying, less time specifically scheduled, not a clear relation between input and result) and the nature of the other cornerstones (rather tightly scheduled; direct and visible relation between input and result) the academic study plays second fiddle. Moelker & Richardson

---

[126] Apart from this, one can argue that the isolation is not beneficial for the academy itself: cadets do not attend the academy because they are interested in the topics that are being taught. For many, the academy a barrier that needs be taken before they can become officers (Kuipers c.s., 1999). As such, the interest for the academic study is structurally undermined.

[127] Cadets with a true interest in academic topics are ridiculed, there are collective efforts to lower norms, an attitude of utter boredom and disinterest is hailed, the abstract nature of academic issues is taken as evidence of their irrelevance, etc.

(2002) concluded that the current structure at the Academy develops a 'gray mice' attitude. Kuipers (2003) suggested furthermore that the fact that the academic study is subjected to the military hierarchy has adverse effects on its status. The result of this is, according to Kuipers (2003), that the academic study is, in the end, not capable of holding on to its own norms. Because cadets recognize the way the power is distributed in the organization, the status of the academic study deteriorates. This state of affairs has, according to Kuipers (2003), also an effect on the culture within the organization (educators with a more significant loyalty towards the military organization than to their profession). According to Kuipers (2003), the academic study should gain an independent status, comparable with the situation in Germany.

18.4 Hypotheses about the influence of leadership

Based on the analyses in this chapter it seems reasonable to suggest the following hypotheses on the influence of leadership structures on the ability of the Army to design self-organizing units:

I.   *The existing leadership structures fit the existing classical structural regime.* That is, the existing leadership structures emphasize the centralistic role of leaders. The existing structural regime leaves few other options than such a role. Furthermore, this role of leaders has been firmly established within the 'leadership culture' of the Army. The elite is perhaps prepared to argue amongst themselves, however, the claim that argumentation with all ranks is important is nowhere to be found.

II. *One can question whether argumentation among officers is truly emphasized.* On the basis of the discussion of the leadership structures one can conclude that emphasis is laid on the role of 'all must come from the leader' and the establishment of leaders as the ruling class within the organization. On the other hand, the classical nature of the organization makes that leaders at many positions in the organization are quite powerless. Indeed, notwithstanding heroic rhetoric one becomes an officer through severe conformity.

III. *The leadership structures discussed here possess the causal potential to hinder self-organization in crisis operations.* The exploration of leadership showed that a crucial element of leadership is not available in the Army's philosophy of leadership. Any thought on doubt, argumentation and a spirit of contradiction is not available. This confirms the hypothesis that the Army is orientated to dealing with dynamic complexity in a top-down manner. For this reason it can be questioned whether the Army aims to train and educate leaders to lead self-organizing units.

The thinking at the operational level, if it is allowed, is supposed to be conducted by the leader, between the borders of a top-down fence. It was shown that leaders in the cases did not portray themselves as stimulators of doubt and contradiction. The only example in which they did so was Logtbat. In this case, however, leaders were, as a result of the rotation policy, put in a powerless position which led them no other option than using insights of the lower levels.

PART VI

It would go too far to consider Part Six truly 'a part' of this study as it only consists of Chapter Nineteen. Nevertheless, this chapter can be logically distinguished from the other parts of this study and is therefore set apart from the rest of this study. Chapter Nineteen reflects on the usefulness of this study. Furthermore, it will explore directions for further research. The conclusions of this study may provoke important discussions for the Army.

Chapter 19

Implications of the reflection

This study has started from the ambition to reflect on the existing case studies, with the problem of dynamic complexity as the starting point of the reflection. In this final chapter I like to examine the outcomes of the reflection. In Chapter Two, three different criteria were formulated for a valuable substantive theory. After restating these criteria, this chapter is mainly orientated to the issue of 'necessary further research'. This will involve addressing issues for further research that can help to develop the Army as a crisis organization.

19.1 The substantive theory

The various chapters have provided many different analyses and different outcomes. The structure of the substantive theory is represented by the conceptual model as it was displayed in Chapter One:

The different resulting hypotheses are the content of the substantive theory. The hypotheses were orientated to the relations between elements of the conceptual model. The theory has been developed by 'working backwards': based on an analysis of the cases, the influence of the mother organization was explored. The most valuable insights into this substantive theory are those that are relevant for operational units and crisis organizations in general. Necessarily therefore, these are the – analytical – hypotheses about the influence of the mother organization on crisis organizations in general. According to a pragmatist orientation, usefulness is the main criterion by which the substantive theory in this study should be judged. Three criteria for a useful substantive theory were formulated in Chapter Two.

1. The insights of the substantive theory are valuable if the resulting insights were not totally obvious beforehand;
2. The insights of the substantive theory are valuable if they provide clear indications for further research;
3. The insights of the substantive theory are valuable if they provide insight into how the Army can improve its ability to deploy units that can deal with dynamic complexity.

Regarding the first point, there are different insights that are certainly not common knowledge. To my knowledge, the present analysis of the doctrine is the first to identify MC as a 'single-loop learning system' and as 'rhetorical'. Furthermore, the described link between the organizational structure of the mother organization and crisis organizations is a first, as far as I know. Furthermore, this link provides clear directions for organizational change and further research. The image of the leadership structures that is presented here is valuable because it shows, contrary to the claims of the Army organization, that a classical view on leadership is 'implicitly' dominant within the Army. One could argue that the valuable insights such as they are presented not necessarily required a complex study as the present one. In other words, afterwards it is clear that one could have known it beforehand. However, they are only acceptable beforehand if they are the result from research afterwards. Furthermore, the value of the present insights is that the analysis shows that the characteristics of the mother organization influence crisis organizations. Regarding the second and third points, the second part of this chapter is orientated to the formulation of proposals for further research. These proposals all share an orientation on 'organizational change'.

19.2 Proposals for future research

The conclusions of this study are quite critical of the Army's potential to design self-organizing units. For this reason one can read this study as an advocate of change within the Army. In the following, I will describe three proposals for further research in the Army, all with 'organizational development and change' as central topic.

Proposal 1: 'further research is necessary'

Given the ambition of this study, there will be little surprise about the first proposal. This study was orientated to reflecting on existing case studies that were never specifically designed for such a reflection. It would be valuable when case studies are devoted to the topic of dealing with dynamic complexity by Army units in crisis operations. Such case studies can be performed from a much clearer analytical framework and therefore with the possibility to look much more specific at Army operations. One can furthermore imagine that also the influence of factors other than 'structure' and 'leadership' could be taken into account. In any case, the conclusions in this study should stimulate further research.

Proposal 2: The Army and self-organization

According to the analysis in this study, self-organization is crucial for dealing with complexity, and therefore Army units that are deployed in difficult operations should be designed to be self-organizing. Considering the rather unequivocal result of the various analyses, it is not controversial to conclude that the Army is not aiming at designing such units. In the foregoing it was concluded that the Army is, in fact, organized to control difficult operations in a top-down manner. An obvious conclusion from this study is that the Army needs to rethink the doctrine, basing it on a more refined idea of complexity and developing a much more clearly formulated philosophy of command. Indeed, that is a proposal for future research. Perhaps the present study has performed theoretical work that can be helpful for such an effort.

Proposal 3: Changing the organizational structure

One of the most important conclusions of this study is that, in different ways, the organizational structure of the Army does not support self-organization in crisis organizations. The logical implication is that this study is in favor of change in organizational structure. The reflection showed that the ability to assemble an organization in such a way that self-organization at the operational level is supported is an important requirement that the new design should be able to meet. Developing a new design is a complex job for specialists. Furthermore, detailed knowledge on the organization is necessary. The issue is therefore much too complex to be dealt with in this section. Here I want to briefly point to a number of interesting topics regarding structural change in the Army.

- One can imagine that one particular category of operations should be used as an anchorpoint in the design of the mother organization. In the design of the current mother organization the anchorpoint is the war-type operation. The distinction in different battalions of artillery, infantry and cavalry is just one example of that. These different distinctions are made because the resulting different organizational parts have a distinctive role to fulfill in a traditional battle. To my mind, however, peace-operations should be the anchor-point of organizational design if only because these operations are the only 'real' operations the Army performs nowadays. The organization is much more frequently occupied with peace operations than with war-operations.

- If peace operations are taken as the anchorpoint of design then there are several ways to split up the Army. It is possible to create specific self-contained units for peace operations on the basis of differences in circumstances in which they may be deployed (f.i. arctic circumstances or desert circumstances); on the basis of difference in 'dangerousness' of missions ('police missions' versus 'peace-enforcing'); or on the basis of size (deployments of companies, battalions), etc. It is also possible to create different organizational parts that are all the same (perhaps this option creates even the most flexibility of deployment for the organization). It is tempting to make this discussion more specific, but at the same time that would make it more speculative.

- In order to enhance the self-organizing potential of crisis organizations, I consider it essential that crisis organizations exist within the mother organization as an integrated whole (compare this with the situation of the SFOR rotation that was the object of study: that crisis organization consisted of 57 parts of the mother organization). The challenge of designing a mother organization is to design an organization that contains such integrated wholes, yet retains the potential as a mother organization to flexibly deploy different kinds of crisis organizations and retains capabilities for all-out war operations.

- In order to lay the basis for self-organizing potential in crisis organizations, the mother organization should be based on the philosophy of minimal division of labor. A philosophy of maximal division of labor is an attempt at establishing a perfect top-down structure, while making a bottom-up structure redundant. By means of a philosophy of maximal division of labor one designs simple tasks. A defining characteristic of dynamic complexity is that exactly this is not possible. Rules for dealing with various problems cannot be designed in advance. Nor are there unequivocal principles of operation on which to base these rules. Therefore a philosophy of top-down command and maximal division of labor is fundamentally at odds with the nature of a dynamically complex environment. Implementing a philosophy of minimal division of labor throughout the organization requires a fundamentally different way of thinking.

- Choosing to split the peace operations up into different categories and assigning organizational parts to them means that a different logic of assembly is chosen. This logic of assembly is more fortunate in my opinion. It is easier to assemble an organization from 'small to large', than from 'large to small'. With this I mean the following. At present the Army is structured to perform large-scale 'war operations'. If an organization is built up for such a (as yet unclear) large-scale operation, then crisis organizations meant for peace operations need to be assembled from this large-scale organization (from large to small). Chapter Fifteen has shown that this logic of assembly leads to particular problems. In the opposite case the organization is built up from smaller units that are constructed to deal with a part of the operations. In case the organization is confronted with a large-scale operation, then it can create a large-scale operation by putting together a certain number of small-scale organizational units[128]. Such logic of assembly (from small to large) is to my opinion implied by the theory of sociotechnical design. A whole organization (large) operates through the collective contributions of autonomous groups that work on a meaningful whole of the total workflow.

Proposal 4: Leadership as a problem

Within the Army, leadership is often seen as a solution to problems. If there is a lack of motivation, leaders should intervene. If soldiers are not convinced of the usefulness of a mission, leaders should adopt the role of explainer and persuader. If the environment is uncertain, the leader should 'present a vision'. This study gives rise to another view on leadership. I want to briefly mention two directions for further research on the topic of leadership in which a 'spirit of contradiction' is at center stage.

In the first place, within the present Army, leadership itself can be perceived as a problem. The different leadership structures that were discussed are designed to put leaders in the position of the top-down ruler, while being powerless at the same time. A suggestion for further research is the topic of redesigning leadership structures in such a way that doubt and argumentation are promoted. There is one particular topic that I like to single out for further discussion: the design of a Military Academy that is orientated to a different type of leader. Within the limited space available here I cannot devote much attention to the details of such an Academy, but there is one particular point that I like to stress. If doubt and argumentation are considered to be important then psychological maturity is important. One can imagine that it takes psychological maturity to be able to view matters from different sides, to challenge existing insights, and to act in spite of a lack of certainty. The discussion in Chapter Sixteen suggests that the current design of the Military Academy is hardly orientated to psychological maturity. On the contrary, there are rituals of introduction which are orientated to humiliation, critical thinking is uninspired, conformity is demanded, and hierarchy is viewed as panacea. Furthermore, the curriculum is designed in such a way that passivity, cynicism, and distaste for intellectual challenge are the result. Ideas that recruits join an elite seem to be in contrast with the reality of the

---

[128] The exact scale of what is to be considered "small" and what is to considered "large" is, of course, as yet unclear as this depends on the more detailed design. A sociotechnical rule of thumb states that groups that should function smoothly should not be larger than 20 people, larger organizational wholes of which the groups are part should not be larger than about 200 people (Kuipers & Kramer, 2002a).

situation cadets are in. They can therefore be interpreted as a luring story to conceal reality, along with ZACVE suggestions. As such, cadets from the Military Academy can be seen as 'powerless heroes'[129]. For these reasons the evaluation study of Kuipers c.s. (1999) advised a fundamental redesigning of the education of leaders.

In the second place, one can discern that within the Army the role of leaders is overvalued. The doctrine, for example, is phrased in the language of leadership. De Sitter (1970) showed that leaders are restricted by the existing organizational regime. In itself an overvalued attention for leadership can be interpreted as a lack of psychological maturity. Fromm (1942) indicated that a yearning for a leader that knows the solution for problems is an example of 'a fear of freedom'. As a matter of fact, this problem stimulated Fromm to take up the study in the first place. A second suggestion for future research is therefore the establishment of a tradition of research that perceives the possibilities and limitations of leaders in a more realistic way.

Proposal 5: A psychoanalytic approach to organizational change

There is one particular trace in the reflection that deserves further attention because it can be the stepping stone for further research in the Army. In Chapter Sixteen it was concluded that the Army doctrine has a powerful rhetorical effect. It appears to be introducing a modern and very liberal concept, while on further examination little of this initial appearance can be retained. As such, the doctrine protects the classical organization by appearing to be modern. I believe that there are many people in the Army that honestly aim for a modern and liberal organization. However, as the analysis of doctrine has shown, the result of their collective efforts can be a shrewd instrument for the protection of the classical organization. This has a psychoanalytic flavor to it because of the element of the unconsciousness. According to Fromm (1970), the idea of unconsciousness is a cornerstone of psychoanalytic thinking. Characteristic of the unconsciousness is that it hides its traces. For example, the severely destructive personality can be frail and overly sensitive in his conscious life. This destructive personality uses evidence of his frailty in order to hide away his destructive side (a 'reaction

---

[129] Frequently it is brought forward that "it is not that bad" and "there are also intelligent cadets". I am the first to note that the problem of the Military Academy is not located in the individual recruit, although one can question whether cadets are selected for their 'critical attitude', or whether they are selected to suit the existing structures at the Academy. However, one cannot blame the individual for this as he is probably partly unaware of what he is getting himself into. Suggestions that "things are not that bad", however, should be valued for what they are. If reality is not as bad as it sounds in theory, it can also be seen as an inability of the current system to reach its goals. Just as an Academy that is orientated at maturity can produce immature cadets, an institution that is orientated at immaturity can produce mature cadets (the system has "causal potential"). In other words, if reality is not that bad, it is a failure of the system.

formation'). Psychoanalytic concepts have been applied to organizations many times before (Klein, 2001). For example, Van der Vlist (2003) aimed to link the topics of organizational change and psychoanalysis, and discussed a case of an organization in which the ethically sublime (a moral code) served to hide and preserve an authoritarian status quo.

An interesting line of research would be the hypothesis that the Army unconsciously preserves its classical nature by appearing to be modern. If it can be confirmed that particular unconscious motives operate in this manner, one can imagine that this is a formidable barrier to change in the Army. There are further ways in which a psychoanalytical perspective can be an interesting line of research that can be pursued. Resistance to change is, of course, a classical theme in both psychoanalysis and organizational change. Resistance to organizational change is known to be fiercer if the structures that need change are tightly coupled to existing power structures (Van der Vlist, 2003). Furthermore, Fromm (1942) pointed to the importance of conformity. Perhaps psychoanalytical insights regarding conformity can help to understand the dynamics at the Military Academy where, as was shown in Chapter Sixteen, conformity is an important theme. Another theme from Fromm, the fear of freedom (which is, in Fromm's theoretical logic, linked to conformity) can be used to shed a light on another matter. It was discussed that the Army is fearful of operational units that act 'out of control'. It was concluded that the Army should accept that it is confronted with environments in which total control is impossible. Perhaps this is an example of a 'fear of freedom'? Of course this referred to a fear that others are free, while Fromm referred to the importance of fear of freedom of the self. I believe that a psychoanalytic perspective can be useful for keeping researchers suspicious of the everyday dealings in the Army.

19.3 Final remarks

The various proposals for further research have the topic of organizational change as a common denominator. Although it is easy to announce the necessity for change, I believe that change is difficult to realize within the Army. It is known that for change to materialize within organizations, more is needed than documents with critical analyses (Van der Vlist, 2003). It is furthermore known that the commitment of top management is necessary in order to make change-projects a success (Kuipers, 1998). I doubt that such a commitment is available in the top of the Army organization. I believe the Army possesses some built-in mechanisms to fend off real or fundamental change. Especially the proposals for a psychoanalytic approach to organizational change are interesting in this respect. This does not mean that change is impossible. I believe that change is inevitable. A 'classic Army' will become politically less and less acceptable. The mere fact that the Army is engaged in peace operations can be interpreted as a demand from the outside. The critique on the Army in the last decennium, and the continuous confrontation with peace operations can be interpreted as a healthy pressure on the organization, which will eventually make 'true change' inevitable.

Appendix I

Because the analytical framework is meant to engage the cases and the mother-organization, it is probably helpful to provide an overview of both the content of the analytical framework and the ingredients used to engage the cases. The following 2 models provide such a schematic overview.

A. The *content* of the analytical framework
The following table presents an overview of the development.

Ingredients	Theoretical elements	
I. Descriptive and normative model	Weick's 'Organizing model'	
II. The normative element in this model	Doubt	
	The process of doubt	Argumentation
III. Organizing the normative element + indicators	External structure of argumentation → Holographic principles	
	Internal structure of argumentation → leadership as 'adding the deficient'	

B. The *function* of the analytical framework

The analytical framework is subsequently used to research the object of study. It has a double function: It is used to select data from the raw material (from the cases and the mother-organization). Subsequently it is used to search for patterns within the data (an interpretative process that is called analytical abduction).

Function		
Selection	*Sets of data*	*The data is selected from the raw material by:*
	A. Dealing with dynamic complexity at the operational level	Searching for practical problems that can be explained according to the logic of Weick's **organizing model**
	B. Design of the operational units by the crisis-organization	Finding information about: **A. The holographic principles** **B. The definition of the role of leaders**
	C. Design of the mother-organization	**A. The philosophy of dealing with dynamic complexity as espoused in the doctrine** **B. Characteristics of the organizational structure of the mother-organization** **C. Leadership structures**
Interpretation		
	The relations to be reconstructed	
	The conceptual model presented in section 1.5	
	Procedure used for interpretation	
	This study searches for relations between the different 'sets' of data. The analytical framework is used here as a heuristic tool to reconstruct the relations in the conceptual model. The result of this process is a collection of hypotheses about the quality of the Army as an organization that deploys units that need to be able to deal with dynamic complexity.	

Appendix II

References to the Logtbat case study

1. Vogelaar, c.s. (1997a), p. 74.
2. See for example: Vogelaar & Kramer (1997).
3. Vogelaar, c.s. (1997a, p. 73).
4. Vogelaar, c.s. (1997a), pp. 133–137.
5. This organizational chart is reconstructed on the basis of a description in Vogelaar, c.s. (1997a), pp. 71–74.
6. Vogelaar, c.s. (1997a), p. 80; p. 110.
7. Vogelaar, c.s. (1997a), pp. 121–124.
8. Vogelaar, c.s. (1997a), p. 75.
9. Vogelaar, c.s. (1997a), pp. 93–96.
10. Vogelaar, c.s. (1997a), p. 78.
11. Vogelaar, c.s. (1997a), p. 85.
12. Vogelaar, c.s. (1997a), p. 126.
13. Vogelaar, c.s. (1997a), p. 76.
14. Vogelaar, c.s. (1997a), pp. 96–110.
15. Vogelaar, c.s. (1997a), p. 12.
16. Vogelaar, c.s. (1997a), pp. 93–96.
17. Vogelaar, c.s. (1997a) p. 113.
18. Vogelaar, c.s. (1997a), pp. 101–109.
19. Vogelaar, c.s. (1997a), pp. 91–93.
20. Vogelaar, c.s. (1997a), p. 92.
21. Vogelaar, c.s. (1997a), p. 94; p. 116.
22. Vogelaar, c.s. (1997a), p. 114.
23. Vogelaar, c.s. (1997a), p. 122.
24. Vogelaar, & Kramer (2004).
25. Vogelaar, c.s. (1997a), p. 73.
26. Vogelaar, c.s. (1997a), pp. 176–179.
27. Vogelaar, c.s. (1996b), p. 82.
28. Vogelaar, c.s. (1997a), pp. 121–124.
29. Vogelaar, c.s. (1997a), pp. 110–111.
30. Vogelaar, c.s. (1997a), p. 113.
31. Vogelaar, c.s. (1996b), p. 82.
32. Vogelaar, c.s. (1997a), p. 96.
33. Vogelaar, c.s. (1997a), pp. 87–90.
34. Vogelaar, c.s. (1997a), pp. 87–90.
35. Vogelaar, c.s. (1997a), p. 111.
36. Vogelaar, c.s. (1997a), p. 110.
37. Vogelaar, c.s. (1997a), p. 74.
38. Vogelaar, c.s. (1997a), p. 41.

39. Vogelaar, c.s. (1997a), pp. 101–109.
40. Vogelaar, c.s. (1996b), p. 45.
41. Vogelaar, c.s. (1996b), p. 87.
42. Vogelaar, c.s. (1997a), p. 94; p. 122.
43. Vogelaar, c.s. (1997a), pp. 103–107.
44. Vogelaar, c.s. (1997a), p. 108.
45. Vogelaar, c.s. (1997a), pp. 176–179.
46. Vogelaar, c.s. (1996b), pp. 63–67; p. 81.
47. Vogelaar, c.s. (1996b), p. 34.
48. Vogelaar, c.s. (1997a), p. 122.
49. Vogelaar, c.s. (1997a), pp. 77–84.
50. Vogelaar, c.s. (1997a), pp. 77–84.
51. Vogelaar, c.s. (1997a), p. 156.
52. Vogelaar, c.s. (1997a).

References to the SFOR case study

53. Vogelaar, c.s. (2001), p. 7.
54. Vogelaar, c.s. (2001), p. 13.
55. Vogelaar, c.s. (2001), pp. 15–19.
56. Vogelaar, c.s. (2001), pp. 9–10; pp. 15–20.
57. Vogelaar, c.s. (2001), pp. 15–20.
58. Vogelaar, c.s. (2001), p. 12.
59. Vogelaar, c.s. (2001), p. 19.
60. Vogelaar, c.s. (2001), pp. 9–10.
61. Vogelaar, c.s. (2001), pp. 10–12.
62. Vogelaar, c.s. (2001), p. 22.
63. Vogelaar, c.s. (2001), p. 15.
64. Vogelaar, c.s. (2001), p. 15
65. Vogelaar, c.s. (2001), p. 16
66. Vogelaar, c.s. (2001), p. 9.
67. Vogelaar, c.s. (2001), p. 22.
68. Vogelaar, c.s. (2001), p. 45.
69. Vogelaar, c.s. (2001), p. 22.
70. Vogelaar, c.s. (2001), p. 62.
71. Vogelaar, c.s. (2001), p. 41.
72. Vogelaar, c.s. (2001), p. 45.
73. Vogelaar, c.s. (2001), pp. 31–33.
74. Vogelaar, c.s. (2001), p. 16.
75. Vogelaar, c.s. (2001), p. 12.
76. Vogelaar, c.s. (2001), p. 23; p. 61.
77. Vogelaar, c.s. (2001), p. 61.
78. Vogelaar, c.s. (2001), pp. 18–19.
79. Vogelaar, c.s. (2001), pp. 65–68.

80. Vogelaar, c.s. (2001), p. 66.
81. Vogelaar, c.s. (2001), p. 12.
82. Vogelaar, c.s. (2001), p. 53.
83. Vogelaar, c.s. (2001), p. 61.
84. Vogelaar, c.s. (2001), p. 62.
85. Vogelaar, c.s. (2001), pp. 69–72.
86. Vogelaar, c.s. (2001), pp. 32–33.
87. Vogelaar, c.s. (2001), p. 19.
88. Vogelaar, c.s. (2001), pp. 71–72.
89. Vogelaar, c.s. (2001), pp. 24–27.
90. Vogelaar, c.s. (2001), pp. 32–33.
91. Vogelaar, c.s. (2001), p. 25.
92. Vogelaar, c.s. (2001), p. 61.
93. Vogelaar, c.s. (2001), p. 60.
94. Vogelaar, c.s. (2001), p. 56; p. 60.
95. Vogelaar, c.s. (2001), p. 19.
96. Vogelaar, c.s. (2001), p. 19.
97. Vogelaar, c.s. (2001), pp. 18–20.
98. Vogelaar, c.s. (2001), p. 16.
99. Vogelaar, c.s. (2001), pp. 15–16.
100. Vogelaar, c.s. (2001), p. 19.
101. Vogelaar, c.s. (2001), p. 16.
102. Vogelaar, c.s. (2001), p. 41.
103. Vogelaar, c.s. (2001) pp. 41–48.
104. Vogelaar, c.s. (2001), p. 62.
105. Vogelaar, c.s. (2001), p. 66.
106. Vogelaar, c.s. (2001), p. 17.
107. Vogelaar, c.s. (2001), p. 56.
108. Vogelaar, c.s. (2001), pp. 56–57.
109. Vogelaar, c.s. (2001), p. 73.
110. Vogelaar, c.s. (2001), p. 43.
111. Vogelaar, c.s. (2001), p. 73

References to the Dutchbat case study

112. Vogelaar, c.s. (1997a), pp. 15–18.
113. Vogelaar, c.s. (1997a), pp. 19–20.
114. Vogelaar, c.s. (1997a), p. 20.
115. Vogelaar, c.s. (1997a), pp. 20–22.
116. Vogelaar, c.s. (1997a), pp. 66–69.
117. Vogelaar, c.s. (1997a), p. 32.
118. Vogelaar, c.s. (1997a), p. 19.
119. Vogelaar, c.s. (1997a), pp. 166–171.
120. Vogelaar, c.s. (1997a), p. 28; pp. 33–35.

121. Vogelaar, c.s. (1997a), p. 25.
122. Vogelaar, c.s. (1997a), p. 27; pp. 32–33.
123. Vogelaar, c.s. (1997a), pp. 27–28.
124. Vogelaar, c.s. (1997a), p. 56.
125. Vogelaar, c.s. (1997a), p. 56.
126. Vogelaar, c.s. (1997a), p. 55.
127. Vogelaar & Kramer (2004).
128. Vogelaar, c.s. (1997a), p. 27.
129. Vogelaar, c.s. (1997a), p. 56.
130. Vogelaar & Kramer (2004).
131. NIOD, 2002.
132. Vogelaar, c.s. (1997a), pp. 38–39.
133. Vogelaar, c.s. (1997a), pp. 140–144.
134. This is a conclusion that is shared by the NIOD (2002).
135. Vogelaar, c.s. (1997a), pp. 25–30.

Appendix III

Organizational Charts

The source for these charts is the local intranet, more specifically the site of DP&O. They were downloaded on 30 Januari 2003.

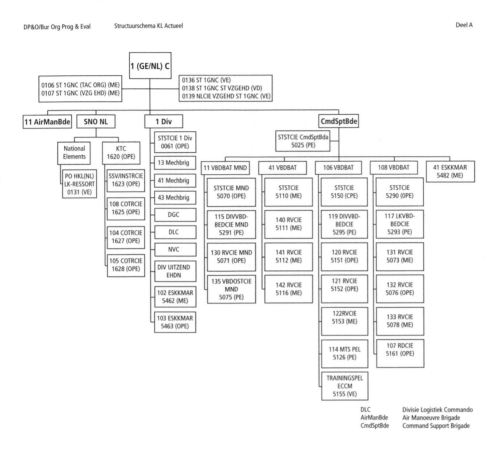

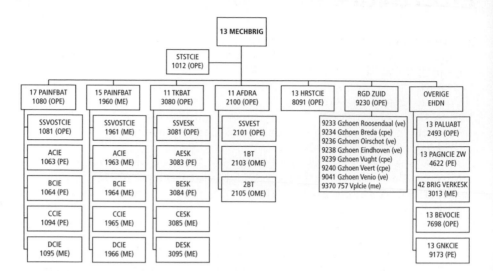

1

262

Literature

Alvesson, M. & Deetz, S. (1996). Critical Theory and Postmodern Approaches to Organizational Studies. In: Clegg, S., Hardy, C. & Nord, W. *Handbook of organization studies*. London: Sage. pp. 191–217.

Archer, M. (1995). *Realist Social Theory: The Morphogenic Approach*. Cambridge: Cambridge University Press.

Argyris, C. On organizational learning. Cambridge, Ma: Blackwell Publishers Inc.

Ashby, W.R. (1969). Self-regulation and requisite variety. In: Emery, F. (Ed.): *Systems thinking*. London: Penguin Books.

Avant, D. & Lebovic, J., (2000). U.S. Military Attitudes Toward Post-Cold War Missions, In: *Armed Forces & Society, 27(1)*, Fall 2000, pp. 37–56.

Bak, P. (1999). *How nature works: The science of Self-Organized Criticality*. New York: Springer Verlag.

Bateson, G. (2002). *Mind and nature. A Necessary Unity*. Cresskill, N.J.: Hampton Press. Original edition published in 1979.

Becker, K.H. (2005). Luhmann's Systems Theory and Theories of Social Practices. In: Seidl, D. & Becker, K.H. *Niklas Luhmann and Organizing Studies*. Copenhagen: Liber & Copenhagen Business School Press.

Bergson, J.R. (1986). *The Control Revolution. Technological and Economic Origins of the Information society*. Cambridge, Ma: Harvard University Press.

Bertalanffy, L. Von (1971). The history and status of General Systems Theory. In: Klir, G.J. (Ed.). *Trends in General Systems Theory*. New York: Wiley Interscience.

Billig, M. (1991). *Ideology and opinions. Studies in Rhetorical Psychology*. London: Sage.

Billig, M. (1996). *Arguing and thinking. A rhetorical approach to social psychology*. Cambridge: Cambridge University Press. 2nd Edition.

Billig, M. (1999). *Freudian Repression. Conversation creating the Unconsciousness*. Cambridge: Cambridge University Press.

Billig, M. Condor, S., Edwards, D., Gane, M., Middleton, D. & Radley, R. (1998). *Ideological Dilemmas. A social psychology of everyday thinking*. London: Sage.

Blom, J.H.C. (2002). Srebrenica, een 'veilig' gebied. Epiloog. In: *Militaire Spectator*, jrg 171, 6, pp. 301–342.

Blom, T. (1997). *Complexiteit en contingentie. Een kritische inleiding tot de sociologie van Niklas Luhmann*. Kampen: Kok Agora.

Bootsma, P. (2002). Srebrenica. *Het NIOD rapport samengevat*. Amsterdam: Boom.

Boxsel, M. van (1999). *De encylopedie van de domheid*. Amsterdam: Querido's Uitgeverij.

Britt, T.W. & Adler, A.B. (Eds) (2003). *The psychology of the peacekeeper. Lessons from the field*. London: Praeger.

Christis, J. (1998). *Arbeid, organisatie en stress. Een visie vanuit de sociotechnische arbeids- en organisatiekunde*. Amsterdam: Het Spinhuis.

Clark, P. (2000). *Organizations in action. Competition between contexts*. London: Routledge.

Clausewitz, C. von (1968). *On War.* London: Penguin Books. Original Edition: Vom Kriege 1832.

Coffey, A. & Atkinson, P. (1996). *Making sense of qualitative data. Complementary research strategies.* London: Sage.

Cohen, E. & Gooch, J. (1990). *Military misfortunes. The anatomy of failure in war.* New York: Vintage Books.

Cox, T.H., Lobel, S.A. & McLeod, P.L. (1991). Effects of ethnic group cultural differences on competitive behaviour on a group task. In: Academy of Management Journal, (34), pp. 827–847.

Creveld, M. van (1985). *Command in war.* Cambrigde (Ma): Harvard University Press.

Cunningham, D.J. (1998). Cognition as Semiosis: The role of Inference. In: *Theory and Psychology,* 1998–6, pp. 827–840. London: Sage.

Dennett, D.C. (1995). *Darwin's dangerous idea. Evolution and the meaning of life.* New York: Touchstone/ Simon & Schuster.

Dixon, N. (1976). *On the psychology of military incompetence.* London: Pimlico.

Egter van Wissekerke F.J.D.C. (1996). Opdrachtgerichte commandovoering als leidend doctrinebeginsel van de Koninklijke Landmacht. In: *Militaire Spectator,* 165, pp. 481–497.

Eijnatten, F. van (1993). *The Paradigm that changed the Work Place.* Assen: Van Gorcum.

Eijnatten, F.M. van (2002). Een introductie in concepten van het Chaosdenken (An introduction in the concepts of Chaos thinking). In: Eijnatten, F.M. van, Poorthuis, J.M.G. & Peters, J. (Eds), *Inleiding in Chaosdenken: theorie en praktijk* (pp. 7–21) *(Introduction in Chaos thinking: Theory and practice).* Assen: Van Gorcum (in Dutch).

Eijnatten, F.M. van (2004). Chaos and complexity: An overview of the 'new science' in organisation and management. *Revue Sciences de Gestion Quarterly, 1* (1), to appear in August 2004.

Emery, F. & Emery, M. (1997). Towards a logic of hypotheses. Everyone does research. In: *Concepts and Transformation,* 2:2, 1997, pp. 119–144. Amsterdam: Benjamin's.

Emery, F. & Trist, E. (1969). Sociotechnical systems. In: Emery, F. (Ed.): *Systems thinking.* London: Penguin Books.

Everts, P. (1998). Command and control in stressful conditions. In: Vogelaar, A., Muusse, K.F. & Rovers, J.H. (Eds). *NL ARMS.* Breda: Royal Netherlands Military Academy.

Franke, V.C. (2003). The Social Identity of Peacekeeping. In: Britt, T.W. & Adler, A.B. (Eds) (2003). *The psychology of the peacekeeper. Lessons from the field.* London: Praeger.

Freud, S. (1960). *Jokes and Their Relation to the Unconscious.* New York: W.W. Norton & Company. Standard Edition, translated and Edited by James Strachey.

Foucault, M. (1975). *Surveiller et punir: naissance de la prison.* Paris: Gallimard.

Fromm, E. (1942). *The fear of freedom.* London: Kegan Paul, Trench, Trubner.

Fromm, E. (1973). *The anatomy of human destructiveness.* New York: Holt, Rinehart and Winston.

Gabriel, R.A. & Savage, P.L. (1978). *Crisis in Command. Mismanagement in the Army.* New York: Hill and Wang.

Galen, M.C. van & Eijnatten, F.M. van (2002). Chaosdenken en dialoog voor cultuurcreatie (Chaos thinking and dialogue for culture creation). In: Eijnatten, F.M. van, Kuijs, M. & Haffmans, J.M. (Eds), *Verdieping van Chaosdenken: theorie en praktijk (Going into Chaos thinking: Theory and practice)* (pp. 110–130). Assen: Van Gorcum (in Dutch).

Gardner, H. (1987). *The mind's new science*. New York: Basic Books.

Garver, E. (1994). *Aristotle's rhetoric. An art of character*. Chicago: The University of Chicago Press.

Giddens, A. (1984). *The constitution of Society*. Berkely: University of California Press.

Glaser, B. (1978). *Theoretical Sensitivity*. Mill Valley: Sociology Press.

Glaser, B. (1992). *Emergence vs Forcing: basics of Grounded Theory Analysis*. Mill Valley: The Sociology Press.

Glaser, B.G. & Strauss, A.L. (1967). *The discovery of grounded theory: Strategies for qualitative research*. Chicago: Aldine.

Goffman, E. (1961). The characteristics of total institutions. In: Etzioni, A. *Complex Organizations. A sociological reader*. New York: Holt, Rinehart & Winston.

Groen, P. & Klinkert, W. (2003). Slotbeschouwing. In: Groen, P. & Klinkert, W. (Eds) *Studeren in uniform. 175 jaar koninklijke militaire academie*. Den Haag: Sdu.

Gustavsen, B. (1996). Is theory useful? In: *Concepts and Transformation*, 1:1, pp. 63–77.

Haerkens, T. (1995). 'Beschuldigingen van wangedrag'. In: *Rotterdams Dagblad*, 05/05/95.

Haley, J. (1986). *The power tactics of Jesus Christ*. Rockville, Md: The triangle press. 2nd Edition.

Hartog, D.N. & Verburg, R. (1997). Charisma and Rhetoric: Communicative Techniques of International Business Leaders. In: *Leadership Quarterly*, 8(4), pp. 355–391.

Hartog D.N. den, Koopman, P. & Muijen, J. (1997). *Inspirerend leiderschap in organisaties*. Schoonhoven: Academic Serevice.

Hedberg, B. (1981). How organizations learn and unlearn. In: Nystrom, P.C. & Starbuck, W.H. (Eds). *Handbook of organizational design*. (Vol. 1, pp. 3–27). New York: Oxford University Press.

Heijster, W. (2003). Pseudo-oplossingen in de KL. Resultaat van de opleiding aan de KMA? In: *Carré*, 2-2003, pp. 33–36.

Hemphill, J.K. & Coons, A.E. (1957). Development of the leader behavior description questionnaire. In: Stogdill, R.M. & Coons, A.E. (Eds). Leader Behavior: Its description and measurement. Ohio: Ohio State University.

Herbst, P.G. (1974). *Socio-technical design: strategies in multi-disciplinary research*. London: Tavistock publications.

Holland, J.H. (1995). *Hidden order. How Adaptation builds Complexity*. Reading, Ma: Perseus Books.

Hosking, D.M. & Morely, I.E. (1991). *A social psychology of organizing*. Prentice Hall: Harvester Wheatsheaf.

Janis, I.L. (1989). *Crucial Decisions. Leadership in policymaking and crisis management*. London: Free Press.

Janis, I.L. & Mann, L. (1977). *Decision Making. A psychological analysis of Conflict, Choice and Commitment*. New York: Free Press.

Josephson, J.R. & Josephson, S.G. (Eds). (1994). *Abductive Inference. Computation, Philosophy, Technology.* Cambridge: Cambridge University Press.

Karels, A. & Hager, P. (2003). 175 jarige KMA: Een open organisatie midden in de maatschappij. In *Trias*: 2003-2, pp. 3–6.

Katz, D. & Kahn, R.L. (1978). *The social psychology of organizations.* New York: John Wiley & sons.

Kauffman, S. (1990). *At home in the universe. The search for the laws of Self-Organization and Complexity.* New York: Oxford University Press.

Kelle, U. (1995). Theories as Heuristic Tools in Qualitative Research. In: Maso, I., Atkinson, P.A., Delamont, S. & Verhoeven, J.C., (Eds). *Openness in Research. The Tension between the self and other.* Assen: Van Gorcum.

Klein, G. (2001). *Sources of Power. How people make decisions.* Cambrige (Ma): MIT Press. Seventh Printing.

Klein, L. (2001). On the use of psychoanalytic concepts in organizational social science. In: *Concepts and Transformation*, 6:1, 2001, pp. 59–72. Amsterdam: Benjamin's.

Klep, C. & Gils, R. van (1999). *Van Korea tot Kosovo.* Den Haag: Sdu.

Klinkert, W. (1998). *100 jaar cadettencorps.* Tilburg: Gianotten.

Knodt, E.M. (1995). Foreword. In: Luhmann, N. (1995). *Social systems.* Stanford University Press. Translated by Bednarz, J. & Beacker, D. Originally published in 1984 in German. pp. ix–xxxvi.

Koninklijke Landmacht (1996). *Militaire doctrine.* (LDP 1). Den Haag: Sdu.

Koninklijke Landmacht (1998a). *Beleidsvisie Leidinggeven.* Den Haag: Sdu.

Koninklijke Landmacht (1998b). *Gevechtoperaties. Grondslagen.* (LDP II. Deel A) Den Haag: Sdu.

Koninklijke Landmacht (1999). *Peace Operations* (ADP III). Den Haag: Sdu.

Koninklijke Landmacht (2000). *Leidraad commandovoering.* (2000) Den Haag: Sdu.

Koopman, P. & House, R.J. (1995). Charismatisch leiderschap in organisaties. In: Vlist, R. van der, Steensma, H., Kamperman, A. & Gerrichhausen, J. (Eds). *Handboek leiderschap in arbeidsorganisaties.* Den Haag: Lemma. pp. 39–52.

Kramer, E.H. & Kuipers, H. (2002). Structuur en flexibiliteit. In: Richardson, R., Verweij, D., Vogelaar, A. & Kuipers H. (Eds). *Mens & Organisatie.* Amsterdam: Mets & Schilt.

Kramer, E.H. & Kuipers, H. (2003). Flexibiliteit en starheid in krijgshistorisch perspectief. In: *Militair Spectator*, sept. 2003. pp. 454–471.

Kroon, W.B., Heesakkers, H.K.J., Jacobs, M. & Van der Veer, J.B.C. (1997). Rules of Engagement and the experiences of Dutch soldiers during UNPROFOR and SFOR. In: Soeters, J. & Rovers, J.H. (Eds). *NL ARMS.* Breda: KMA.

Kuipers, H. (1989a). *Zelforganisatie als ontwerpprincipe.* Eindhoven: TUE.

Kuipers, H. (1989b). *Het wankele evenwicht tussen management en leiderschap.* Breda: KMA.

Kuipers, H. (1998). The sociotechnical designer as Wizard and Juggler. In: *Concepts and Transformation*, 3:3, 1998, pp. 229–254. Amsterdam: Benjamin's.

Kuipers, H. (2003). Opleiding en vorming op de KMA. In: *Carré* 2-2003, pp. 22–25.

Kuipers, H. & Van Amelsvoort, P. (1990). *Slagvaardig Organiseren. Inleiding in de sociotechniek als integrale ontwerpleer.* Deventer: Kluwer bedrijfswetenschappen.

Kuipers, H. & Vogelaar, A. (1995). Leidinggeven aan teams. In: Vlist, R. van der, Steensma, H., Kamperman, A. & Gerrichhausen, J. (Eds). *Handboek leiderschap in arbeidsorganisaties*. Den Haag: Lemma. pp. 131–155.

Kuipers, H., Richardson, R., Dulfer, M., Hoeks, T., Heijnsdijk, J., Poll, I., Scheepers, H., Verweij, D. (1999). *Eindrapport Evaluatie Opleidingsmodel '92. "Kiezen en Delen"*. Breda: KMA.

Kuipers, H., Kramer, E.H. & Richardson, R. (2001). *Structuur, motivatie en prestatie in de krijgsmacht. Dictaat ten behoeve van MB4*. Breda: KMA.

Kuipers, H. & Kramer, E.H. (2002a). Het mensbeeld in de sociotechniek. In: *Tijdschrift voor arbeidsvraagstukken*. 2002-1, pp. 54–69.

Kuipers, H. & Kramer, E.H. (2002b). Het Herontwerp van organisaties. In: Richardson, R., Verweij, D., Vogelaar, A. & Kuipers H. (Eds). *Mens & Organisatie*. Amsterdam: Mets & Schilt.

Lakoff, G. (1987). *Women, Fire and dangerous things. What categories reveal about the mind*. Chicago: The University of Chicago Press.

Latour, B. (1999). On recalling ANT. In: Law, J. & Hassard, J. *Actor Network Theory and after*. Oxford: Blackwell Publishers.

Law, J. (1999). After ANT: complexity, naming and topology. In: Law, J. & Hassard, J. *Actor Network Theory and after*. Oxford: Blackwell Publishers.

Layder, D. (1997). *Modern Social Theory. Key debates and new directions*. Padstow, Cornwall: UCL Press.

Lindesmith, A. (1947). *Opiate Addiction*. Bloomington, Ind.: Principia.

Lorenz, E. (1996). *The essence of chaos*. Seattle: University of Washington Press.

Luhmann, N. (1995). *Social systems*. Stanford University Press. Translated by Bednarz, J. & Beacker, D. Originally published in 1984 in German.

McCaskey, M.B. (1982). *The executive challenge: Managing change and ambiguity*. Marshfield, Ma: Pitman.

Metsemakers, Van Amelsvoort & Van Jaarsveld, (2002). *Het organiseren van kennisintensieve processen*. Vlijmen: ST-groep.

Miles, M.B. & Huberman, A.M. (1984). *Qualitative data analysis. A sourcebook of new methods*. London: Sage Publications.

Miller, L. (1997). Do Soldiers Hate Peacekeeping? The Case of Preventive Diplomacy Operations in Macedonia. In: *Armed Forces & Society, 23(3)*, Spring 1997, pp. 415–449.

Ministerie van Defensie (2000). *Defensienota*. Den Haag.

Moelker, R. & Richardson, R. (2002). Socialisatie op de KMA. In: Richardson, R., Verweij, D., Vogelaar, A. & Kuipers H. (Eds). *Mens & Organisatie*. Amsterdam: Mets & Schilt.

Moelker, R. & Richardson, R. (2003). Grijze muizen knagen aan de pilaren van de Koninklijke Militaire Academie. In: *Carré* 2-2003, pp. 11–17.

Morgan, G. (1997). *Images of Organization*. Thousand Oaks: Sage. New edition.

Moskos, C. (1976). *Peace Soldiers. The Sociology of a United Nations Military Force*. Chicago: The University of Chicago Press.

Myerson, G. (1994). *Rhetoric, reason and society*. London: Sage.

Naveh, S. (1997). *In pursuit of military excellence. The evolution of operational theory*. London: Frank Cass.

Nederlands Instituut voor Oorlogsdocumentatie (NIOD), (2002). *Srebrenica, een veilig gebied. Reconstructie, achtergronden, gevolgen en analyses van de val van een Safe Area*. Amsterdam: Boom.

Parker, I. (Ed.). (1998). *Social Constructionism, discourse and realism*. London: Sage.

Peirce, C.S. (1955). *Philosophical writings of Peirce*. New York: Dover Publications, Inc; Selected and edited by Buchler, J.; first published in 1955.

Perrow, C. (1985). The short and glorious history of Organizational Theory. In: Lynch, B. (Ed.). *Management strategies for libraries. A basic reader*. (pp. 232–247). New York: Neal-Schuman.

Perrow, C. (1999). *Normal Accidents. Living with high-risk technologies*. Princeton (NJ): Princeton University Press. 2nd Edition, first published by Basic Books 1984.

Pettigrew, A.M. & Fenton, E.M. (Eds) (2000). *The innovating organization*. London: Sage.

Prigogine, I. (1996). *The end of certainty. Time, chaos and the new laws of nature*. New York: The Free Press.

Rapoport, A. (1968). General systems theory. In: Sills, D. (Ed.). *The international Encyclopedia of the Social Sciences*. Vol. 15. New York: The MacMillan Company & The Free Press.

Ramakers, F. (2002). Omgaan met orde en chaos. Is het kritisch leervermogen van de krijgsmacht toereikend? In: Richardson, R., Verweij, D., Vogelaar, A. & Kuipers H. (Eds). *Mens & Organisatie*. Amsterdam: Mets & Schilt. pp. 149–186.

Ramakers, F. (2003). Van 'Stier' tot officier? In: *Carré* 2-2003, pp. 38–42.

Reason, J. (1990). *Human Error*. Cambridge: Cambridge University Press.

Reed, M. (1999). Organizational Theorizing: a Historically Contested Terrain. In: Clegg, S. & Hardy, C. (Eds). *Studying Organization*. London: Sage. pp. 25–50.

Rescher, N. (2000). *Realistic Pragmatism. An introduction to pragmatic philosophy*. New York: SUNY.

Roemers, M. (2002). Groepsprocessen. Srebrenica. In: *Psychologie Magazine*, juni, pp. 14–17.

Sagan, S. (1993). The limits of safety. Organizations, Accidents, and Nuclear Weapons. Princeton, NJ: Princeton University Press.

Sayer, A. (2000). *Realism and Social Science*. London: Sage.

Scott, R.W. (2001). *Institutions and Organizations*. London: SAGE publications.

Segal D.R. & Tiggle, R.B. Attitudes of Citizen-Soldiers toward Military Missions in the Post-Cold War World. In: *Armed Forces & Society, 23(3)*, Spring 1997, pp. 373–390.

Senge, P.M. (1992). *The fifth discipline. The art and practice of the learning organization*. London: Century Business (reprint; original version 1990).

Shank, G. (1998). The Extraordinary Powers of Abductive Reasoning. In: *Theory and Psychology*, 1998-6, pp. 841–860. London: Sage.

Shotter, J. (1993). *Conversational Realities. Constructing Life through Language*. London: Sage.

Simon, H.A. (1997). *The sciences of the artificial*. Cambridge (Ma): MIT press. 3rd edition.

Sitter, L.U. de (1970). *Leiderschapsvorming en leiderschapsgedrag in een organisatie*. Alphen a/d Rijn: Samsom.

Sitter, U. de (2000). *Synergetisch Produceren*. Assen: Van Gorcum. 2e editie.

Snook, S. (2000). *Friendly Fire. The accidental shootdown of U.S. Black Hawks over Northern Iraq*. Princeton: Princeton University Press.

Soeters, J. (2003). Hoeveel toekomst heeft de KMA na 175 jaar? In: *Carré* 2-2003, pp. 6–7.

Spruijt, R. (2000). *Opdrachtgerichte commandovoering. Bij een artillerie-eenheid onder verschillende operationele omstandigheden* (unpublished paper).

Stacey, R.D. (1992). *Managing the unknowable. Strategic boundaries between order and chaos in organizations.* San Francisco: Jossey-Bass.

Strauss, A. & Corbin, J. (1990). *Basics of Qualitative Research. Grounded Theory Procedures and Techniques.* Newbury Park: Sage.

Strauss, A. & Corbin, J. (1998). *Basics of Qualitative Research. Techniques and Procedures for developing grounded theory.* London: Sage. 2nd Edition.

Strien, P.J. van. (1986). *Praktijk als Wetenschap. Methodologie van het social-wetenschappelijk handelen.* Assen: Van Gorcum.

Trist, E.L., Higgin, G.W., Murray, H. & Pollock, A.B. (1963). *Organizational Choice. Capabilities of Groups at the Coal Face Under Changing Technologies.* London: Tavistock Publication.

Vaughan, D. (1996). *The Challenger Launch Decision. Risky Technology, Culture, and Deviance at NASA.* Chicago: The university of Chicago Press.

Veld, J. in't (1987). *Analyse van organisatieproblemen.* Leiden: Stenfert Kroese.

Vlist R. van der (1981). *De dynamiek van sociale systemen.* Alphen aan den Rijn: Samsom Uitgeverij.

Vlist, R. van der (1991). *Leiderschap in organisaties.* Den Haag: Lemma.

Vlist, R. van der (1996). Niet per sé wetenschap; Stekelbaarzen en organisaties. In: *Journal of Soap.* Leider: RUL, vakgroep S&O psychologie.

Vlist, R. van der (2000). Psychology: Between Science and Practice. In: *Concepts and Transformation*, 5:2, 2000, p. 213–236. Amsterdam: Benjamin's.

Vlist, R. van der (2003). *Het veranderen van de narcistische organisatie.* Utrecht: Lemma.

Vlist, R. van der & Breukelen, W. van (2002). Participatief leiderschap. In: Richardson, R., Verweij, D., Vogelaar, A. & Kuipers H. (Eds). *Mens & Organisatie.* Amsterdam: Mets & Schilt.

Vogelaar, A., Bosch, J., Kuipers, H., Metselaar, M., Nederhof, F., Witteveen, A. Van den Berg, C., De Bruin, E. & Van der Vlist, R. (1996a). *Leiderschap in Crisisomstandigheden.* Breda: Research Paper FMB. 96–32.

Vogelaar, A., Kramer, F., Witteveen, A., Bosch, J., Metselaar, M., Kuipers, H., Nederhof, F., Kensmil, N. & De Bruin, E. (1996b). *Leiderschap in Crisisomstandigheden, Deel 2.* Breda: KMA, Research Paper FMB. 96–36.

Vogelaar, A., Kramer, F., Metselaar, M., Witteveen, A., Bosch, J., Kuipers, H. & Nederhof, F. (1997a). *Leiderschap in Crisisomstandigheden. Het functioneren van pelotons- en groepscommandanten in UNPROFOR.* Den-Haag: Sdu.

Vogelaar, A., Soeters, J. & Born, H. (1997b). Working and living in Bosnia: Experiences of Dutch IFOR soldiers. In: (Soeters, J. & Rovers, J.). *Netherlands Annual Review of Military Studies 1997: The Bosnian Experience*, Breda, The Netherlands: Royal Netherlands Military Academy, 1997), 113–132.

Vogelaar, A.L.W. & Kramer, F.J. (1997). Mission-orientated command in ambiguous situations. In: *Netherlands Annual Review of Military Studies*, I, pp. 475–493.

Vogelaar, A.L.W., Kramer, F.J., Op den Buijs, T.P. & Peters, N.C.W. (2001). *Leiderschap bij vredesoperaties.* Breda: KMA/ FMB/ KOC, researchpaper 01–59.

Vogelaar. A.L.W. & Kramer, F.J. (2004). Command in Dutch Peace Support Operations. In: *Armed Forces & Society*, Vol. 30, Spring 2004, pp. 409–431.

Vroom C. (2003). De geest van Kilacadmon groet u allen. In: *Carré* 2-2003, pp. 18–19.

Waldrop, M. (1992). *Complexity. The emerging science at the edge of order and chaos*. New York: Simon & Schuster.

Wallace (Ed.). (1969). *Sociological Theory. An introduction*. New York: Aldine Publishing Company.

Weathers, F.W., Litz, B.T. & Keane, T.M. (1995). Military Trauma. In: Freedy, J.R. & Hobfoll, S.F. (Eds), *Traumatic Stress: From Theory to Practise*. New York: Plenum Press.

Weick, K.E. (1979). *The social psychology of organizing*. New York: McGraw Hill.

Weick, K.E. (1993). The collapse of sensemaking in organizations: The Mann Gulch Disaster. In: *Administrative Science Quarterly*, 38 (4).

Weick, K.E. (1995). *Sensemaking in Organizations*. London: Sage.

Weick, K.E. (2001). *Making sense of the organization*. Malden, Ma: Blackwell Business.

Weick, K.E. (2004). Normal Accident Theory As Frame, Link, and Provocation. In: *Organization & Environment*, Vol. 17, No. 1, pp. 27–31.

Weick, K.E. & Roberts, K. (1993). Collective mind in organizations: Heedful inter-relating on flightdecks. *Administrative Science Quaterly*, 38 (3).

Weick, K.E., & Westley, F. (1996). Organizational learning: Affirming an Oxymoron. In Clegg, S.R., Hardy, C. & Nord, W.R. (Eds), Handbook of Organization Studies (pp. 440–458). London: Sage.

Weick, K.E. & Sutcliffe, K.M. (2001). *Managing the unexpected. Assuring high performance in an age of complexity*. San Francisco: Jossey Bass.

Wester, F. (1993). *Strategieën voor kwalitatief onderzoek*. Bussum: Coutinho.

Wester, F. & Richardson, R. (1989). *Kwalitatieve analyse in de praktijk en handleiding bij KWALITAN 2.1*. Nijmegen: ITS.

Wester, F. & Peters, V. (2004). *Kwalitatieve Analyse. Uitgangspunten en procedures*. Bussum: Coutinho.

Wilson, J.Q. (1989). *Bureaucracy. What government agencies do and why they do it*. New York: Basic Books.

Winslow, D. (1997). *The Canadian Airborne regiment in Somalia: A socio-cultural inquiry*. Ottawa: Canadian Government Publishing.

Zwaan, A. van der (1999). *Organising work processes. Engineering work & Managing workers*. Assen: Van Gorcum.

Name & Subject Index